KT-368-200

Empowerment
HR strategies for service excellence

Conrad Lashley

NORWICH CITY COLLEGE LIBRARY		
Stock No.	181469	
Class	647. 940683 LAS	
Cat.	Proc.	IWL

OXFORD AUCKLAND BOSTON JOHANNESBURG MELBOURNE NEW DELHI

Butterworth-Heinemann
Linacre House, Jordan Hill, Oxford OX2 8DP
225 Wildwood Avenue, Woburn, MA 01801-2041
A division of Reed Educational and Professional Publishing Ltd

A member of the Reed Elsevier plc group

First published 2001

© Conrad Lashley 2001

All rights reserved. No part of this publication may be reproduced in
any material form (including photocopying or storing in any medium by
electronic means and whether or not transiently or incidentally to some
other use of this publication) without the written permission of the
copyright holder except in accordance with the provisions of the Copyright,
Designs and Patents Act 1988 or under the terms of a licence issued by the
Copyright Licensing Agency Ltd, 90 Tottenham Court Road, London,
England W1P 0LP. Applications for the copyright holder's written
permission to reproduce any part of this publication should be addressed
to the publishers

British Library Cataloguing in Publication Data
Lashley, Conrad
   Empowerment: HR strategies for service excellence
   1. Service industries – Personnel management
   I. Title
   658.3

ISBN 0 7506 5244 6

> For information on all Butterworth-Heinemann
> publications visit our website at www.bh.com

Composition by Genesis Typesetting, Rochester, Kent
Printed and bound in Great Britain

FOR EVERY TITLE THAT WE PUBLISH, BUTTERWORTH-HEINEMANN
WILL PAY FOR BTCV TO PLANT AND CARE FOR A TREE.

Contents

Contents

Hospitality, Leisure & Tourism Series

Introduction

This volume is in effect a second edition of the text originally published under the title, *Empowering Service Excellence: beyond the quick fix*, by Cassells (Lashley, 1997). As series editor for Butterworth-Heinemann's Hospitality, Tourism and Leisure Series, I was keen to publish this empowerment book under the series heading. In planning the current edition, I have been concerned to use the opportunity to update my thoughts and understanding of empowerment. In particular, I want to make a more robust case for an understanding of empowerment at work that extends beyond the somewhat narrow relational dimensions of empowerment. That is, in a way that considers more fully the 'state' of being empowered.

Although a critical analysis of the literature on empowerment does communicate an array of meanings that I have attempted to encapsulate in this text, published material overwhelmingly assumes that empowerment is fundamentally about addressing the relationship between managers and employees. A dominant strand for advocate writers is that empowerment is essentially a democratic process, allowing 'disempowered employees' more say in the decisions currently made by managers in traditional command and control structures. For these writers, democratic structures are more relevant to the learning organization capable of responding quickly to a fast moving and changing world (Senge *et al.*, 1999). Interestingly, those who criticize empowerment (Wilkinson, 1998; Collins, 1999) frequently do so for precisely the opposite reason, that is, empowerment is *not* democratic. These writers challenge empowerment's democratic credentials because empowerment is a management-inspired initiative that limits employee involvement in decisions to task level, and that managerial and owner power is rarely challenged by empowerment.

Both the advocate and critical accounts can be seen as flawed. First, neither considers empowerment to cover a range of initiatives that alter the relationship in different ways. Not all initiatives said to be empowering, involve employees making decisions formerly made by managers. Some are more con-sultative. There is even variation amongst these forms; quality circles, team briefings and suggestions schemes are consultative but in different ways. One takes a representative form whilst the other involves direct participation by all employees in the team(s), and the other is largely passive. Yet all of these have been described as empowerment. In some cases, initiatives involving empowerment are set within a traditional command and control structure and are aimed at developing an employee's sense of engagement in the service encounter, through training, rewards and promotion prospects. Flowing from this, few of these accounts consider the impact of context on the form that empowerment might take and the outcomes that empowerment is designed to achieve for management. Bowen and Lawler (1992); Rafiq and Ahmed (1998b); Lashley and Taylor (1998) all suggest that variations in the service context require different performances from front-line service employees and this impacts on the way they 'fit' with how managers manage them. Managers are likely to want different forms of empowering service employees, depending on their perceptions of the performance required to meet customer service expectations.

A second common flaw in these accounts of empowerment is that they rarely consider the psychological state of empowerment or how it feels to be empowered. So some of the more evangelical advocates largely assumed that initiatives called empowerment will be *empowering* and that all employees are just waiting to be empowered. There is rarely any consideration of the conditions likely to lead to feeling empowered or the barriers to effective empowerment. Nor is there consideration that individuals in the workforce may vary in their need to feel empowered at work. Similarly, the critics of empowerment rarely consider the benefits of feeling personally more effective and that employees may gain emotional comfort from feeling valued enough to be trusted to make some decisions or even just asked what they think.

The psychological and emotional dimensions of empowerment need more consideration, and to that end I have edited what was

Chapter 8 and moved some of the content to a new Chapter 2 dealing with the psychology of empowerment together with recent research on how the organizational and managerial context contribute to having a sense of empowerment. The chapter dealing with feeling empowered now sits in Chapter 9, and includes new material dealing with emotions at work. This later work builds on the seminal work of Hochschild (1983), particularly suggesting that service workers suffer stress by having to supply *'emotional labour'*, that is, displaying emotions in the service interaction with customers that they don't actually feel. Potentially empowerment may create emotions that are consistent with what Mann (1999) describes as the 'Have a Nice Day' culture, and thereby reduce the emotional labour required.

This edition of the book includes a wide array of case study material, but primarily focuses on case study material from three key service organizations, which have many similarities. All three are branded service organizations that supply food and drink to customers through a multi-unit organization where units are located close to their markets. To varying degrees, all are 'McDonaldized' (Ritzer, 1993), but each represents a different service offer to customers. Each is therefore following a different service strategy, which results in different operational processes and ultimately in different approaches to empowering employees. The three core case studies were not chosen at random. They were chosen to represent different approaches that would inform the development of an understanding of empowerment in service organizations.

McDonald's Restaurants Limited is the eponymous ideal type of Ritzer's somewhat bleak forecast for the future of the society. This text argues that whilst there are trends in approaches to the branding of services, which involve some similar features, McDonald's represents one form of service offer that satisfies particular consumer needs. The standardized, reliable, largely tangible nature of the offer to customers goes some way to meet customers' anxieties about the nature of the service encounter. McDonald's operating systems, quality assurance techniques and management of human resources are designed to deliver consistency and reliability. 'One best way' informs much of the organization's approach to the managerial processes. Within the context of this book, these marketing, operational and human resource approaches ultimately impact on the intentions and forms of empowerment introduced.

McDonald's Restaurants has provided two foci for the study of empowerment. In the first, the organization introduced an initiative on a pilot basis that merged two layers of management

Hospitality, Leisure & Tourism Series

and 'empowered' both restaurant managers and the new General Area Supervisors. I was invited to conduct a study of the pilot and produced a report for the company, which then fed into the subsequent reorganization of the management structure. The second focus explores the extent and potential 'empowerment' of front-line service employees. This work has been informed by detailed work with the company through the study of the use of National Vocational Qualifications, and by the work of Tony Royle who has conducted detailed studies of the organization's employment practices in both the UK and Germany.

TGI Fridays, the second company in the study, has many features in common with McDonald's. It is a branded service organization that also delivers standardization and reliability to customers. Hence production service manuals, standardized menus and building design ensure that the offer to customers is explicit and assures customers of consistency. That said, the offer to customers varies from McDonald's in that it is aimed at a targeted and narrower market segment. In particular the offer aims to meet both the customer's security needs through the standardized and consistent offer, and at the same time respond to customer needs to be treated as individuals. Customers are provided with opportunities to personalize the service which they purchase. An extensive food menu and cocktail list (100 items on each) allows customers a fair degree of freedom to 'design' their lunch or dinner. The intangible element of the offer allows a range of types of experience – intimate dinner, celebration, party. Given the potential variety, the offer to customers could be described as typifying 'mass customization'. Operating systems and approach to the management of human resources, therefore, involve the delivery of elements of standardization that are tailored to personalized customer needs. Employee performance requires employees to act as advisors and consultants to customers and then to provide the performance desired by the customer. The management of employees, and the form of empowerment, aims at engaging the employee in providing the performance through developing a sense of personal efficacy in the employee.

Harvester Restaurants provides the third case study. Like the other two, Harvester offer a branded product. Standardized menus, production methods, pricing and promotional methods aim at providing customers with a clear message as to what they are offering. In this case the offer is quite tightly focused on a particular market segment requiring a standardized service based on a 'traditional' British country pub and British food menu. Although providing a standardized service, the offer to customers relies a great deal on the intangibles. The quality of service, based on a homely atmosphere, all support the offer of 'tradition' and continuity in a world of change. Operating systems create a standardized offer in both the tangible and intangible aspects. Like McDonald's and TGI Fridays, the food production process and menu, format of the premises and general ambience are standardized. Unlike, McDonald's however, the offer in the intangibles involve more elaborate interactions and employees must be caring, courteous and willing to help customers. Employees are encouraged to develop both a sense of personal efficacy and a willingness to meet the customer's emotional needs for homeliness and 'informal formality'. The management of human resources and form of empowerment attempt to build the necessary sense of efficacy and engagement in the service offer to customers.

The three case studies display both similarity and difference. The organizations concerned are similar in that they deliver much that is standardized in the brand offer to customers, and have operational systems which assist in the delivery of consistency and similarity in to their customers. These organizations differ in the wider service offer made to customers, particularly in the extent that they meet customer needs in the intangible elements of the service. In turn this affects the manner in which employee performance is managed in each organization.

Each of the case studies help to build a picture of empowerment of service employees in context. Through these studies the following book aims to show how different managers interpret the operational needs of the organization differently and this results in different approaches to the management of employees. Different forms of empowerment are employed and different working arrangements are practised. Particularly, employees in these organizations are required to exercise different amounts of discretion in the service of customers. Employees working under these arrangements experience different feelings about their work and empowerment represents different benefits to the employees concerned.

These case studies provide a valuable vehicle for, not only witnessing different approaches to empowerment, but also helping to show how a complex of factors are likely to influence the introduction of empowerment and its successful application within the service organizations. A holistic picture of empowerment is built in which the behaviour of managers and employees are interdependent with the context in which the initiative is introduced. Through the study of these cases it has been possible to deduce some generally applicable influences on service operations and the fit between the cluster of service attributes which make up the customer offer, the characteristics of the service operational process, and the management of employee performance.

The issue of fit also suggests that empowerment needs to be carefully considered within the context of the wider organizational environment and the ingredients needed for empowerment to work. The history of management ideas is littered with applications of techniques that appeared successful in one organization, which, when adopted in another, do not produce the same successful results. The empowerment of service employees requires critical appraisal through which to understand the ingredients necessary for success, and the barriers that can hamper it. Uncritical advocacy by the enthusiasts together with equally uncritical application by practitioners are likely to lead to empowerment being regarded as yet another management fad. The promise of a quick fix to complex management problems is appealing, but unlikely to result in long term solutions.

Fundamental to a critical appraisal of empowerment is that the meanings and perception of empowerment will not only differ between managers in different organizations, there may also be different perceptions, meanings and experiences of empowerment between the empowering and the empowered. As a managerially originated initiative, empowerment reflects managerial concerns, but impacts on what people do in the workplace, and most importantly how they feel about work, the organization and customers. These case studies were therefore constructed through interviews with a variety of organization members at different levels and at different position in the empowerment relationship: senior managers responsible for business strategies, middle and unit managers responsible for direct relationships with the empowered, and the empowered themselves. In addition to visits to head offices and units to interview these various stakeholders, the case studies were also informed by site visits to the various units so as to simulate customer experiences. These visits attempted to gauge how these various arrangements impacted on customer service.

Findings from the case studies are present in two ways throughout the text. First, each case study is used to illuminate different forms of empowerment and described in the relevant chapters that highlight different approaches to empowerment. Second, the findings from the case studies are interwoven through the text so as to illustrate the variations in responses and approaches under each facet of the analysis of empowerment.

Chapter 1 explores the claims for empowerment as articulated by those advocating it for the future of business organizations. The chapter includes attempts made by various advocates to define empowerment and the nature of the empowered organization. It concludes by suggesting a framework for the investigation of empowerment within an organizational context.

Chapter 2 highlights the psychological dimensions of empowerment outlining first an overview of how empowered employees might be moved through a state of being disempowered to being empowered. The chapter also shows how social psychology can assist in understanding how employee attitudes at work might be changed through the experience of being empowered. Finally the chapter discusses the context of empowerment and the importance of management actions in providing the necessary support likely to assist in the development of the psychological sate of empowerment.

Chapter 3 aims to provide some insights into relational aspects of employee empowerment set within a history of concerns to engage employees in a way that encourages more job satisfaction, reduces industrial conflict, or develops more employee commitment. The framework of analysis is used as a tool for describing each form of empowerment in the ensuing chapters, and locates each within traditions of employee management that are essentially participative, consultative or directive.

Chapters 4–7 explore each of the four managerial meanings of empowerment in greater depth. The primary case studies are used to explore differences in approach to empowerment of both front-line employees and managers, and these are supplemented by reference to other examples. Chapter 4 explores initiatives, which, though a variety of forms, involve employees making decisions that traditionally might be made by managers. Chapter 5 explores initiatives that take forms designed to gain employee involvement through a variety of techniques to gain employee suggestions and improve performance in the service encounter. Chapter 6 explores employee empowerment that is chiefly concerned with winning employee commitment to the service encounter, and that includes little by way of formal decision making or suggestion gathering. These three earlier chapters examine initiatives that empower employees; Chapter 7 considers those initiatives that are concerned with empowering managers and 'flattening' the organization structure.

Chapter 8 suggests a five-dimensional model through which to analyse the nature of the changes introduced under empowerment. These are designed to establish objective boundaries of the changes that have been introduced. As stated earlier, what is it that the empowered can do now that they could not do before? How has the organization changed in its structure, distribution of power and culture? The change in the arrangements that have been introduced impact on the subjective feelings of being empowered experienced by those who are empowered.

The nature of this 'state of empowerment' is the subject of Chapter 9. In particular it focuses on the limits and boundaries that different forms of empowerment may have in producing the required emotional state of being empowered that is said to be so beneficial. In particular it explores the role of emotions at work in general and specifically the management of emotions in service contexts. The case studies chiefly reported throughout tend to require the 'Have a Nice Day' culture mentioned earlier, but Mann reminds us that emotional labour is not only concerned with presenting happy emotions to customers. Some jobs, like debt collectors or 'bouncers' in pubs and clubs, need to communicate a 'Have a Nasty Day' culture. Each of these, and other emotional states, present employees with a need to provide 'emotional labour', and empowerment may have a role to play in assisting employees both feel and display the emotions required by the job.

Chapter 10 is concerned with links between employee performance and improved organizational performance. The advocates of empowerment suggest that empowered employees will deliver a range of benefits in organizational performance – for example, improved service quality, increased customer repeats, reduced labour turnover, etc. Managers in the case study organizations all felt that improvements had ensued from their approach, but there was rarely any detailed study to show precisely how performance had changed as a direct result of the initiative, rather than as a consequence of some externally, and thereby uncontrollable, factor.

Chapter 11 examines the particular role the employee empowerment is said to play in resolving the difficulties experienced by service organizations. The personal nature of the service encounter, the key element of intangible elements of the encounter, create difficulties and limits on the ability of service organizations to predict and systematize consistent service quality. Employee performance and thereby employee commitment to service quality become fundamental and employee empowerment appears to be a mechanism for achieving commitment and performance.

Chapter 12 builds a model of contextual influences that under the normative model should be influential in shaping the human resource strategies, and the form of empowerment that best fits the organization's business strategy and the offer to its customers. The three case studies that have been used to illustrate various aspects of the book reflect different approaches to the introduction of empowerment and also reflect different approaches to empowerment, though each might be described as a 'hospitality retail organization'. McDonald's Restaurants Limited, TGI Fridays and Harvester Restaurants each makes a different service offer to its customers and this is reflected in the form of empowerment at work in each organization. The chapter illustrates a range of key drivers and influences on the service offer, the operational processes involved and the best fit with approaches to the management of employees.

Finally Chapter 13 explores the extent that empowerment is a universalistic answer to the future of service organizations. It suggests that there are a number of potential futures, depending on the contexts in which individual service organizations operate and the labour market conditions that are operating at the time.

Conrad Lashley
School of Tourism Hospitality Management
Leeds Metropolitan University

CHAPTER 1

Understanding empowerment: a framework of analysis

- **Definitions and meanings**
- **Empowering the organization**
- **Researching empowerment**

It is true to say that the 'age of empowerment' (Senge *et al.*, 1999: 11) has become a key rhetoric of the last decades of the twentieth century. Whether in social, political or employment fields, commentators use empowerment in a variety of contexts and with a variety of intentions. Indeed, empowerment is used by so many people, in such a variety of ways, that the term is almost becoming meaningless. Certainly, any serious discussion of the topic needs to define terms and establish the assumptions upon which the commentary is based.

In the employment field there has been a burgeoning literature on employee empowerment, mostly written from a 'normative' perspective. That is, a perspective that identifies the functions that empowerment 'serves' or 'should serve' in organizations (Senge *et al.*, 1999).

These texts provide guides as to the aspirations of academics and/or practitioners who advocate empowerment as an approach to organizational management in the current competitive environment (Johnson and Redmond, 1998).

'Empowerment is about achieving organizational goals; it means getting everyone involved in making a success of the business.' (Johnson and Redmond, 1998: xv). According to the advocates, empowered organizations will gain commercial advantages and will be more competitive. Furthermore, they suggest that more traditional command and control structures disempower organization members (Belbin, 1998). Empowered organizations will become the norm in the modern, or 'postmodern', age and the traditional disempowered organizations will be driven from business under the weight of competitive pressure, inflexibility and atrophy.

This chapter explores these arguments and approaches by first establishing a range of meanings provided by the various writers and practitioners, the organization adjustments needed by empowered organizations and the benefits seen to be achieved by firms that empower their workforce. Finally, the chapter introduces a model for understanding the impact of empowerment and aims to provide a corrective to the more evangelical claims of many commentators.

Definitions and meanings

Some definitions of empowerment start with a discussion of empowerment in relation to delegation of authority. In fact, one definition of 'empower' given in the *Oxford English Dictionary* suggests that it means 'to invest legally or formally with power: to authorize, license.' On the other hand some writers (Foy, 1994) are keen to distance the definition from merely intensifying the delegation of authority. Nancy Foy provides a nice example that both helps with the distinction between empowerment and delegation, and reveals something of the assumptions and mind set underpinning many aspirations for empowerment. She says 'If you give your 12-year-old daughter money to buy jeans, that's delegation . . . If you give her a clothes allowance which she can spend as she chooses, that's empowerment' (p. 4).

Stewart (1994) suggests that managers need to draw distinctions between being *in* authority and being *an* authority. Again she uses a child–parent example to explain differences between being in authority and thereby having the power to make decisions that are to be obeyed, 'as when telling a child to go to bed' (p. 2), and being an authority 'on the sleeping habits of children'. Empowering managers act as authorities for empowered employees.

Apart from the normative content of both these definitions, the examples employed reveal much about the assumptions that underpin some definitions of empowerment, namely that the *empowerer* is in a more powerful position than the *empowered*, and the empowered have empowerment done to them. This is not a negotiated process. Hence there is an implicit imbalance built in to the notion of empowerment. The example by Nancy Foy implies that empowerment is determined by the more senior authority and the empowered operate within the boundaries set. So in her case, the child is given a clothing allowance. The budget head is defined, the money is to be spent on clothes, rather than being given an allowance with the freedom to spend the money as she sees fit.

This draws a parallel with the definition of empowerment given by several other writers, namely that empowerment is about deciding on the boundaries of what the empowered are able to do (van Outdshoorn and Thomas, 1993) and the empowered operate within the boundaries laid down. van Outdshoorn and Thomas also provide another insight into empowerment in that they make a distinction between the objective facts of what the empowered are 'given authority or permission' (p. 4) to do, and the subjective feelings of power, energy and ability generated within the supposedly empowered. This presents some possible differences in perceptions, which will be discussed more fully later. In the first instance the potential difference between subjective feelings and the objective limits on empowerment hints at political processes involved. Decisions about what the empowered are allowed, and not allowed, to do suggests potential differences in perceptions between those deciding on the boundaries and those who have to work within them. Second, the presence of subjective feelings implies that there may be subjective differences between individuals. Both these aspects require much more discussion than is usual in the more 'evangelical' literature. For these commentators the notion that political processes are involved is rarely discussed, and there is little recognition that people may differ in their orientations to work or expectations for power and a sense of personal worth associated with work.

Where the responses of the empowered are discussed, they often slide into humanistic generalizations. There is an implicit and explicit assumption that the empowered are just waiting to be liberated from the oppressive experiences. 'Empowerment is the realization and actualization of potential and opportunity just waiting to be unleashed,' (Johnson, 1993: 32).

Traditional organization structures based on Weberian formal rationality, Taylorist work organization, and command and control power relations (Johnson and Redmond, 1998) are 'disempowering' (Potterfield, 1999) because traditional structures create feelings of powerlessness (Johnson, 1993). Setting this within the context of the justification for empowerment, these traditional structures are seen as representing the source of many organizational and even social problems. Thus problems of worker alienation and generally low levels of employee commitment, and feelings of anomie in society are all caused by feelings of disempowerment and a sense of powerlessness. For writers such as these, empowerment goes beyond the needs of the current business climate; it is essential to resolving the tensions in the employment relationship, and in society at large.

Some writers, (Senge *et al.*, 1999) define empowerment as persuading employees to take total responsibility for their own job satisfaction. In these cases the organizational task is to encourage employees to consider what they like and dislike about their jobs and 'probe their own motives and discover what would make their jobs more interesting' (Barry, 1993: 24). The empowerment of employees through releasing their talents and abilities, meeting their inner needs, and generally engaging employees with moral commitment (Etzioni, 1961) is deemed to be an essential feature of organizations in the 'Information Age'. Barry reminds readers of the example of the future organization provided by Drucker (1988). In this view future organizations will resemble orchestras comprised of highly trained and skilled individuals each with specialist skills. Their efforts are orchestrated but the conductor cannot control the sound made by any one individual player. The whole is dependent on the sum total of the individual players exercising their own skills and talents. Hierarchies are minimal and there are no status differences between the various instrument sections. There is, of course, no mention of potential disagreements over the programme to be played and the different workloads that might be involved for various sections of the orchestra.

The link between employee emotional and psychological needs, their untapped abilities and future organizational performance is an important strand in the rhetoric of empowerment. Some writers (Johnson and Redmond, 1998) make specific mention of the need to improve employee commitment to organizational goals and objectives, particularly highlighted in connection with organizational strategies relating to product and service quality (D'Annunzio-Green and Macandrew, 1999). Empowerment is thus frequently linked with total quality management (Rodrigues, 1994), 'customer oriented organization' (Bowen and Basch, 1992), a 'total quality culture' (Simmons and Teare, 1993), or a 'service driven culture' (Hirst, 1992); the assumption being that employee commitment is an essential feature of achieving quality objectives. This particular resonance for service industries will be discussed in more detail later.

Others draw the link between the need for improved employee commitment in the context of increased global competition (Johnson, 1993; Nixon, 1994), and rapid technological change plus the need for greater organizational flexibility (Barry, 1993). In each case it is assumed that empowered employees will be committed to organizational success, and will bring their full range of talents and experiences to play in the achievement of organizational goals. The unitary assumptions underpinning these aspirations for empowerment are not far from the surface in many of these writings. It is taken as axiomatic that there is a community of interests between owners, managers and employees, with all organizational stakeholders having shared aspirations, goals and objectives. Indeed many of these accounts can be accused of being simplistic in their understanding of organizational life and the political dynamics which shape decision making and policies. Typical is a statement by Nancy Foy (1994) in relation to managerial concerns and the need to empower. '*Empowering* people is as important today as *involving* them in the 1980s and getting them to *participate* in the 1970s' (p. xvii).

Such statements reveal little of the environmental, economic and industrial circumstances that have led to differences in focus and terminology (Rafiq and Ahmed, 1998a). Nor do they consider the continuity of concerns that they reveal about employing organizations. The discourse on employee empowerment in fact reflects both continuity and change in employer concerns. The abiding concerns are to generate employee commitment and ensure optimum effort from employees (Marchington and Wilkinson, 2000). The changing circumstances relate to the changes in labour market conditions whereby organized labour is no longer perceived as a collective threat to managerial prerogatives. And empowerment reflects an attempt to engage employee individually and emotionally. Empowerment represents an attempt to establish moral involvement, '. . .which means that the person intrinsically values the mission of the organization and his or her job, and is personally involved and identifies with the organization' (Schein, 1988: 45).

It is not accidental that both the terminology used to discuss empowerment, and examples of arrangements that claim to be empowering overlap with these other initiatives. Thus some writers use empowerment and employee involvement (Plunkett and Fournier, 1991) and empowerment and employee participation (Cotton, 1993) interchangeably. There is rarely a recognition of, let alone an attempt to explain or define, the boundaries between them. Similarly, an examination of initiatives that claim to be empowering covers a wide array of arrangements that are also discussed under the headings of participation and involvement.

In the hospitality industry, for example, employee empowerment is a term that has been used to describe quality circles (Accor Group), suggestion schemes (McDonald's Restaurants), customer care programmes (Scott's Hotels), employee involvement in devising departmental standards (Hilton Hotels), autonomous work groups (Harvester Restaurants) and delayering the organization (Bass Taverns). All these different forms are likely to represent different intrinsic and extrinsic rewards to employees and thereby different levels of intensity with which they will be engaged by the organization's objectives.

Table 1.1 Examples of forms of empowerment in hospitality services

Form	Organization
Quality circles	Accor Group
Suggestion schemes	McDonald's Restaurants
'Whatever it takes' training	Marriott Hotels
Autonomous work groups	Harvester Restaurants
Delayering the organization	Bass Taverns

Even within the normative notions of what empowerment is supposed to achieve it is possible to evaluate various initiatives and forms of empowerment according to the 'state of empowerment' that they generate in the empowered. The likely elements present in the state of being empowered will be discussed more fully in Chapter 2, but having a sense of personal efficacy and worth, individual control together with a sense of power with the freedom to use that power in the achievement of valued goals are likely to be important ingredients (Conger and Kanungo, 1988; Sparrowe, 1994; Siegall and Gardner, 2000).

Whilst the supposed congruence of employee needs and organizational goals is one important strand in the rhetoric of empowerment, it is possible to detect differences in the nature of empowerment in socio-political terms. For some writers (Barbee and Bott, 1991) employee empowerment is defined as 'the act of vesting responsibility in the people nearest the problem' whilst for Bowen and Lawler (1992) empowerment covers 'management strategies for sharing decision making power'.

These two sets of emphases reflect quite different assumptions about the nature of empowerment. In the first case, vesting responsibility can be seen as being concerned with intensification of work. Thus if an employee is told that they are not only responsible for their duties to serve customers, but also for ensuring customer satisfaction or product quality, they may well be brought to account for things which are beyond their control. For example, company policy, customer moods and expectations may impact on perceptions of satisfaction and may be areas beyond the server's control. Dealing with customer complaints, which is frequently a feature of empowerment in service operations, puts the server in difficult and potentially stressful situations. They have to try to placate the customer, or anticipate customer needs. Many service organizations talk about employees aiming to *'delight the customer'*, that is, provide a level of service beyond the customer's expectations of the service they will receive. In other cases, company policy may put contradictory pressures on employees – *'give customers attentive service and maximize sales'*.

Adding extra responsibilities to a person's job can increase the burden of work, produce more stress and represent in intensification of work. In a real sense the individual is having to achieve more within a given work period. Often they are having to manage their feelings to more closely match how they are expected to feel (Mann, 1999). For some workers, empowerment in the form of added responsibilities can be an unwelcome development and, as will be discussed further later, generates resentment from those who 'only want to work as a waitress' (Ashness and Lashley, 1995). For others, however, added responsibilities can bring new dimensions to work experiences and exert welcome demands on the empowered. Adding responsibilities can develop a sense of personal ownership and attachment to a specific aspect of the work. Having said that, empowering people by extending responsibilities for a wider range of performance measures does have its limits, not least of which being that operational decision making structures are still left intact. There are still some significant limits on the power of the empowered.

Definitions which reflect Bowen and Lawler's notion that empowerment involves sharing decision making implies that more authority is delegated to the empowered employee. Clearly this means that employees will be given some power to make certain decisions and resolve certain issues themselves. Frequently service firms empower employees to deal with customer complaints or do 'whatever it takes' to ensure customer satisfaction. In restaurant situations front-line staff are often empowered to replace meals, provide new meals or provide complimentary bottles of wine where accidents or complaints occur. In other circumstances empowered employees make decisions about reordering stock, work organization, and the means of achieving organizational sales targets. Giving employees more authority to make the decisions about their immediate tasks can increase organizational effectiveness, and improve employee satisfaction. Problems and complaints are dealt with more quickly and operational decisions are shaped by immediate operational experiences. Frequently, however, the authority is limited to operational immediate task matters and rarely does empowerment extend to decision making about company objectives or targets within which the empowered operate.

The act of giving authority for employees to make decisions is likely to meet a different set of intrinsic needs than merely making them responsible, and thereby accountable, for operational performance (Siegall and Gardner, 2000). These feelings will be discussed more fully later, but interviews with employees who had been given authority to make decisions, where previously a supervisor had held this authority, showed that for many employees the experience was satisfying and increased their own sense of personal worth. Typical of the favourable comments which we registered was the waitress who said, 'I wanted to do more than just come in as a waitress' (Ashness and Lashley, 1995).

There can be a sense that empowering employees through an extended authority, although limited to operational issues, does at the very least counter the sense of powerlessness and disempowerment mentioned earlier. Certainly the expectations of those writing from a normative perspective expect that increased responsibility and/or increased authority are essential ingredients in empowerment as a means of gaining the commitment to organizational goals. The work of Conger and Kanungo (1988), and Kelly and Kelly (1990) show in different ways that such links are not inevitable.

At root, much of this discussion rests on the answers to questions that relate to the amount of power being given by whom, to whom, to do what? Fundamentally, differences in definitions of empowerment rest on the degree of power associated with an initiative. Those definitions that stress extensions of responsibility tend to imply that limited power and authority is delegated to the empowered. It is possible for existing power and authority structures to remain intact, unchanged by the initiative. In the second definition, there is an assumption that some degree of power to make decisions is delegated to the empowered. In this case there is an assumption that as the empowered are given more authority to make decisions, there is a corresponding reduction in the direct authority exercised by supervisors and managers. Indeed as the extent of empowerment increases, there is a change in the nature of the roles of managers and supervisors. As highlighted above, there is said to be a change from being in authority to being an authority.

A final strand in the discourse about empowerment relates to the extent that employee empowerment represents an extension of employee democracy. Again with other aspects of the common definitions of empowerment, there is no clear agreement amongst those who adopt the normative approach to empowerment. For some writers (Plunkett and Fournier, 1991) empowerment has 'nothing to do with democracy' whereas for other writers empowerment involves 'newer more democratic organizations' (van Outdshoorn and Thomas, 1993: 10). 'According to the advocates, empowerment involves the relocation of power form the owners and managers of corporations to the lower-level rank and file workers' (Potterfield, 1999: 2). The link between empowerment and industrial democracy will be drawn in more detail, the key issues relate back to the power issue and the nature of the boundaries set, within which the empowered operate. Typically the expanded boundaries that allow employees to make decisions previously made by supervisors or managers, involve decisions related to task organization and operations. Thus in one example we encountered employees were given a target to increase restaurant sales by 50 pence per head and were given the freedom to organize the achievement of the target as they saw fit. The restaurant team came up with a range of ideas which they implemented, and subsequently achieved the target. In the past, managers would have decided on the target, how to operationalize it, and told employees what to do. Under the new arrangements a democratic style of leadership allows individuals and teams to make decisions about the implementation of policy objectives that have been set by more senior organization members. Clearly, the answer to the question as to whether empowerment is essentially democratic or not depends on both how democracy is defined, which form of empowerment is implemented and the definition of empowerment being used.

Attempts to establish an agreed definition show that there are a number of different sets of assumptions and aspirations for empowerment, which are at times mutually exclusive or at least contradictory. Indeed this lack of precision and overlap with employee participation and employee involvement, might explain its appeal to a wide range of commentators and practitioners alike. It provides a rhetoric which can be applied to different intentions and underlying assumptions. Furthermore it has the appeal of sounding progressive and reflecting a modernity (or postmodernity) in relation to organizational design and conduct. It holds out the promise that it will deliver employee involvement and commitment to organizational goals and objectives. It will tap the reservoir of employee abilities and experiences in a way not achieved by traditional command and control structures. The quality of organizational outputs in goods and services will be improved. Communication processes will be improved and organization decision making will better reflect the realities of the grass roots organization and the customer needs.

The normative discussion of empowerment is, therefore, one which makes an array of sweeping claims without clear definition or, most importantly, any recognition of the limits and boundaries to the application of empowerment within different organizational contexts. Some of these limitations will be discussed later in this chapter. Before this there is a need to highlight some of the features of the empowered organization according to the normative model.

The empowering organization

Nancy Foy (1994: 3) reminds her readers that 'Organizations are not empowered, people are'. This is an important point because it reveals much about the assumptions of many commentators, namely that organizations are things that exist at an extra level to the people who comprise their members. This tendency to reify organizations is one that accompanies the more apolitical discussions about empowerment and the accompanying claims for its success as an approach to the management of organization members. The following section highlights some typical claims for empowerment.

At heart most of the claims for the benefits of empowerment are centred round the need to win greater commitment from employees. Much of the comment tends towards universalistic claims, namely that circumstances have changed and that employment practices based round low trust, low discretion job design, have to change (Potterfield, 1999). For these writers, organizations need to prioritize employee commitment. According to this view, the empowered organization allows a faster response to environmental change and allows the organization to benefit from the harnessing of the strengths of the whole workforce in the effective satisfaction of customer needs. For writers such as these, empowerment meets a universal need that traditional organizations don't satisfy. It is stressed that the source of future competitive advantage is in the dedication, commitment and competence of the workforce (Nixon, 1994). Empowerment is the 'new fuel for the growing workplace' (p. 25).

Employee empowerment is said to offer those concerned about greater employee commitment to the organization's goals a technique which provides a 'win-win' situation. Employees gain greater job satisfaction through the use of a wider range of skills and abilities together with an increased sense of worth, whilst employers gain a more committed, better informed and more focused workforce. Employees develop themselves in a learning environment. Employers are able to gain from the experiences and ideas from those working at the 'sharp end'. Employees gain a greater sense of ownership through the added responsibility and authority. Employers gain by increased productivity, better quality and reduced labour turnover. For employees satisfaction comes from being more involved and participating in decisions, because empowerment meets power needs and develops a sense of personal efficacy. The benefits for employers result in improved organizational performance, through an improved 'bottom line', more satisfied customers and improved competitiveness. The ultimate goal of empowerment is, '. . .a committed workforce with everyone whole-heartedly devoting their full energies and talents to the achievement of a common vision' (Nicholls, 1995: 9). Johnson and Redmond (1998: 5) say, 'An organization is empowered when people have the information they need to make decisions about the organization in which they are engaged, the motivation to make the decision in the best interests of the organization and the authority to make these decisions. . .'

For both employees and employers empowerment is said to offer a chance to overcome the wasteful rigidities of traditional disempowering organizations. Table 1.2 summarizes some of the claims for employee empowerment and the shortcomings consequent on organizations which 'disempower' their employees.

Empowered employees have a sense of belonging and excitement in their jobs. They are 'engaged' by the organization on an emotional level. Personal capabilities are enhanced in an environment where they are encouraged to enhance the scope of their job. They have responsibilities and authority delegated to them and are empowered to get with on their work in their own way (Johnson and Redmond, 1998). By continuing to extend the scope of jobs, the manager supports the employee with appropriate training until employees reach their full potential.

Empowered organizations have structures and cultures which encourage and facilitate empowerment (van Outdshoorn and Thomas, 1993; Nixon, 1994). The empowered organization has a

Hospitality, Leisure & Tourism Series

Table 1.2 States of empowerment and disempowerment

Empowerment	Disempowerment
Accepting responsibility	Avoiding taking responsibility
Being active	Being passive
Boldness	Timidity
Creative	Conventional
Energetic	Lethargic
Enjoys life	Gets little joy out of life
Happy	Depressed and miserable
Healthy	Many health problems
Imaginative	Dull and unimaginative
Independent	Dependent
Individualistic	Conforming
Innovative	Sticks to routines
Interesting	Dull and boring
Motivated	Unmotivated
Prepared to take risks	Reluctant to take risks
Observant	Unobservant
Satisfied with job	Frustrated in job
Sensitive to subtleties	Not sensitive to subtleties
Uses intelligence to the full	Does not use intelligence to the full
Uses full potential as a human being	Uses only a fraction of potential

Source: van Outdshoorn and Thomas, 1993

'flatter' structure. It requires less immediate supervision than a traditional organization because decision making is passed down the line. Senior and middle managers need to spend less time on control of subordinates and can focus on increasing customer satisfaction and market share (Barry, 1993). People are self-managing and the consequence is that the span of control can be wider. Managers act as coaches, facilitators and enablers, assisting subordinates to be more effective. To use Stewart's term, they become *an* authority, not *in* authority.

Cultures are more trust orientated and generate a sense of self-confidence and courage. Employees in the empowered organization are encouraged to take risks and learn from mistakes, which, when they occur, are regarded as learning opportunities (Senge, 1990). The whole organization is dedicated to learning and empowerment. Above all, empowerment cannot be grafted on to an organization. It must have the full support of managers at all levels. Indeed it is recognized that one of the barriers to the successful implementation of initiatives that are empowering comes not from operatives but from managers (Hopfl, 1994).

The relationship between employees and managers changes.

Managers need to change their expectations and styles of dealing with subordinates. Nicholls (1995) describes this as moving from the TDC to the TLC model, that is, from 'thinly disguised contempt' to 'tender loving care' (p. 7). Managers have to be prepared to explore their own experiences and expectations so as to be clear about the real limits of employees' abilities and capabilities. They must be able to communicate vision and justify the limits and boundaries that are imposed. They must be able to deal with conflicts that 'might arise because of the limits of the subordinates empowerment' (van Outdshoorn and Thomas, 1993: 11). They must create both an 'anxiety free environment' in which individuals will talk freely about their problems and difficulties; and a 'non-threatening environment' in which individuals will be prepared to take risks. They will look for lessons to be learned from mistakes and coach employees through a learning process that enhances self-confidence.

A review of the applications and uses of empowerment as an employment strategy in service industries reveals concerns that correspond with many of the key issues regarding the management of human resources, namely a concern to gain competitive advantage through improved service quality (Rafiq and Ahmed, 1998b; Siegall and Gardner, 2000). Particularly, it has been held that service deliverers (front-line people; Horoviz and Cudenne-Poon, 1990) play a crucial role in determining the extent and quality of customer experience and satisfaction.

Attempts to gain competitive advantage through service quality can be problematic for service operators. Customers may vary considerably in their personal definitions of what is a successful service encounter (Rust and Oliver, 1994). Indeed individual customers may well define and re-define their needs from service deliverers as their circumstances and expectations change. This, in turn, is likely to create situations where customer expectations are pivotal in shaping customer evaluations of service, and thereby future decisions to return to, or reject, particular service operators (Foulkes, 1994).

Whilst there are problems in establishing universal definitions, and thereby universal standards, of service quality in service operations, it is true to say that positive interpersonal contact, service deliverer attitudes, courtesy and helpfulness are closely related to customer evaluation of service quality (Adelmann et al., 1994). Employee performance, involvement and commitment to quality service delivery are, therefore, fundamental. Human resources and strategies to engage employees emotionally in the objective of customer satisfaction take a new and urgent meaning (Mann, 1999).

Hochschild's (1983) work with air stewardesses reveals much in common with the 'commercialization of feelings' in many service operations. 'Seeming to love the job' becomes part of the job; and actually trying to love it, and to enjoy the customers, helps the worker in this effort' (p. 6). Fineman (1993) also comments on the interplay between feelings and performance in service interactions. Enabling employees to sense their own power and significance of their part in the service dramas may help employees to manage the emotions required of their performance. Thomson (1998: 1) sets these concerns at the centre of organizational performance in future years, 'In the next few years emotional capital will be an asset on the balance sheet of any major business'.

Empowerment of employees has particular attractions for service organizations, because employee commitment and customer service quality are seen as interwoven. As WJ Marriott Snr is famously reported as saying, 'It takes happy employees to make happy customers' (Barbee and Bott, 1991: 30). Thus employee commitment to meet service quality pledges to customers results in more responsive service interactions, because employees are committed to 'delighting the customer' and will do whatever it takes to ensure successful service encounters. Given the unpredictability of customers, service employees are best placed to respond to customer wants. Thus rather than the organization attempting to second guess customer needs, the empowered employee is ideally placed to both interpret and deliver the service needed (Potterield, 1999).

Indeed empowerment meets both the need to gain greater commitment and allows the flexibility and responsiveness needed in service encounters where it is difficult to predict customer requirements (Barbee and Bott, 1991). Thus organizations which prioritize customer service quality objectives and the value of the customer repeat visit (Parson, 1995) turn to empowerment as a valuable technique. The series of advertisements by Marriott Hotels, which are discussed later in Chapter 3 (Figure 3.1), is a good example of the aims and aspirations of employer organizations. Idealized stories demonstrate the link between employee and organizational ambitions to 'do whatever it takes', and the result is customer service which exceeds the expectations of the customer.

Researching empowerment

It is possible to criticize these claims for the benefits of employee empowerment both for industry in general, and to service operators in particular, on two levels. First, even with a normative frame of reference these more evangelical claims for empowerment need further analysis. The model itself seems to offer a simple two-stage notion of the process. Empower the employee and organizational gains will ensue. This is, at best, over-simplistic; it fails to recognize that empowerment is being used as a term to describe many different initiatives that represent different experiences for the empowered. On a second level, these claims assume that all employees are motivated in the same way and come to work with same sets of needs and wants. For some people work represents a central part of their lives and plays a key role in defining who they are; for other people work is at the periphery of their lives and interests. It is unlikely that all individuals will react equally to initiatives that claim to be empowering. There is a need to both understand that empowerment has a motivational dimension (Conger and Kanungo, 1988) and to understand the psychology of empowerment (Siegall and Gardner, 2000).

The normative approach to human resource management in general and empowerment in particular can be criticized because it is informed by a 'unitarist perspective' (Legge, 1995) and provides little by way of critical analysis within the employment relationship. Thus, much of the normative and evangelical claims build on assumptions about the employment relationship that take as read a community of interests between employee and employer. Bassett (1986: 174) has provided a useful insight into these assumptions, 'It is no longer us the workers against them the management, it is now us our company against them the competition'.

These normative approaches to employee empowerment provide plenty of advice about how employees should be empowered, but they fail to consider issues of stakeholder difference in organizations. They rarely discuss issues about power and conflict, nor consider the sources of commitment; rarely do they discuss the tensions inherent in the setting of boundaries within which the empowered operate. The analysis of empowerment will be better informed if it is assumed that there is naturally a conflict of interest amongst organization members and that co-operation between people at different positions in the hierarchy is unlikely.

Having said that, it is necessary to study and develop the normative model of empowerment for several reasons. The normative model provides a model of expectations and aspirations for empowerment on which to base any analysis of empowerment in practice. Thus it is necessary to establish what empowerment *'should be like'*, before we study what empowerment is, or is not, in service organizations. Without this, researchers are in danger of treating empowerment as that which is labelled empowerment, with little sense of the difference from that which was previously practised in the management of employees.

A further reason for studying the normative model is that it does provide a managerial rhetoric that does guide – whether deliberate and planned or processual and pragmatic – the perceptions and actions of managers. In turn these actions shape the experiences of those who work within service industries, and is of sociological interest in the study of work. Particularly, it provides the basis for critical evaluation of initiatives introduced by management in service operations.

Finally, the normative model as expressed by writers in mainstream HRM is flawed and limited in its analysis of service industries specifically. The service encounter and the key role of front line staff, the recent emergence of a rhetoric espousing service quality as a now vital business strategy (Pannel Kerr Forster Associates, 1991), and the cluster of service features, particularly the role of intangibles; is largely ignored. Potterfield (1999: 6) affirms the need to adopt a critical approach to the study of empowerment, 'The critic strives to create an understanding of the texts that captures both the positive (i.e. freedom enhancing) and negative (i.e. dominance reinforcing) aspects, ideas, elements and influences'.

Criticism of some of the claims made by those who are promoting employee empowerment suggests the need to develop a multi-staged model for researching management initiatives that empower employees. Given the variations in meanings and definitions of empowerment, the need to explore both the form of empowerment being introduced and the state of being empowered as well as perceived organizational benefits that are supposed to flow from these changes, it becomes necessary to establish the meanings, perceptions and feelings of those immediately involved in initiatives that claim to be empowering. Figure 1.1 provides a visual representation of the key elements in the research agenda that has been developed (Lashley, 1996).

Many claims for empowerment fail to recognize the potential differences between individuals and their managers in perceptions of empowerment, and between individual employees in their needs to be empowered. Critically, these claims rarely address contextual factors in which managers and employees operate. They fail to address differences in the nature of the businesses and the markets in which they operate. This can be shown to have particular relevance when considering the nature of employee empowerment in service industries. The nature of the service offer being made to customers, the various competitive strategies, and the components of the brand are all likely to impact on the employment strategies that best 'fit' the organization's business context, and thereby the form that empowerment takes in particular businesses. Thus, even within the framework of a normative discourse, these models of empowerment are flawed and need refinement. Figure 1.1 suggests an alternative to the standard 'evangelical' two-stage model. This will be discussed more fully later because it provides a structure for some of the early chapters of the book.

The model outlined in Figure 1.1 assumes that there are many different meanings, interpretations and expectations of empowerment, but as the initiatives which claim to be empowering are derived and introduced by management to meet organizational and commercial objectives, it is necessary to develop an understanding of the meanings and myths that managers use when referring to empowerment.

The intentions and perceptions of managers vary and consequently the form of empowerment introduced will also vary and should, according to the normative model, fit with the managerial intentions. In particular the nature of the services on offer, discussed further in Chapter 12. In turn this should lead to some changes in the nature of the work undertaken by the empowered. At root the key question is, *'what can the empowered employees do now that they could not do before?'* The analysis needs to address issues about the nature of the changes – what decisions are employees able to make, are decisions limited to the task level, etc.,? Here the opportunity for a number of rhetorics to be at work becomes manifest. Managers may well label something as empowerment that is in effect regarded as an imposition of increased work responsibilities, or empowerment to make marginal decisions. Conger and Kanungo's (1989) relational aspect of empowerment is useful and the early chapters of the present book provide a discussion of examples of different forms of empowerment and suggested changes in working arrangements can be analysed.

Fundamentally, the feelings of the empowered have to be examined. If a key concept is that empowerment meets employee needs for power, and for personal efficacy, then employee feelings and responses to initiatives that claim to be empowering are crucial. These considerations are important in establishing differences between employees, their prior experiences, their expectations about and orientations to work, and their different needs for personal effectiveness and control (Siegall and Gardner, 2000). Also these considerations assist in exposing the potential tensions between employer aims and ambitions for empower-

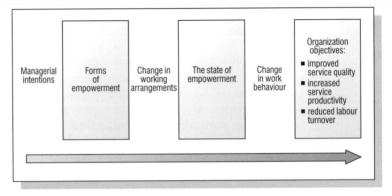

Figure 1.1 Key stages in empowerment in service organizations

ment and employee responses to the experience of being empowered.

Flowing from employee feelings about being empowered, is the response that this generates in employee performance. Even if employees do feel that changes introduced are empowering and improve their feelings of personal worth, does this result in changes in work behaviour? Do more committed workers increase their efforts, or do they just feel better about their work? To what are employees committed – is it the organization and its goals, local management, fellow workers, or the work itself? If a key assumption is that empowered employees are more committed, these questions need to be followed through.

Finally, even if empowered employees are committed to the organization, its goals and policies, and work harder, deliver improved quality, etc., what impact does this have on organizational performance anyway? The issue about the relationship between the management of human resources and subsequent improvements in organizational performance is an extremely complex one. It is frequently difficult to prove with any certainty that there is an absolute causal link between HRM policies and improved profitability, etc. Even the measures themselves are difficult to define because the definition of effective organizational performance depends to some extent on who is asking the question and the priorities that they apply. Different organization stakeholders may use different measures, and wider cultural assumptions may shape assumptions and perceptions. Manager perceptions and expectations about the perceived benefits of empowering employees are crucial, because the immediate organizational management will evaluate the success, or otherwise, of the initiative depending on whether the experience of empowerment matches expectations.

One of the key assumptions about the normative approach to human resource management in general, which can be applied to the specifics of employee empowerment within service industries, relates to the notion of fit with the organization's business strategy. Based round a 'classical' rational model (Whittington, 1993), the normative model of HRM as espoused by writers such as Guest (1987) and Storey (1992) sees the formulation of the organization's business strategy in relation to its trading environment resulting in strategies being 'cascaded downstream' to HRM strategy. The precise form and nature of the empowerment of the organization's employees should therefore be shaped by a match with the organization's strategies for dealing with its customers and gaining competitive advantage.

In service industries the precise nature of the service offered, the importance of tangibles and intangibles, the degree of standardization and customization of the service offered, the amount of contact between the service deliverer and customers, and the level of discretion to be exercised by employees shape the potential 'best fit' or match between the management of human resources manifest through the form of empowerment adopted within the firm. Thus any consideration of the normative approach to empowerment in service organizations must develop a model based on a thorough analysis of the organization's service offer to its customers, the marketing strategies being followed, together with the operational strategies.

On the basis of the development of a robust model of what empowerment *should* be like it will be possible to study what it is like in service organizations. From this systematic analysis it is possible to detect the forms and nature of the various rhetorics at work in an organization. As Watson (1994b) and Legge (1995) show, it is somewhat misleading to discuss human resource policies and behaviours as differences between 'rhetoric and reality', because it suggests that somehow the rhetoric is something unreal and that reality objectively exists. Both reality and rhetoric are social constructs (Keenoy and Anthony, 1992). In Watson's (1994a) account of practising managers it is possible to see a number of rhetorics at work in the organization. Thus a rhetoric of empowerment may exist alongside a rhetoric of profit maximization, with managers slipping from one rhetoric to the other.

Conclusion

This chapter has outlined many of the key themes of this book. Empowerment is a term widely used to mean a variety of different things. In the employment relationship, employee empowerment is said to be an essential feature of future work organizations. In the increasingly competitive future, organizations will be much more dependent on committed employees operating in flatter and more customer-focused structures. This set of claims is said to be of particular relevance to future service organizations, because the intangible aspects of service put much more reliance on the performance of front-line staff in meeting and exceeding customer service needs.

Investigating empowerment beyond these functional claims reveals that the empowerment has been used to describe a wide variety of forms, many of which overlap with initiatives which are said to be about employee involvement and participation, and which reveal many different managerial motives and intentions for their introduction. Chapter 3 attempts to resolve these overlaps and differences by developing a framework for both analysing employee involvement, employee participation, industrial democracy and employee empowerment; and for understanding the different forms and meanings for empowerment being applied by managers.

Finally this chapter has suggested that the somewhat simple links drawn by many advocates of empowerment need a more sophisticated and multi-staged approach. Clearly there are some important barriers to the introduction of empowerment, which, even in its own terms, may limit the benefits of empowerment. A process that fails to recognize precisely what form of empowerment best suits the organizational context, or one that merely removes layers of management and renames the new relationship as empowerment will create tensions, which may well have negative effects. However, even if the approach is carefully planned, consistent with organizational business strategies and introduced into a sympathetic organizational culture, empowerment will not necessarily result in improved organizational performance. Managerial intentions, the form introduced, the changed working arrangements, impacts on the empowered and resulting changes to employee commitment will not automatically result in improved organization performance. Each step needs to be investigated in detail, exploring both the objective nature of the changes and the subjective responses of managers and employees to them.

CHAPTER 2

The psychology of empowerment

- **Motivational empowerment**
- **The empowerment process**
- **Attitudes and empowerment**
- **The context of empowerment**

Initiatives in the management of employees that claim to be empowering have much in common with other techniques, such as employee involvement and employee participation (Siegall and Gardner, 2000). Many of the forms that are introduced under the name of empowerment are both varied, covering a wide range of initiatives, and shared by forms which claim to be involving and participatory. That said, one of the defining features of empowerment, and a core feature of any claim to be different from involvement and participation, is that empowerment is supposed to produce a psychological state. Empowerment by definition needs people to feel empowered (Heslin, 1999).

Empowered employees are supposed to feel in greater control (Koberg *et al.*, 1999), have a greater sense of personal power together with the freedom to use that power (Potterfield, 1999), a sense of personal efficacy and self determination (Alpander, 1991). They have to feel that they have power and can make a difference; that they have choices and can exercise choice (Johnson, 1993). Unlike disempowered or powerless employees, empowerment provides employees with a sense of autonomy, authority and control (Heslin, 1999) together with the abilities, resources and discretion to make decisions. Empowerment, therefore, claims to produce an emotional state in employees from which the additional commitment and effort stem.

Certainly the increasing requirement of service sector employers for employees to manage their emotions in meeting customer service expectations does intensify the inputs that employees bring to the work (Rafiq and Ahmed, 1998a; Mann, 1999). Thus in front-line service jobs employees not only have to provide the physical labour and skills required for serving the customer, they must also supply the appropriate emotions and body language that will encourage customers to feel welcome, wanted and delighted (Hochschild, 1983). The provision of emotional labour has intensified, particularly in the service sector, as firms have recognized that effective competitive strategy via service quality enhancement requires employees to provide more than standardized and scripted interactions with customers. Effective service delivery requires employees to genuinely feel a commitment to the customer, that goes 'beyond smiling' (Adelmann *et al.*, 1994) and this requires the employee to manage their feelings so as to achieve the required state (Hochschild, 1983).

Whilst these general ambitions are clearly stated in the literature, there is little discussion of how the state of empowerment might be created, nor the *contextual factors* likely to enhance or inhibit its development (Corsun and Enz, 1999). Similarly, the processes through which employees develop attitudes more positive to the organization and its management are rarely discussed. Finally, what is required of the management and organizational context to produce the psychological state of empowerment? Indeed, many of the discussions and case studies rarely consider the psychological or 'motivational dimension' of empowerment. The following sections attempt to provide some discussion of the concepts that help to develop an understanding of how empowerment might bring about changes, and highlight those contradictions both within the conceptual models themselves and within the realities of organizational life that might inhibit the required changes.

Motivational empowerment

Aspirations for empowerment include a change in employees' feelings of personal power and control, together with more positive attitudes to the organization and increased commitment to its policies and goals (Heslin, 1999). In particular, in service organizations, it is hoped that empowered employees will display sufficient confidence to do whatever is necessary to meet customer service needs, they will understand and manage potential tensions between organizational commitments to customer service quality, brand rigidities and profits; and will be loyal employees who will 'pay back' training costs by remaining with the organization. Much of the more evangelical and normative literature takes these benefits as axiomatic. The empowerment of employees will result in the desired outcomes (Barry, 1993; Johnson and Redmond, 1998). There is little by way of an explanation of how these changes in working relationships will result in changes in feelings, attitudes and behaviour.

Conger and Kanungo (1988: 471) do, however, attempt to provide some explanations of the *empowerment process* and signal up those contextual factors that are likely to influence the development of feelings of powerlessness and feelings of empowerment in organizational life. First they draw a distinction between concepts of empowerment that are *relational* and those that are *motivational*. Relational constructs stress the power relationships between managers and employees. The following chapters (4, 5, 6 and 7) engage with some of these dimensions of empowerment by exploring different forms of empowerment. Conger and Kanungo state that this focus has led to the development of approaches to the relationship between employees that equate, even out or redistribute, power between managers and employees. Techniques involve more participation and involvement, and the merging of terms where empowerment is said to mean the same as participation and involvement (Cotton, 1993). The key problem, they suggest, is that these meanings do not address the experiences of empowered employees. Hence, empowerment can be used as an operational rhetoric to cover quite different degrees of involvement, forms, levels, ranges of issues to be covered, and power to influence decisions.

Empowerment as a motivational construct relies more on an understanding of empowerment through individuals' internal needs for power and control (McClelland, 1975) and feelings of personal efficacy (Bandura, 1986). Under this model, individuals perceive themselves as having power when they are able to control events or situations and deal effectively with the

Hospitality, Leisure & Tourism Series

environments and situations that they encounter. Conversely, individuals are likely to feel powerless in situations that they cannot influence or where they do not have the time, resources or skills to be effective. From a motivational perspective, power is intrinsicly based on a need for self-determination, and managers should adopt techniques that strengthen employees' needs for self-determination and personal efficacy. Sparrowe (1994) adds that to be effective in generating feelings of empowerment, the empowered have to both value that which they have been empowered to do, and feel that their empowerment encompasses meaningful actions.

Under this motivational construct of empowerment, employees are enabled through the development of employee personal efficacy. Implicitly this means that employee perceptions of their ability to cope in situations in which they value success – by exercising a range of judgements and skills that they themselves value – become paramount. Effective management needs to be aware that heightened motivation to complete organizational tasks and aspire to greater organizational goals, such as increased customer satisfaction, will be achieved through the development of a 'strong sense of personal efficacy' (Conger and Kanungo, 1988: 474). Using the motivational construct, Conger and Kanungo define empowerment 'as a process of enhancing feelings of self-efficacy among organizational members through the identification of conditions that foster powerlessness and through their removal by both formal organizational practices and informal techniques of providing efficacy information' (1988: 474).

For them, relational models of empowerment may or may not provide the necessary conditions for the empowerment of employees. Thus a redistribution of power over organizational resources with more participative forms of empowerment or the ability to influence decisions via empowerment through involvement may provide an environment in which employees develop a sense of personal efficacy; they are not guarantees of feelings of empowerment in themselves.

Whilst this view of empowerment can be criticized because it takes for granted much about organizational life and plays down the tensions inherent in empowerment, it does provide a useful explanation of how empowerment *should* work. It provides a model against which organizational practices can be compared with experiences of the empowered. If the analysis of empowerment is to move beyond the face value of initiatives that are labelled empowerment, it must provide a robust model of the conditions in which employees develop their sense of personal efficacy.

Conger and Kanungo (1988) identify feelings of powerlessness as the key target of initiatives designed to empower employees. Although this may be an important motive, and one consistent with the suggestion that empowerment is a necessary ingredient to the management of organizations in modern internationally competitive economies, it is not the only motive. Service organizations have a particularly urgent need to engage employees on an emotional level. The nature of service requires that employees are committed to delighting the customer and this requires the display of the appropriate emotions of welcome, care, and concern for customer needs. To be most effective, employees need to both believe in their own efficacy and central significance in making the service encounter a success, and in summoning up the appropriate feelings required of the interaction. The 'empowering process' has a key role in developing feelings of efficacy and in managing the feelings required.

The empowerment process

Figure 2.1 reproduces Conger and Kanungo's representation of the five stages in the process of empowerment. **Stage 1** involves consideration of those aspects of the organization and its operation that are leading employees to feel disempowered. This might include a range of bureaucratic procedures, an overly tall organization structure that limits their ability to take decisions, or a command and control culture that imposes decisions from above. It could be that supervisors operate in an autocratic manner, or treat employees with the 'thinly disguised contempt' mentioned by Nicholls (1995). In other situations, the reward system limits initiative because such a system is arbitrary and does not reward employees who are effective. The nature of the work itself may be restricted and standardized in such a way as to limit opportunities for discretion or for the employee to feel that they can make a difference.

Stage 2 involves a range of managerial techniques that will assist the employee to enhance their feelings of efficacy. This might include the introduction of more participatory management techniques, though these again need to be set within a framework of analysis that recognizes the range of diversity of these arrangements. It involves setting goals, providing adequate systems of providing feedback, reward systems that reward competence, management styles that are supportive and design jobs to involve diversity, variety and allow the application of discretion.

Stage 3 provides self-efficacy information to subordinates from a variety of sources. Providing information about how the individual's personal efficacy is developing is deemed to be an important feature in developing the individual's perceptions and belief in their own efficacy. Information on personal efficacy comes from the personal evaluations of their own development, from watching others, from verbal feedback and through a supportive emotional environment that stresses trust and builds confidence. This in turn leads on to **Stage 4,** in which empowered employees strengthen their efforts and develop an expectancy of personal efficacy. This in turn leads to behavioural change which results in continued efforts to achieve organizational goals (**Stage 5**).

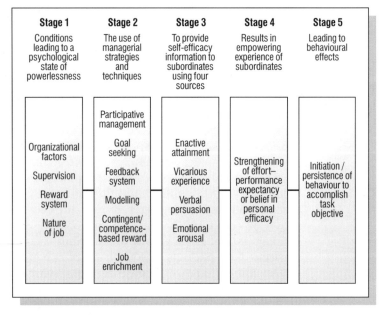

Stage 1	Stage 2	Stage 3	Stage 4	Stage 5
Conditions leading to a psychological state of powerlessness	The use of managerial strategies and techniques	To provide self-efficacy information to subordinates using four sources	Results in empowering experience of subordinates	Leading to behavioural effects
Organizational factors	Participative management			
	Goal seeking	Enactive attainment		
Supervision	Feedback system	Vicarious experience	Strengthening of effort–performance expectancy or belief in personal efficacy	Initiation / persistence of behaviour to accomplish task objective
Reward system	Modelling	Verbal persuasion		
Nature of job	Contingent/ competence-based reward	Emotional arousal		
	Job enrichment			

Figure 2.1 Five stages in the empowerment process. *Source:* Conger and Kanungo (1988)

This focus on the motivational concept of empowerment does allow a consideration of the possibility of employees developing a sense of personal efficacy, even in situations where there has been no alteration to relational power. The notion of 'empowerment via commitment', or Lockwood's (1996) enabling empowerment are consistent with this. Organizations can develop this sense of personal efficacy in employees if there is an organizational commitment to identifying those policies and practices that create barriers to its development, changes are made so as to overcome the barriers and employees are encouraged to track their development. It also allows empowerment to be seen as a tool for developing individuals, even in situations where the structure and context do not encourage extensive employee participation or involvement in the decision-making process.

Again, this model can be criticized because it fails to recognize some of the contradictions inherent in the empowerment of employees, particularly in branded service organizations. For example, many organizations in the service sector who have introduced employee empowerment have done so in circumstances where the organization is making a tightly defined branded offer to its customers. In these cases, employees may be encouraged to 'delight the customer' by meeting customer service needs as they arise, but they may not do anything 'out of brand' where customers might become confused because they are getting different experiences in different establishments. In these situations empowered employees are in a difficult position and have to manage the tension inherent in their relationship to both customers and the organization. If tips, or commission, are also elements in these relationships, the positive benefits of employee empowerment and the associated sense of personal efficacy may be counter balanced by negative feelings of pressure and stress. Thus managers may be constrained by the nature of the service offer being made to customers in the extent that they can manipulate job design and rewards so as to generate feelings of personal efficacy.

A further difficulty with the general sweep of Conger and Kanungo's model is that it fails to recognize the complexity of the chain that they are attempting to build. There is no consideration of the contextual factors that may restrain managers in their analysis of the benefits of empowering employees – labour market conditions, business strategy and the nature of the service offer to customers are all likely to influence the way managers perceive empowerment and the benefits supposedly generated. Similarly, some of the linkages are not foregone conclusions whereby one step leads naturally to another. For example managers introduce a form of empowerment that changes working practices, but employee experiences of these many not result in the development of a sense of personal efficacy. Even if employees do develop this sense of personal efficacy and permanently change their work behaviour as in Stage 5, there is no guarantee that organizational effectiveness will be increased, because there may be factors internally or externally that are more influential in determining the organization's success.

These reservations limit the overall utility of their observations, but Conger and Kanungo do provide a model for understanding how personal efficacy might be developed at an individual level.

Whilst recognizing the significance of content theorists in suggesting that discomfort with disempowerment may stem from inner need states, for example, the need for power (McClelland, 1975) and the need for self actualization (Maslow, 1954), they look to process theory for explanations of how variations in the strengths of these needs might occur. Lawler's (1973) expectancy theory and Bandura's (1977, 1986) self-efficacy theory provide a model for suggesting that feelings of empowerment will develop by employees' evaluating the situation in which they find themselves. Put simply this assumes a two-stage process empowerment to result in changes in employee behaviour. First the employee has to believe that their efforts will result in an improvement in their performance and second, that their improved performance will produce valued outcomes.

Thomas and Velthouse (1990) also suggest that employee expectancies are likely to be key to the development of feelings of empowerment. They suggest a four-dimensional model based on a cognitive assessment of their own *competence* to operate effectively in the situation, the *impact* that they as individual employees can make to effective performance, the *meaningfulness* that they attach to the tasks they undertake as empowered employees, and the *choice* that they can exercise. In other words the state of empowerment is likely to be a consequence of the individual's assessment of their ability to be effective, the feeling that they can make a difference in a task which they perceive as worthwhile, and that they have some degree of freedom to act as they see fit in the situation.

Empowerment involves both the objective facts of what a person is empowered to do and the subjective feelings that the individual experiences as a result. Initiatives introduced by management will, therefore, be tested against the experience of being empowered and the sense of personal efficacy created. No matter which form empowerment takes, initiatives entitled empowerment will be exposed as empty rhetoric if they do not produce feelings of being empowered in the recipients of empowerment. Thus the 'boundaries set for the empowered' (van Oudtshoorn and Thomas, 1993), the organizational processes in which the empowered work and the management of those processes become crucial factors in the development of personal efficacy and empowerment.

This raises another issue rarely discussed about empowerment. Individual differences between employees are also factors that need to be considered. Orientations to work and needs are likely to be important factors in the way an individual interprets and responds to a particular change (Alpander, 1991). Personal experience and previous status may shape the approach to an initiative. Thus one employee may see empowering initiatives as a positive development allowing greater scope for personal growth, whilst others might view the same initiative as an increased burden, demanding an unacceptable increase in emotional contribution to the job.

There are therefore likely to be a number of problems in assuming that a given set of changes is likely to produce a state of empowerment. Changes will be judged in so far as they deliver responsibilities and authority that are worth having to individuals who have the competence to be effective and value the outcome of their efforts. Individuals will approach empowerment with different personal experiences and different affiliations to work, and these will all influence the way that individuals achieve the state of empowerment.

Finally, the form of empowerment introduced does have an impact on the development of feelings of personal efficacy because they represent different experiences for employees and are not equally effective in removing powerlessness. The degrees of involvement in different schemes vary in the passivity and activity which employees experience. The receiving of information may help employees better understand the organization's policies and objectives, but employees are less involved in actively practising personal efficacy than in schemes in which they jointly make decisions. Similarly, schemes vary in the extent that all employees take part. Representative forms may develop personal efficacy in the employee representatives who participate, but those whom they represent may be largely untouched by the experience. Task level empowerment may allow greater personal efficacy over immediate work experiences, but in circumstances where both immediate operational targets and long term strategic decisions are made by managers and 'handed down', employees may feel that the boundaries within which they operate and the range of issues over which they are empowered are too narrow or constraining. Finally where employees are empowered to make suggestions, or have limited power to make their decisions stick, it will be difficult to develop personal efficacy, particularly where managers intervene to countermand decisions or do not act on suggestions.

Attitudes and empowerment

Although focused on a range of management techniques introduced in the 1980s and described by the authors as the 'new industrial relations', the work of Kelly and Kelly (1990) casts some interesting insights into both the aspirations of managers when introducing an array of more participatory and involving techniques (many in common with those discussed in later chapters) for managing employees, and the reaction that these initiatives had on employee attitudes. As with initiatives entitled employee involvement, participation and empowerment, the initiatives studied were frequently introduced with the aspiration that they would lead to changes in employee attitudes and behaviour, and these would lead to changes in quality, productivity and support for company policies. Ultimately, the aspiration for these changes was the 'replacement of the class struggle with the struggle for markets' (1990: 26) and a reduction in 'Us and Them' attitudes.

The findings of their analysis from an array of studies suggests that whilst workers often hold positive attitudes about the form of the changes – share ownership schemes, quality circles, etc. – 'this positive response does not generalize to more affect the underlying climate of management–worker relations' (1990: 26). Thus, while initiatives introduced under the name of empowerment may well produce a positive response in employees and may well increase satisfaction with the working environment, there is no guarantee that employee commitment to the organization or its policies will increase.

Using models from social psychology, Kelly and Kelly suggest that the development of 'us and them' attitudes can be located in the relationships between group memberships to which individuals belong. In most organizational contexts, operatives and managers belong to different groups. Any one individual belongs to an 'in-group' and through group membership develops attitudes to individuals who belong to other groups – 'out-groups'. Attitudes are likely to become more conflictual in situations where there appear differences in status and rewards and competition over scarce resources. Kelly and Kelly examine the conditions necessary to bring about change in these circumstances using the discipline of social psychology and attitude change in inter-group contexts.

Figure 2.2 highlights three possible routes to the change of attitudes that would reduce notions of 'us and them', and thereby the development of shared goals and commitment to the organization. The **first route** suggests that increased worker–management contact might help to shift attitudes away from stereotypes and produce more positive attitudes between inter-group memberships. Some initiatives that claim to be empowering do involve operatives and managers working together in quality circles, or in teams. Potentially, these have the possibility to develop favourable attitudes to the organization amongst employees. However, it is worth remembering that not all these initiatives involve employees equally with managers – thus representative forms of empowerment only involve a section of the workforce and unless they are particularly powerful opinion-formers, the majority of employees would have attitudes unchanged. Similarly in service organizations, multi-unit businesses have particular problems in the focus of commitment. Work group operation, team briefings, etc., may well develop positive attitudes between the immediate unit managers and workforce, but attitudes to the wider organization remain unchanged because there are limited opportunities to overcome the 'us and them' attitudes at unit/head office level.

The **second route** suggests that attitudes between conflicting groups will change if they are both faced with a challenge, or goal, that is common to both groups and that neither can overcome, or achieve, on their own. Clearly, appeals to common competitors, nationally or internationally, are attempting to persuade employees that they have a common goal and threat. These claims can be seen as unconvincing in situations where the benefits and rewards of international success are perceived to be unequal or where employees have little choice in the initiative. For empowerment to be successful in changing attitudes, there needs to be a high level of trust between members of different groups. Thus managers and employees need to trust in each other's motives and that they will mutually benefit from co-operation.

The **third route** to attitude change suggests that changes in behaviour lead to changes in attitudes. Thus more participatory management techniques that involve working co-operatively between managers and employees may result in changes in attitudes, because it is difficult to maintain attitudes that are in conflict with behaviour. Hence employees and managers who experience working arrangements based on co-operation would find it difficult to hold adversarial attitudes because of the psychological tension caused. Thus cognitive dissonance theory suggests that when attitudes are in conflict with behaviour it is easier to amend attitudes to come in line with behaviour. Empowered employees might, therefore, develop more positive attitudes to the organization through the experience of working co-operatively with managers in work groups, work teams and quality circles. That said, attitude change is unlikely to occur if individuals feel that they have no freedom of choice in the behaviour.

These three possible routes to attitude change are useful in showing how empowerment could help to change employees' attitudes to the organization, and thereby generate more employee commitment to the organization. They also suggest that their analysis of studies of a range of initiatives having much

Hospitality, Leisure & Tourism Series

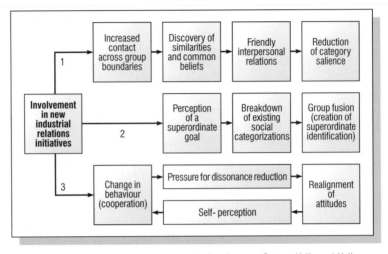

Figure 2.2 Three possible routes to attitude change. *Source:* Kelly and Kelly (1990)

in common with empowerment shows that changes in employee attitudes to the organization have largely not occurred. The reason they suggest is due to the presence of several barriers to attitude change within the context in which these initiatives are introduced.

- A *lack of choice* for employees about the adoption and form of the initiative, together with a lack of choice as to whether they are involved once the initiative is introduced, limits the power of persuasion. This lack of choice is unlikely to result in attitude change because cognitive dissonance mechanisms will not come into play. Workers compelled to act in a certain way do not experience the psychological tension likely to result in attitude change. Thus an important ingredient in the successful introduction of empowerment that results in attitude change has to be choice, negotiation and developing a sense of employee ownership of the changes.
- Similarly, a *lack of trust* between the parties can be a considerable barrier to attitude change. Organizations that have experienced conflict between managers and the workforce, or rapid organization change say via redundancies or changes in working practices, may find it difficult easily to overcome the hostility felt by members of different groups. Perceptions of the motives for the change are likely to be important. Thus if one group, say operatives, perceive the change as being brought in because the other group (manage-

ment) genuinely want to improve relations and share benefits with employees, attitude change is likely to ensue. If, on the other hand, employees feel that empowerment is being introduced as an underhand way of making them work harder or reducing costs, attitude change is less likely.

- *Unequal status and outcomes* is a barrier to a change in attitudes. If employees perceive themselves and managers as having unequal status in the form of empowerment – say as in quality circles, team briefings, suggestion schemes – employees are less likely to change attitudes. Similarly if they perceive imbalance of either the inputs in effort or benefits resulting from the initiative, attitude change is less likely to occur. The introduction of empowerment can be perceived as involving the intensification of work without a compensatory increase in rewards. For some, the experience may produce more negative attitudes to the organization. Several published case studies (Cunningham and Hyman, 1999; Collins, 1999; Holden, 1999) show how a failure to manage these changes can produce the opposite effect than the one intended.

- *Lack of institutional support* is also identified as presenting a barrier to attitudinal change. To be successful in generating positive attitudes and commitment to the organization, empowerment needs to be part of an established and long term approach to the management of people. As Chapter 5 shows in the discussion on quality circles, these initiatives often fail because they are introduced as a quick fix to a problem, but are not sustained over a long period. Once managers stop acting on the suggestions, or fail to give the initiative the resources needed, employees quickly get the message and they too lose interest.

This section has argued that for initiatives that claim to be empowering to result in employees changing their attitudes about the organization, social psychology provides a means of explaining how these processes might occur and the obstacles that might prevent the desired changes taking place. That said, this is a somewhat mono-causal explanation of attitude development and behavioural change. Again, it is possible to criticize the approach for having a simplistic view of organizational life, and the conflict pressures on managers. It could be argued for example that managers are only interested in empowerment so long as it preserves their status and rewards. The contradictions inherent in empowering employees, or managers, within limits or where individuals are required to balance a range of mutually contradictory objectives do present systematic difficulties for attitudinal change. Hochschild (1993) criticizes social psychology for studying employee attitudes and job satisfaction whilst leaving employee emotions untouched. Yet the management of emotions and emotional labour is 'a large part of what trainers train and supervisors supervise' (1993: xii). It is true of organizational life in general, 'but is far more true in the rapidly expanding service sector – department stores, airports, hotels, leisure worlds, hospitals, welfare office and schools' (1993: xii).

The context of empowerment

The work of both Kelly and Kelly, and Conger and Kanungo have suggested that attitude and motivational empowerment are likely to succeed or fail as a result of the actions of managers and the organizational context in which an initiative is set. They have both suggested that managerial blind faith in an initiative, whatever the name, that fails to address the experiences of the people working under the new arrangement is bound to fail.

Spreitzer (1996) found that middle managers who were the subjects of empowerment were more likely to develop a sense of being empowered in circumstances where they understood their role and the boundaries within which they operated. They needed a strong supportive, trust based, and participative culture in which their immediate bosses acted as mentors. Having access to appropriate information and a good level of communications through the organization were all necessary ingredients. In another study (Spreitzer *et al.*, 1997), it was maintained that no one dimension was important; all were important. Siegall and Gardner (2000: 706) conclude, 'If an organisation wants all the benefits of empowerment, it needs to provide an environment that will help create all the components of empowerment'.

Taking the Thomas and Velthouse (1990) model and building in Spreitzer's (1995) refinements, Siegall and Gardner (2000) tested the links with immediate supervision and management relations with employees. Thomas and Velthouse claimed that the internalized state of being empowered is multi-dimensional. Empowered employees need to feel that they are undertaking meaningful work and exercise choice in tasks that allows them to be personally effective, with a sense of competence. Siegall and Gardner suggest that organizations could have a positive impact on employees' *sense of competence*. 'Effective person-job match, a good training programme, and more opportunities for feedback built are but three ways that employers can contribute to this important aspect of empowerment' (p. 713). They also establish that *meaningfulness* is associated with contextual factors. A working environment that values all contributions and values collective success is likely to build a sense that each contribution is meaningful. Similarly, building in Spreitzer's dimension relating to communications with both the immediate supervisor and the company, they conclude that 'supervisory behaviour that increased subordinate's self-worth and negotiating latitude increased a person's sense of control and empowerment' (p. 713). Thus in each of the cornerstone dimensions, organizations can influence employees' sense of empowerment. It is necessary for organizations wishing to gain from the benefits of empowerment to recognize the crucial concept here. As Siegall and Gardner summarize, 'In order for one to act empowered, one needs to perceive that he or she is empowered, and that perception is influenced by organizational context' (p. 715).

Cunningham and Hyman (1999) provide a useful case study of an approach that reflects the problems that can occur when an organization attempts empowerment in a half-hearted manner and fails to address these dimensions. Parcelco, a national parcel distribution service, introduced an initiative aimed at empowering line managers and supervisors. They introduced empowerment during a period of intense competition from national and local firms. As a way of trying to cut costs and make the service more locally sensitive to service needs, the company went through a period of decentralization and cost cutting. There had been job losses and a strategy to cut costs as a way of meeting financial targets immediately prior to the introduction of empowerment. In these circumstances, training programmes, support systems and monitoring and evaluation were minimal. The consequences were that both managers and employees interviewed by the researchers were highly dissatisfied with empowerment. Most importantly narrow financial priorities tended to prioritize operations at the cost of quality and employee development. They quote the personnel manager as saying, 'Line managers face a lot of basic pressures like getting the parcels out. There is also conflict between operations and training. IiP had gone by the wayside because of other priorities' (1999: 201). A line manager interviewed also reinforced this view; he is reported as saying, 'I have to get the job done as easily and cheaply with as little resources' (p. 201). This pressure to prioritize operational and financial goals is a barrier to the success of empowerment because resources are not made available to ensure success.

These findings are consistent with general approaches to managing people within the service industries. Many firms operate what Johnston (1989a) has described as 'cost leader competitive strategies'. In these circumstances firms aim to compete on the basis of cost minimization. In particular, labour costs as measured by direct costs of labour through wages, hours worked, and training are kept to a minimum. Training is a crucial means by which employees develop the skills and confidence to bring about a sense of being empowered. Self-efficacy regarding one's job is one of the key dimensions of developing a sense of empowerment, using Thomas and Velthouse's (1990) model mentioned earlier. Yet in the UK in general, and amongst service sector firms in particular, cost leadership drives HR strategies that minimize training, or in some cases, cut it completely.

For example, the Hospitality Training Foundation (1999) survey of training in the UK confirmed that, although there had been improvements since their earlier study (HTF, 1996), much training was still largely aimed at simple induction and meeting statutory requirements. The 1999 survey claimed that, whilst many firms were providing training, not all employees were receiving training, and management, supervisory and craft employees were more likely to be trained by their employers. Eaglen *et al.* (1999) show that these approaches are not without cost. They argue that there is a cost to not training people in the sector. So cutting the training budget may appear to be a cost reduction but may incur added, though hidden, extra costs. Certainly, failing to provide training and support will cause a major barrier to empowerment.

This has a particularly British context, a consequence of business strategies that Armstrong (1987) claims are due to the dominance of the financial community in the UK, and Keep and Rainbird (2000: 187) call a 'shareholder rather than a stakeholder model of capitalism'. In the past, short-termism and immediate bottom-line considerations dominated. More recently, consistent service quality and employee development become more central, giving a 'quality leadership strategy' (Johnston, 1998a) or a 'learning organization strategy' (Keep and Rainbird, 2000). In particular, personal development is essential if managers and employees are to develop a sense of personal efficacy and commitment to the service encounter.

These contextual factors relating to general management strategies and priorities will create considerable barriers to empowerment and require firms to adopt quite different approaches than those currently practised in many service firms (Corsun and Enz, 1999). Strategies aimed at quality leadership or at creating a learning organization put employee contribution to business success in a more central role. It is difficult to envisage empowerment being successful in an organization that does not have a total commitment to empowering employees. For empowerment to be effective it requires the appropriate culture and climate of trust that allows employees to grow and learn from their mistakes.

At a more practical level, managers themselves are part of the hierarchy that had created the sense of disempowerment, or that is to be changed as a result of altering the relationship between management and front-line staff, and as such are key making empowerment work. The work of Siegall and Gardner (2000) mentioned earlier stresses the relationship with the immediate supervisor as having an important impact on developing the psychological state of empowerment. Heslin (1999) also demonstrates that management action in developing the psychological state of empowerment is crucial in empowered organizations. In fact Kizilos (1990) sees managers as a key barrier, because often empowerment of subordinates changes the nature of their role and removes some of their power, or at least requires a different style of managing that is more consultative and participative than directive. Interestingly initiatives that empower elements of the management structure but leave the tiers above and below unchanged experience difficulties. Proctor *et al.* (1999) show how attempts to empower some managers in a Health Service Trust failed because senior managers did not appreciate the changes needed in their own approach. Similarly, my own study of empowering multi-unit managers in McDonald's Restaurants (1995a) experienced difficulties because senior managers intervened whenever problems occurred and the immediate 'empowered' manager was not allowed to solve the difficulties as he/she saw fit.

That said, managers, at all levels, play a crucial role in developing the context in which empowerment can be developed. As discussed earlier, the provision of training, communication processes, and a culture of trust are some of the necessary ingredients for the psychological state of empowerment to be created. Furthermore, Figure 2.3 highlights a process that can be used to bring on the individual to reach a state of empowerment by taking individuals successively through a series of stages that alter the relationship and builds confidence. The key point here is that this process can be aimed at individual employees and can therefore be helpful in a traditional command and control structure. It is taken and adapted from a model promoted in McDonald's Restaurants' management development programme.

The approach does not necessarily change the relationship between managers and employees, but it does show that individuals can be developed to take on more responsibility and be given more authority for specific projects or aspects of the business. Careful scrutiny shows that the stages move through the directive, consultative and participative processes that are discussed more fully in Chapter 3. The key point that is reflected

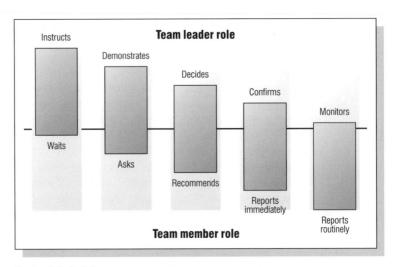

Figure 2.3 Building empowerment

in this and other chapters is that managers need to carefully consider the state of empowerment and how it will be created. All the case study evidence suggests that this is the key to success or failure.

Conclusions

Empowerment of all employees, whether they be management or operative level, assume as a defining feature, a change in their feelings. Empowered employees are said to develop a sense of their personal efficacy, and hold positive attitudes to the organization that will provide more commitment to the organization's goals and objectives. Furthermore, techniques that empower employees are said to correct negative feelings that are a consequence of organizational life in Western organization structures. In particular it is hoped that service organizations will benefit from the use of empowerment because it engages the employee in such a way as to assist them to manage their feelings so as to contribute the desired emotional response to customers.

A sense of personal efficacy needs to be nurtured by management. The conditions for the development of employees' awareness of efficacy is said to be congruent on both the existence of internal conditions which create the desired environment for efficacy to develop, and processes which require employees to build up the necessary competences to be effective and which inform them of their development. Thus those initiatives that do not consider issues of job design, organization structure, rewards, etc., are likely to be less effective in developing a sense of efficacy.

The form of empowerment introduced frequently involves changes in the relationships between managers and employees. The assumption being that changes to the traditional command and control relationships is a necessary condition for developing more commitment. The work of Kelly and Kelly (1990) throws some interesting light on the conditions that are required to produce attitudinal change. Though their work is not specifically about empowerment, many of the initiatives that they investigated have much in common with empowerment. They claim that changes in the relationships between managers and employees do not necessarily result in positive attitudes to the organization, because the necessary conditions for attitudinal change are rarely considered by managers when they introduce new management practices that are designed to empower employees.

Finally this chapter has argued that organizations wishing to gain from the benefits of empowerment need to address the psychological needs of empowered employees. In particular, the organization has to recognize the need to consider employee feelings. The organization can help develop its employees' needs to feel competent and exercise choice undertaking tasks that they feel are meaningful and make an impact, with appropriate training, communication and feedback on performance in a trust culture that celebrates growth and development. Crucially, it is management's actions that determine how the initiative works in practice.

CHAPTER 3

The relational dimension of empowerment

- Common ground
- Participation, involvement, democracy and empowerment
- A framework of analysis
- Managerial meanings of empowerment
- Empowerment and rhetoric

A review of accounts of the applications of empowerment in service organizations reveals that the term covers a wide array of initiatives that are likely to represent different experiences and benefits to both employers and employees. Clearly, empowering employees to 'take responsibility for the service encounter' (Corsun and Enz, 1999), setting quality circles in the Accor Group, and organizing autonomous work team in Harvester Restaurants (Ashness and Lashley, 1995) may all be described as empowering employees but they ask different things of employees and clearly serve different expectations of employers.

A common feature of case studies and much of the academic literature is that they assume empowerment is largely a 'relational construct' as defined by Conger and Kanungo (1988). That is, they describe empowerment as being chiefly concerned with changing the relationship between managers and employees. These comments are true of both Foy (1994) as an enthusiastic advocate, and Collins (1999) as an ardent critic. For Foy empowerment represents a way of democratizing the working relationship, whereas Collins and the other critics are concerned for precisely the opposite reason, namely that it is *not* an extension of industrial democracy. The common feature of these and most other writings is that they miss the motivational and psychological dimensions discussed in Chapter 2 and the feelings of being empowered highlighted in Chapter 9.

This chapter discusses the relational dimensions of empowerment within the wider context of discussions of initiatives that take forms that are similar to those introduced under the broad heading of human resource management. Some notions of HRM identify empowerment within the 'soft' approach to the management of human resources (Storey, 1992). Indeed, many are also discussed under the headings of employee involvement (Marchington *et al.*, 1992), and employee participation (Geary, 1994). Other writers use the terms of employee empowerment and employee involvement (Cotton, 1993), and employee empowerment and employee participation (Rodrigues, 1994) almost interchangeably, with little attempt to define the boundaries between them. This chapter locates employee empowerment within this range of initiatives, particularly showing where the initiatives are both similar to and different from each other.

Interest in employee empowerment is inextricably linked with a number of initiatives in management stemming initially from the United States that coincided with the growth in the use of the term 'human resource management' in US and British literature relating to the management of people in work organizations. It is not the intention here to enter into the debates about the significance of HRM as a distinct set of practices (Guest, 1987) or whether this is merely a new title for personnel management with little difference in practice (Sissons, 1994). Chapter 12 will touch on these issues in more depth as a strand in the discussion of empowerment and the strategic integration of the management of human resources with wider business objectives. This chapter is concerned with developing a framework for understanding the 'relational dimension' of empowerment discussed by Conger and Kanungo (1988). This relational dimension describes the form that manager/employee relations take under empowerment.

Common ground

The key point is that initiatives that claim to be empowering share many assumptions and roots with employee involvement, employee participation and increased industrial democracy (Bach and Sissons, 2000). They reflect both continuity and change in ideas about the management of employees. Concern for ensuring employee commitment and to improve motivation so as to improve employee performance at work can be traced back to the beginnings of the Industrial Revolution (Hyman and Mason, 1995), with a series of cycles of interest and fashion in the forms taken (Ramsay, 1977). Foy's (1994) comments about participation in the 1970s, involvement in the 1980s and empowerment in the 1990s reflects these trends in fashion and perceived problems which the initiative is supposed to address.

Much of the debate about current initiatives overlap and intermingle because they also share many assumptions about the contribution employees can make to organizational success. In recent years the ideas flowing from the Harvard School have tended to stress that employees are a valuable asset to be nurtured and developed. This 'developmental humanism' (Legge, 1995: 66) suggests that competitive advantage is achieved in part through the commitment, flexibility and skills of employees. Employees are capable of development and can be trusted. Employees have talents which remain untapped in many organizations, and managers need to discover new ways of managing that will enable the organization to benefit from employees' experiences and expertise. With roots in the human relations school, these initiatives stress the importance of communication, motivation, leadership and a cluster of techniques designed to win greater employee commitment.

Figure 3.1 highlights aspirations for employee empowerment specifically, but which are typical of much comment on the benefits supposedly to be gained from employee involvement, employee participation and more 'democratic' practices in the management of employees. Here the offer made by the company to its customers specifically market the benefits of employee empowerment in providing high quality service. In a series of advertisements similar in type and tone to the one displayed in Figure 3.1, Marriott Hotels provide a number of vignettes in which 'customers' praise employee performance because it exceeds their expectation of service. In this case employee empowerment has resulted in employees who can be said to 'delight customers'. The employee's commitment to providing service that exceeds customer expectations, and

Hospitality, Leisure & Tourism Series

> "It was more than considerate of the Marriott night porter to trace my lost wallet – it meant he had to re-trace my entire journey through Vienna. All I could remember was that I'd been travelling on a Southern District streetcar. Miraculously, from this tiny piece of information, the night porter from the Marriott hotel managed to trace the route I'd travelled, the particular streetcar I was on, and my wallet. I was astonished that he went out of his way so much to help me. But, as I now know, everyone at Marriott works this way. Personally assuming responsibility for the needs of every guest. It's called *Empowerment*. And thankfully, they never seem to find anything too much trouble."

Always in the Right Place at the Right Time   Marriott

Figure 3.1 Marketing feelings of empowerment

delights customers, matches the organization's policies and marketing offer to its customers, and is used as a device for gaining competitive advantage.

Marchington and Wilkinson (2000) suggest that recent interest in employee involvement and these 'softer' commitment oriented forms of employee management is due to a cluster of factors. Increased competition, particularly from newly industrialized and industrializing countries, has increased concern to manage employees differently. The supposedly different management practices of Japanese companies have been regarded as a source of advantage to oriental companies not available to their more bureaucratic, controlling and restrictive Western counterparts. Restructuring of British industry has resulted in the decline of many of the country's traditional heavy industries and the growth of service industries, together with the growth of more part-time and numerically flexible forms of employment (e.g. contract working, sub-contracting) means that traditional forms of participation are no longer appropriate.

The decline in trade union membership, both within the UK and USA, and internationally (with a few exceptions), has resulted in reduced collective influence over employment policies and practices. In part this decline is due to the growth of the service sector and changed working arrangements, because they present organizational difficulties for trade unions. In part, relatively high levels of unemployment in the 1990s reduced the potential bargaining power of trade unions.

The consequence is that management faced limited restrictions on the introduction of more individualistic, less collectivist approaches to the management of employees. These market driven developments were further compounded in the UK by successive Conservative governments that supported supposedly individualistic and unitary forms of involvement and discouraged collectivistic forms of participation, particularly where these might involve a formal role for trade unions. Apart from a programme of legislation to restrict trade union activities at home, the Conservative government consistently opposed the more collectivist and participatory interventions emanating from the European Union.

The growth of the service sector and the introduction of new technology have also been influential on the nature of job design and management structures within large service organizations. Apart from the difficulties that service interactions present for employers, the location characteristics of most service organizations present difficulties for controlling unit management. Many service organizations have to locate service points close to their customers. Fast food restaurants, betting shops, banks, retail shops have, with varying degrees, to be located near local markets. There are limited opportunities for vast economies of scale and many of these organizations manage hundreds, if not thousands, of units. Traditionally these businesses would have exercised quite narrow spans of control over the management of units. McDonald's Restaurants, for example, typically had one area supervisor for every three restaurants, and a consequent hierarchy which had eleven tiers of management between customers and the senior vice president in the UK. More empowering and involving approaches to management have provided employers with a means of reducing the layers of management and 'empowering' managers to manage with less direct control (Lashley, 1995b). The advent of new information systems have also played a part in providing senior managers with more direct information and control, which has also enabled the seeming paradox of allowing more local discretion whilst at the same time extending more central control.

While aspirations for these various initiatives share many common roots and contexts, and some writers, commentators and practitioners use the terms interchangeably, it is possible to develop a framework for defining each and drawing some boundaries between them. The following section attempts to provide a definition for each of these terms and thereby a means by which initiatives can be analysed that goes beyond rhetoric.

Participation, involvement, democracy and empowerment

Although some writers (Cotton, 1993) claim that the terms are interchangeable, employee participation, employee involvement, employee empowerment and workplace democracy do have different origins and are responses to different situations by managers and employees. In the first instance it is important to distinguish between those initiatives which have been introduced by managers to meet some need perceived by management from those which have been advocated by employees as a campaign to extend industrial democracy (Poole, 1986). Employee empowerment and many initiatives that are receiving attention tend to have been introduced by management with little or no consultation with employees (Marchington *et al.*, 1992). The aim has largely focused on gaining employee commitment to organizational objectives.

If employer concerns to motivate employees to maximize their output and performance have long been an issue for employers, then concerns to extend democratic control over the organizational policies and the organization of work have an equally long tradition. Concerns with priorities and policies pursued by managers working in the interests of owners in capitalist enterprises led some to advocate socialist alternatives. These either regulated the production process through the intervention of the state, or set up alternative organizations through worker co-operatives (Poole, 1986). Concern with the organization of work in capitalist organizations and the potentially exploitative nature of power relations between owners and employees influenced the growth of a variety of arrangements. Whenever possible employees sought to restrict or limit employers' power in the workplace. Collective bargaining over pay and conditions, staffing, apprenticeship schemes and the allocation of jobs are all examples of employee attempts to intervene in management's power to organize and reward employees as they see fit.

In addition to initiatives that were largely about workers' control of industry and work organization, there have been calls for an extension of democracy in the workplace as a natural extension of democratic society. Without necessarily altering the private ownership of commercial enterprises, there have been those who argue that there are a plurality of interests in these organizations and these need to be recognized in formal arrangements in the management of work organizations. The Bullock Committee (1977) major and minor reports were variations along this theme. The John Lewis Partnership involves a pluralistic assumption that employees should have some say in running the organization. The German system of 'codetermination' with works councils, worker directors and supervisory boards is also an example of this more pluralistic approach where the key 'stakeholders' are said to have a voice, and are involved in decision-making processes.

Given that there are potential disagreements about the form of, and requirements for these initiatives, the precise form introduced in an individual organization or favoured at a particular moment in history is likely to be an outcome of the relative power of the two principal actors in the employment relationship to impose, or amend, the introduction of a specific form of employee involvement in managerial decision-making. Labour market conditions are one important factor in determining the relative strength of the parties to impose or resist. High levels of unemployment in the 1980s and early 1990s, and the structural changes mentioned above, gave employers a dominant position to impose forms of involvement and participation which meet their needs with little organized opposition. These forms of involvement are therefore aimed at engaging employees in individualistic schemes that are not primarily concerned with industrial democracy or giving employees a share in decision-making at a strategic level (Marchington and Wilkinson, 2000).

A second issue that is important in shaping the forms of initiatives introduced in a given situation are the views held by the principal actors the employment relationship. Fox's (1974) unitary, pluralist and radical pluralist perspectives provide a useful starting point. Many initiatives currently being introduced by management are both unitary in perspective and have the effect, either intentionally or unintentionally, of redefining the perceptions of the employment relation in unitary terms (Keenoy and Anthony, 1992). That said, some managers and organizations perceive their relationship with employees in more pluralistic terms and forms of employee involvement in decision-making will reflect concerns to ensure employees as 'stakeholders' have their views formally expressed. The work of Purcell and Sissons (1983) further extended understanding of the 'styles' with which managers manage their relationships with employees, and thereby assumptions about employee involvement in decision-making. Later, this work was extended by Purcell and Gray (1986) to take account of individualism and collectivism as managerial concerns. Here, individualism and collectivism are not seen as two ends of the same continuum but rather two aspects of employer considerations. Individualism refers to those aspects of employment policy that concern the belief in the individual and his/her contribution to the organization. Collectivism expresses the recognition of the collective interests of employees, the role of union or non-union mechanisms within decision-making processes and the value accorded to contributions made. Both the dimensions of individualism and collectivism were expressed as a continuum from high to low, crosscutting to produce four quadrants.

Figure 3.2 reproduces Purcell and Gray's (1986) model of styles of employee relations. The quadrant representing a low concern for the collective interests of employees and low concern for the individual contribution of employees is called *'traditional'*. Labour is strongly regarded as a cost to be minimized, trade unionism is strongly opposed and employees are typical of the secondary labour market representing high proportions of ethnic minorities, women, and younger workers. Like the traditional style, the *'sophisticated human relations'* style shares a unitary orientation, but presents a more caring approach to the management of employees. Employees are regarded as valued assets and personnel policies aim at building employee loyalty and commitment though internal promotions, good pay and conditions, and training, etc. Employee involvement in decision-making may be via suggestion schemes, quality circles, and an array of communications techniques.

The second two styles reflect an approach in which the collective interests of employees are recognized. The *'consultative'* style has similarities with sophisticated human relations approaches in that the contribution made by employees to organizational success is highly regarded by managers. Thus many of the practices in relation to pay and conditions, training, and other personnel management techniques are used, but in addition trade unions are recognized and used as a source of consultation and, in some cases legitimization of management's policies and agenda. In the final quadrant, the *'constitutional'* approach involves a low regard for the contribution made by individuals to organization success, though the collective interest is recognized. Trade unions are recognized but with limited enthusiasm, and management tends to hang on to decision-making. Hence the potential contribution to be made by trade union representatives to decision-making is not highly regarded and is given low esteem. Often the key concerns are to maintain industrial peace through a recognition of the potential disruptive power that employee collectives represent. These organizations display low trust of employees and their involvement in decision-making.

This model of styles of employee relations has been developed and amended by Purcell (1987) and Storey and Bacon (1993). The important point, however, when building a picture of employee empowerment and other initiatives, is that

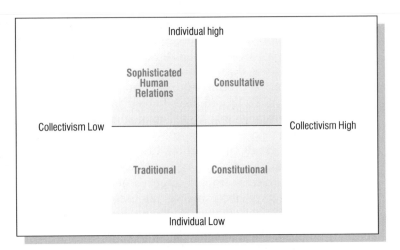

Individual high

Sophisticated Human Relations

Consultative

Collectivism Low

Collectivism High

Traditional

Constitutional

Individual Low

Figure 3.2 Purcell and Gray's model employer relations styles. *Source:* Purcell and Gray (1986)

employer approaches vary. Each approach is based on a set of assumptions about employees and the contribution they might make to organizational success in general and decision-making processes in particular. These assumptions and ideas may well be reflections of both internal political processes and organizational culture, and external factors such as the labour markets, government legislation, product market conditions, and, in service industries, the nature of the service offer to customers. As we saw in Chapter 2, many service organizations adopt a cost leadership strategy and adopt employment practices that are *traditional* using this model. Hence there is often a low investment in training and these organizations experience high levels of staff turnover. Both are likely to create barriers to empowerment, because employees are unlikely to develop feelings of being empowered.

Although these models suggest that organizations tend to have reasonably consistent styles, there have been general changes in approaches to employee involvement in Britain. Marchington *et al*. (1992) identify five distinct phases of interest in involving employees. They claim that this current phase commenced in the early 1980s and is different from most earlier phases.

'The most recent manifestation of EI is individualistic (as opposed to collective and conducted via representatives), it is championed by management often without any pressure from employees or trade unions (as opposed to earlier incarnations where employee or union pressure was influential), and it is aimed at securing greater employee commitment to and identification with the organization and its success' (p. 6)

Employee empowerment is, therefore, one of a range of initiatives that appears to have common foundations, but which differ in content and managerial intentions, as well as the amount of employee influence in shaping them. Definitions of employee participation, employee involvement and industrial democracy vary and as was stated earlier are used by some writers interchangeably. Marchington *et al.* (1992) do attempt to provide a definition that uses employee participation as an 'umbrella term' including all forms of employee influence, including collective bargaining; employee involvement is used as a term to describe managerially inspired initiatives aimed at winning employee commitment, and industrial democracy as those practices whose aim is to increase the rights of employees to participate in management decisions. There are still some problems with these definitions because initiatives that claim to be empowering have a range of motives and overlap with these terms. The last section of this chapter expands on this point. Before turning to this, the precise nature of various initiatives can be better understood by using a framework of analysis through which to describe each initiative.

Analysing changes in working practice

Marchington *et al.* (1992) provide a useful four-dimensional matrix through which to 'deconstruct the different components of employee involvement' (p. 7). They suggest that various techniques can be located against the dimensions that cover *'degree'* of involvement, the *'form'* which involvement takes, the *'level'* in the organization hierarchy in which involvement takes place, and the *'range'* of subjects dealt with under the arrangements. A framework for analysing initiatives that claim to empower employees is given later. However, this four dimensional model is a useful starting point and one that helps to establish similarities and differences between initiatives called employee participation, employee involvement, industrial democracy and empowerment.

The **degree of involvement** refers to the extent that employees are able to influence decisions made within the organization. Several writers have produced continua of involvement of employees in decision-making. Poole (1986) distinguishes between schemes via which 'workers influence decisions but are

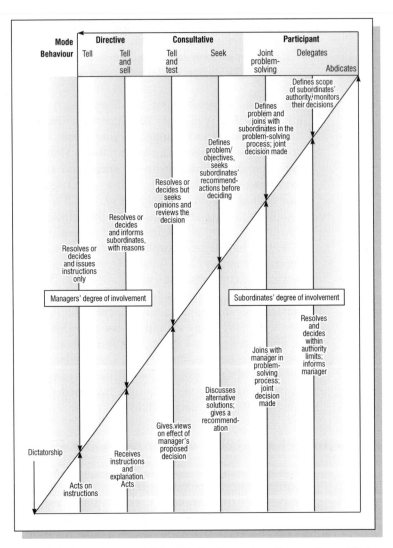

Figure 3.3 Tannenbaum and Schmidt's involvement continuum. *Source:* Biddle and Evenden (1983)

not responsible for them' (p. 18), and those where 'workers have actual control and authority over particular decisions' (p. 18). Earlier, Tannenbaum and Schmidt (1973) identified a continuum of employee involvement in managerial decisions, which involves three broad relationships. Figure 3.3 reproduces their model. At one end the ***directive style*** involves managers *'telling'* or *'telling and selling'* a decision to employees. Employees are required to act on the instructions given and have little opportunity to influence them. Moving from this the managerial style is **consultative** and managers *'tell and test'* out potential decisions or *'seek'* employee views on alternatives but managers ultimately make the decision. Under the more ***participative style*** managers either *'jointly solve problems'* with employees, or *'delegate'* some decisions completely to subordinates (Biddle and Evenden, 1980). Marchington *et al.* (1992) use a similar model though fashion it in the form of an escalator with employee control as the 'upper stage'. Figure 3.4 reproduces this 'escalator model' because it assists in developing an understanding that different forms of employee empowerment involve different relational dimensions.

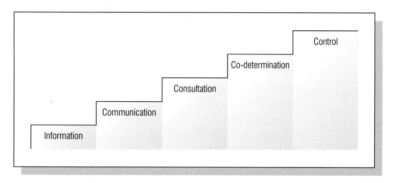

Figure 3.4 The escalator of employee participation in decision-making. *Source:* Marchington *et al.* (1992)

In this model *information* involves providing employees with information in an essentially 'top down' direction – company magazines and some forms of team briefing are examples. *Communication* includes schemes that involve two-way processes. Extended forms of team briefing that allow questions to be asked and clarification sought are examples – perhaps close to tell and test. Schemes that aim to gain from employees' ideas and experiences are described as *consultation*. Managers continue to make the ultimate decisions but quality circles, suggestion schemes and joint consultative committees assist in making decisions with inputs from employees. *Codetermination* involves schemes whereby employees and managers may jointly make decisions. Works councils and employee directors are examples, but issues of relative numbers are important. For example in the German system of codetermination employee directors have nominal parity with owner directors, but in practice can be out-voted by the casting vote of the chairman. Employee owned organizations occupy the top step on the escalator. *Control* involves those organizations in which employees retain ultimate decision-making powers, usually in the form of workers' cooperatives. The Mondragon cooperatives in Spain are some of the most successful examples. In this case employees own the organization and vote in the management and make key strategic decisions.

The second dimension identified by Marchington *et al.* (1992) relates to the **form of involvement** in a particular initiative. They identified three forms through which individuals are involved – direct, indirect and financial. In the *direct form* individual employees are personally involved themselves. Usually all employees in an organization, unit or department directly take part. Work organization through autonomous work groups, say as in Harvester Restaurants (Ashness and Lashley, 1995), involved employees directly in team organization. Other initiatives involve team briefings, house journals, suggestion schemes or similar arrangements for downward information giving and upward problem solving, which involve direct communications between managers and individual employees.

The second involves *indirect forms* of involvement where individuals are represented in the involving process. Usually, one or more individuals are elected, volunteered or are appointed by managers to represent employees. Quality circles rarely involve all departmental employees and usually involve representatives who participate on behalf of the workforce as a whole. Works councils, employee directors, and various forms of joint consultation committees involve representative involvement. The experiences of those involved in representing the workforce as a whole are likely to be different from the workforce. That is, the experiences and feelings of involvement will vary between those actively involved in the initiative and those of the bulk of employees for whom the initiative represents a conduit for involvement.

The third form of involvement is the *financial form* which relates employees having some economic benefit linked to the performance of the organization or their performance within it. Typically, and the model favoured by the British Conservative Government in the 1980s and early 1990s, was the use of share ownership and profit sharing schemes. In most cases the proportion of total income that came from these sources was relatively small and in many organizations difficult to link to individual performance. Thus in many schemes individuals found it difficult to link their own performance with an immediate material benefit. In many service industries it is difficult to identify the individual contribution and many profit-related pay schemes related to annual performance. In the case of

TGI Fridays, total pay is made up from two principal sources – a 'commission' on sales paid by the company and 'tips' paid by customers. For food and drink service employees, commission is directly related to personal sales, whilst for the kitchen staff, the group on duty shared a commission based on total food sales. Restaurant and bar staff receive tips from customers but kitchen staff do not (Lashley, 2000).

The level of involvement relates to the point in the organization in which employees are involved in decisions. Employees may be involved in task level activities that may be individual, say as Marriott Hotels, or in autonomous work groups, as found at Harvester Restaurants. The key point with both these is that in both cases 'workers have some rights to organize his or her activities within some discretionary limits' (Poole, 1986: 16). Involvement may be at the level of the department or unit, say in quality circles or team briefings. More widely seen in mainland Europe, works councils may operate at unit or corporate level. Employee directors are involved at board level. Collective bargaining may span task, department, unit or company, and in some cases spans all four levels. Financial involvement round share ownership and company profit sharing schemes occur at company level, though bonus schemes based on personal sales occur at task level whilst other forms of financial involvement may be based on departmental or unit level.

The fourth dimension identified by Marchington *et al.* (1992) is the **range of subjects** covered by involvement. In some cases, the range of topics being covered is limited to aspects of the tasks or interpretation of service delivery. In many service firms, the employee is constrained in what he or she can do with tangible aspects of the business, but may be encouraged to interpret the service delivery as they see fit. In other cases, employees may be involved in decisions about the general conditions of the employment relationship, involving negotiations over pay and conditions of employment. In other cases decisions may well take on a more strategic nature and thereby incorporate decisions that affect the business as a whole. *Prêt à Manger*, the UK-based sandwich bar and snack business, involves employees making recruitment decisions. All new recruits work a probationary shift with their would-be workmates who then vote, at the end of the shift, as to whether the recruit should be employed. There are few other aspects of the organization's decisions that involve employees in the same way.

A fifth dimension, not covered by the Marchington *et al.* (1992) model, needs to be added to aid our understanding of the nature of this range of initiatives and to assist in distinguishing between them. In my view, **the power dimension**, needs to be added.

Without wishing to enter the numerous debates about power in work organizations, it is necessary to comment on the power of the employees on the one hand and managers on the other to make decisions stick. Who makes the final decision has to be a key question. Is involvement constrained with limits placed on the authority which has been delegated, and who has decided what those limits should be? In whose interests has the proposal been initiated – managers and owners, or employees? To what extent has the proposer been able to impose the initiative without opposition, or to what extent have processes of consultation and negotiation ameliorated and amended the proposal? To what extent are employees, or employers, able to resist proposals or decisions made by the other party?

This final dimension is necessary to arrive at definitions that assist in distinguishing between employee involvement, employee participation and industrial democracy. As with Marchington *et al*. (1992), employee involvement is best understood as a term to describe a range of techniques which are largely concerned with improving communications and commitment. They are based on initiatives largely restricted to providing information, improving communications and consultation. Employees are typically directly involved, and chiefly concerned with task level involvement within a range determined by management. In relation to empowerment, these latter two points will be separated out and discussed in the next section. Initiatives described as employee participation are best understood where employees are involved in some form of decision-making that might traditionally be the domain of management, inspired largely for operational reasons because the nature of the business cannot second guess the needs of customers. Employees need to be 'empowered' to make some of the decisions, though within boundaries laid down by management. In these cases, the initiatives are designed largely, if not exclusively, by management to meet operational needs or deal with problems perceived by managers as being unresponsive to traditional command and control management styles. Hence they again tend to involve elements of codetermination. Most, if not all, employees are directly involved but decisions tend to be restricted to 'task participation' (Geary, 1994) and constrained within limits determined by management. Industrial democracy on the other hand, defines a range of initiatives that are deliberately designed to ensure employees make more contribution and have more control in decisions which impact on the organization (Poole, 1986). They may be introduced by management during periods of industrial conflict as a way of mollifying employee demands for more say in the decisions that affect them, or because managers share a pluralistic frame of reference which identifies these arrangements as providing greater industrial stability. Demands for greater industrial democracy, however, are more likely to originate with employees. They are a means of protecting employees from decisions that are employer orientated; or as a general ambition to extend democratic control in the workplace.

Employee empowerment can be seen to overlap several of these initiatives. This is why claims to empower employees often include initiatives that appear under employee involvement, employee participation, and employee democracy in the literature (Cotton, 1993; Potterfield, 1999). The next section of this chapter follows this point further and provides a model for understanding managerial meanings and motives that suggests four separate but overlapping meanings of empowerment in service industries.

Managerial meanings

Changes in working arrangements that claim to be empowering for employees cover a diverse set of arrangements, which can be analysed as representing a variety of levels of empowerment and forms. At the operational level, empowerment as a management rhetoric provides a convenient device for labelling a variety of changes as being universally beneficial, and for obscuring the experiences of the empowered. Some of these different forms are listed in Table 3.1. As stated in Chapter 2, the effectiveness of a particular initiative in producing the necessary changes in employee feelings and work performance will be largely dependent on the experiences of the empowered of the 'state of empowerment'. That is, the extent that particular initiatives generate feelings of personal efficacy and control over situations in which the empowered can make a difference.

Table 3.1 Some forms of empowerment in service operations

Initiative
Quality circles
Total quality management
Suggestion schemes
Autonomous work groups
Whatever it takes training
Team briefings
Delayering

Table 3.2 Managerial meanings of empowerment

Managerial meaning	Initiatives used
Empowerment through participation	Autonomous work groups Whatever it takes training Job enrichment
Empowerment through involvement	Quality circles Team briefings Suggestion schemes
Empowerment through commitment	Employee share ownership Profit sharing and bonus schemes Quality of working life programmes, job rotation, job enlargement
Empowerment through delayering	Job re-design Re-training Autonomous work groups Job enrichment Profit sharing and bonus schemes

This chapter went on to suggest that it is possible to generate an analytical framework through which to describe initiatives in the degree, form, level, range and power involved – irrespective of whether the initiative was called involvement, participation, democracy or empowerment. In addition, the use of empowerment to describe very different initiatives reveals that managers, whilst attempting to employ the rhetorical advantage of the term, can have different needs and intentions for the arrangements. It has been suggested (Lashley 1995a; Lockwood, 1996) that depending on the nature of the service encounter, managers may require employees to exercise varying degrees of discretion in the encounter. This is discussed further in Chapter 12. In turn these intentions will shape the form of empowerment included. Table 3.2 provides an overview of the managerial intentions for empowerment and suggests appropriate forms that empowerment might take.

Empowerment through participation

Where an organization delegates some of the decision-making to employees, which in a traditional organization would be the domain of management, it can be said to be empowering through participation. Using the Tannenbaum and Schmidt model they involve participant styles of management and employees are involved in making decisions jointly with management or have some decisions delegated to them. Employees are participating in identifying and satisfying customer needs, as in the cases of Marriott Hotels (Hubrecht and Teare, 1993); or are making decisions about work organization or scheduling, as in the case of Harvester Restaurants (Pickard, 1993); or joint planning in a Swedish bank (Holden, 1999). This form of empowerment is discussed more fully in Chapter 4.

In continental Europe particularly, employees may participate in decision-making at non-operational levels. Here the use of works councils or worker directors may involve representatives of the workforce in decisions that are more concerned with matters of business policy and strategy. In this situation, European participants can be said to be empowered to make decisions at strategic levels, and initiatives are often motivated by democratic or pluralistic motives.

Empowerment through involvement

Where the managerial concern is to gain from employees' experiences, ideas and suggestions, it may be the intention to empower employees through their involvement in providing feedback, sharing information and making suggestions. Front-line service employees are in a unique position to contribute to problem resolution, and communicate trends in customer service needs and the impact of company policies on service delivery. In Tanennbaum and Schmidt's model these managerial styles are consultative and involve managers gaining feedback from employees or seeking ideas from them.

The use of quality circles in the Accor Group (Barbee and Bott, 1991), or team briefings in Hilton Hotels (Hirst, 1992) and TGI Fridays (Lashley, 2000a) are techniques that attempt to include the ideas and experiences of employees in the managerial decision-making process. Suggestions made may range from the nature of the immediate task, involving both tangibles and intangibles, through to more business strategy and employment policy issues. Essentially, managers continue to make the decisions. Employees who choose to participate are directly involved, but participation in these programmes is usually voluntary. The intention is that organizational effectiveness is improved through better communication with front-line employees; employees feel empowered through being involved in consultation and problem solving processes and, it is hoped, are thereby more committed to organizational objectives and service quality improvement. This form of empowerment is discussed more fully in Chapter 5.

Empowerment through commitment

By empowering employees through greater commitment to the organization's goals, employees take more responsibility for their own performance and its improvement (Barry, 1993). Inherent skills and talents within the employees can be realized and put to work for the benefit of the organization (Antonacopoulou and Kanampully, 2000), to produce more satisfied customers (Hubrecht and Teare, 1993), and greater profits (Cotton, 1993). They will be more adaptable to change (Barry, 1993) and perhaps even accepting of organizational downsizing and redundancies (Shirley, 1993).

Attempts to achieve greater employee commitment overlap and inter-relate with both empowerment through employee participation and employee involvement. However, some initiatives are quite specifically aimed at greater employee commitment. In these cases, it is hoped that greater commitment will result in the development of attitudes which are positive to the organization, employee performance more closely matched to organizational and customer needs, and more stability amongst the workforce. The managerial style may remain largely be directive (Tannenbaum and Schmidt, 1973) and employees may be told what to do or give reasons for why they should undertake certain actions, but nevertheless the organizations is wanting to build employee commitment.

Other forms of empowerment intend to gain greater employee commitment through improvements in job satisfaction and feelings of worth to the organization. Thus, changes in job design through increased job rotation, together with techniques mentioned earlier under both employee participation and employee involvement are intended to change attitudes and reduce feelings of 'them and us'. Bearing in mind the psychological dimension of empowerment discussed in Chapter 2, it is possible to build feelings of being empowered even in these essentially command and control, directive structures given the organizational support required. This form of empowerment is discussed more fully in Chapter 6.

Empowerment through delayering

Since Peters and Waterman (1982) first talked about excellent companies being 'flatter' and 'close to the customer' there has been increasing interest in reducing the number of tiers of management in organization structures. Service sector operators, like their counterparts in manufacturing, have been keen to explore the possibilities of delayering their organizations. The benefits of delayering an organization are found both in cutting overheads by reducing administrative costs, and in making the organization closer to its customers. Hence quality gains and greater responsiveness to environmental change might ensue.

The multi-unit nature of many service outlets, located close to their businesses, have added particular problems for service organizations. If they retain a reasonable span of control across hundreds, or thousands, of units they inevitably involve large numbers of management tiers, as witnessed by McDonald's Restaurants mentioned earlier. On the other hand, increasing the span of control reduces the potential control of each individual business and this could cause major problems for a branded business that is selling consistency to its customers. Empowerment of decision-making by allowing lower levels of the organization's management to make decisions formerly made at senior levels has seemed to be the answer to many service organizations. This form of empowerment is discussed more fully in Chapter 7.

The intentions of managers, and their perceptions of the nature of the offer to customers, is likely to shape the form of empowerment introduced. That said, managerial intentions may not always be singly motivated nor consistent. The above suggested framework of meanings does not exclude the possibility, if not likelihood, that managers may have intentions covering one, or all, of the motives above. As a consequence, initiatives may incorporate a variety of forms. Secondly, it is important to remember that management decision-making does involve degrees of choice, and forms selected need not always be based on a 'rational fit' with circumstances. The ideology, prior training, and vision of managers together with the internal political processes, culture and history of the organization may be powerful determinants in the selections made by managers as to the form introduced.

Rhetoric and empowerment

Watson's (1994a) text on management in action provides some useful insights into the role of rhetoric in shaping management actions and behaviour. Rhetoric has an important role in engaging individuals in normalization through the provision of a series of metaphors with which individuals engage. Legge (1995) shows how the different groups of managers in organizations have adopted the rhetoric of human resource management as a means of protecting their interests. In particular, links with customer quality and empowerment create a rhetoric that 'protects their position and status which is eroded by delayering, outsourcing and the like' (Legge, 1995: 322). The lack of precision in the term and the fact that it covers a wide range of meanings and intentions is an element in its attraction as a current rhetoric. Empowerment represents rhetoric that operates on three levels, operational, strategic human resource management, and at the level of the employment relationship.

On an operational level empowerment provides a rhetoric for using the same concept to describe quite different working arrangements, employer motives and benefits to employees. As discussed earlier, empowerment has been used to describe different arrangements such as autonomous work groups, quality circles, and employee suggestions schemes. Each of these represents different degrees, forms, levels, range and power associated with involvement in decision-making, and overlap with initiatives described as employee involvement and employee participation with echoes of industrial democracy. As a rhetoric it can be applied without being over-prescriptive in what empowerment requires. Therefore, the contradictions inherent in some applications, or where there are other rhetorics, such as cost reduction and profit making, which may be contradictory, these contradictions remain unexposed in the discourse (Watson, 1994b).

The rhetoric of concern for employee control and concern for employee commitment overlay Storey's 'hard' and 'soft' models of human resource management. These emphasize different priorities set with organizations and theoretical origins. The hard model suggests a 'utilitarian instrumentalism' (Legge, 1995: 66), given recent voice by the Michigan School, and stresses the management of human resources as factors of production and the need to control. It is also possible to detect approaches adopted within other organizations where the strategy is to 'treat labour as a variable input and a cost to be minimized' (Legge, 1995: 67). Firms operating in cost-competitive markets and adopting cost leadership strategies are typical of this approach. Typically, employee discretion is designed out of the job and employment practices stress both numerical and functional flexibility A case brought to industrial tribunal in the mid 1990s is typical. Burger King Restaurants was perhaps an extreme example but reveals much that is typical (Bowcott, 1995). Here the manager asked employees to clock on and off the shift as demand fluctuated. Again, a study of labour turnover at a small hotel (Lashley and Chaplin, 1999) confirmed that many part-time employees were being sent home after just one hour of the shift as a way of controlling labour costs.

The 'soft' model, including employee empowerment, on the other hand involves, as we have seen, a general concern for employee commitment. Some writers (Watson, 1986) have suggested that managerial priorities wax and wane between concern for the control of employee performance and concern to build commitment to organizational objectives. Whilst this is helpful in suggesting variability and choice in the employment relationship, it does also illustrate an important rhetoric which the 'soft' model of strategic choices in the management of human resources represents. Managers are seen to be exercising a choice in their approach to employment issues which are more caring and concerned for the personal development of the employee as an individual. Empowerment provides the ideal metaphor.

In fact there are numerous tensions within both hard and soft aspects of the model (Noon, 1992; Legge, 1995). The notion that 'hard' and 'soft' are ends of the same employment strategy continuum is questionable. One manager whom I interviewed in my research with Harvester Restaurants talked about the approach as being based on 'hard love'. This matches with Legge's reference to 'tough love' (1995a: 89). The phrase suggests a preparedness to apply the hard perspective in controlling the labour cost, and exercise caring concern in the management of the human resource. Indeed this merging of 'hard' and 'soft' is further evidenced in Harvester Restaurants (Ashness and Lashley, 1995) where employees will frequently decide to 'send someone home' when the business is quieter than anticipated. Here the 'hard' controls required by Burger King are delivered by 'soft' (committed?) employees themselves. In reality this is not a choice between commitment and control, it is about getting the employees to internalize control.

The empowered and committed employee, therefore, appears to offer management the promise of control *and* commitment and provide a rhetoric of choice within strategies for the management of people which has moved to much 'softer', caring, commitment seeking approach. Rather than control and commitment being two ends of a continuum, empowerment represents a shift in the locus of control from externally imposed directive control to internally imposed self-control. The work of Edwards (1979) and Edwards *et al.* (1975) suggests that an array of control strategies may be exercised according to the market situation of the company. Within the context of this array empowerment represents a recognition that 'Workers do not always need to be overtly controlled. They can control themselves' (Thompson and McHugh, 1990: 153). Paradoxically, empowerment means greater control of employees because of the shift of the locus of control from externally supervised control to internalized self-control. In essence employee empowerment 'has the effect of increasing [top] management control whilst creating the impression of reducing it' (Robbins, 1983: 67).

As stated at the beginning of the book, the rhetoric of empowerment has entered most aspects of social and organizational life. Before discussing the role of empowerment in creating a rhetoric about the employment relationship it is useful to touch on some of these wider issues. On a social and political level, empowerment was traditionally linked to 'enlightenment values of universalism and rights, such as franchise, the rise of the trade union movement, housing initiatives, employment contracts and access to education' (Morley, 1995: 36). The current usage of the concept has been taken over by the New Right (Morley, 1995) as an important element in a 'control culture and new authoritarianism masquerading in the language and philosophy of progressivism' (p. 36). In social service provision Morley argues that empowerment could be client centred and liberatory, a recognition that the less powerful are supported by the more powerful. In effect, she argues, the current rhetoric of empowerment 'is a new regulatory discourse, an extension of the new panopticon of modern public services (p. 36).

In the field of employment, empowerment too has the potential for a variety of meanings applied within different philosophical perspectives. Indeed, Collins (1999) makes the point that 'empowerment is a powerful tool for management precisely because it is ambiguous' (1999: 219). The notion of empowering the disempowered has an attraction to those concerned about the inequalities of power with existing capital structures. Indeed the claims that empowerment is about developing talents that are just waiting to be tapped has an attraction as a liberatory experience. It promises a new kind of order in which work is more humane and more ennobling. Indeed some of the more idealistic evangelists (Johnson and Redmond, 1999) hail empowerment as a technique for the new millennium and a new order.

Employee empowerment provides a powerful rhetoric which goes beyond articulating the view that 'people are a valuable asset' whilst legitimizing 'management practice which treats them as a cost' (Keenoy and Anthony, 1994: 238); it represents an important metaphor in shaping the social construction of the employment relationship. In effect it is a device to legitimize a unitary perspective of the organizational relationship between employer and employee. It delegitimizes trade union collectivist and pluralist perspectives of organizational priorities.

This metaphor stresses the team relationship, the commonality of interests and the need for all employees to recognize and take responsibility for their part in the collective success of the organization. At the same time this attempt to build team spirit amongst work groups and the organization is a rhetoric that by definition denies the existence of sectional interests with specific interests. The narrative is politically sterile, it has no room for the recognition of differences in employer and employee priorities. Thus, empowered employees will happily accept redundancy and downsizing, even when it includes their own job (Shirley, 1993).

Conclusion

This discussion of the relational dimensions of empowerment (Conger and Kanungo, 1988) has suggested that the confusion about the meanings of empowerment, the forms introduced and similarities with initiatives that are called employee participation and employee involvement is not entirely accidental. Autonomous work groups, quality circles, and suggestion schemes, for example have been used as management techniques for decades. They have represented a range of concerns by managers working within a variety of organizational environments and labour market contexts. As the earlier quotation from Foy (1994) shows, employee participation and employee involvement have both had their moments as the current panacea for managing the employee commitment. In many cases, the forms of the initiative remain the same, only the generic term changes. Lawler has suggested that employee empowerment is merely recycling old ideas and on one level there is truth in that, because these initiatives reflect different styles in the management of employees, which move away from directive styles of decision-making, to those that are more consultative and participatory. On another level it is possible to see empowerment as representing both continuing concerns of employers to optimize employee performance, and change in the rhetoric about how best to go about it.

It is possible to build a framework of analysis in which it is possible to locate various forms of participation, involvement, workplace democracy and empowerment. By examining the style by which managers and employees are involved in organization decision-making, the degree of employee involvement, the form, level and range of issues to be considered, and the power that managers and employees have to impose or resist decisions, it is possible to identify and define a range of relationships which all bear the name of empowerment.

Certainly, an examination of initiatives that claim to be empowering reveals the existence of a number of managerial meanings and intentions. Some initiatives empower employees to make decisions that might traditionally be the domain of management. Others empower employees through their involvement in exercises that consult them over operational performance. In some cases, managers perceive empowerment as a motivational concept, where there are few changes to the relationships between managers and employees, but the aspiration is to build the employees' sense of personal efficacy and commitment to the organization's policies and objectives. Finally, some initiatives are directed, not at employees as in the preceding cases, but at the management structure itself. Here the intention is that junior managers are empowered as layers of middle management are removed. Chapters 4–7 discuss these in more detail, but is important to recognize that empowerment performs an important role as a rhetoric in management discourse.

Taking the view that rhetoric provides a means through which discourse can happen, the managerial rhetoric of empowerment operates on three levels. It provides a means whereby different operational variations of empowerment can be discussed without consideration of the variations in employee experiences that they produce. It operates within the realm of strategies in the management of human resources, by being one ingredient in the 'soft' approach to the management of people at work; and empowerment is one of an array of terms being used by employers to build a unitary view of the employment relationship. On this level, it is assumed that employees and employers have overcome their conflictual behaviours of the past; all organization members – employees and managers – are faced with common challenges from competitors and must aspire to ever increasing customer satisfaction. Empowerment, therefore, performs an important role in suggesting that management practice and its relationship with employees has changed as a result of this new employment technique.

CHAPTER 4

Forms of empowerment through participation

- Task level empowerment
- Work groups and empowerment
- Job enrichment and empowerment
- Participation beyond the task

The forms of empowerment that empower employees to make decisions formerly made by managers, or to 'share decision making' (Bowen and Lawler, 1992), are best described as empowerment through participation. These initiatives cover a variety of arrangements, in the context of empowerment, that are introduced by managers, though with a wider definition might also include arrangements initiated by the workforce aimed primarily at extending democracy. The concern of this book is primarily with forms of empowerment introduced by management, but these wider issues will be touched on later in this chapter. At root many of the case studies and literature assume that empowerment is fundamentally concerned with participation (Foy, 1994; Sosteric, 1996; Marchington and Wilkinson, 2000).

Geroy *et al*. (1998: 15) define typically, empowerment 'as the act of giving people the opportunity to make workplace decisions by expanding their autonomy in decision making.'

This chapter discusses two principal levels at which empowerment through participation takes place. Task level empowerment is concerned with employees having the authority to make decisions relating to the immediate tasks of their jobs (Marchington and Wilkinson, 2000). In service industry situations this has relevance to the discretion needed by employees in meeting customer service where such needs are difficult to anticipate and standardize (Rafiq and Ahmed, 1998b). At non-task level, employees might be said to be empowered through the exercise of some control over the more strategic decisions of the organization. In most cases, these initiatives tend to towards a more 'democratic' relationship between employers and employees, though do not involve full blooded workers' control of the enterprise. These non-task examples of employee empowerment will be briefly touched upon, because they form part of the range of meanings of empowerment, and provide an important strand in the rhetoric of empowerment. However, they are not subjected to substantial discussion because the core focus of this text is managerial applications of employee empowerment as a means of resolving some tensions in the service encounter.

Task level empowerment

As was shown in the preceding chapter, many initiatives that are now being discussed as providing employees with empowerment have much in common, both with earlier initiatives say in autonomous work groups and with recent forms which claim to be 'problem solving groups' or total quality management (Geary, 1994). Like Foy (1994), Geary has an account of the shifts in fashion of the initiatives over recent decades. 'In the 1970s, for instance, autonomous work groups were hailed as a key innovation, in the 1980s it was quality circles, and more recently it has been total quality management, team working and continuous improvement' (1994: 635). Marchington and Wilkinson (2000: 340) also set these initiatives in a context of continuity of concerns and note a recent change in emphasis, 'Employee involvement has focused on direct participation by small groups and individuals, it is concerned with information sharing at work-group level and it has excluded the opportunity for workers to have an input into high-level decision making'. Their description of these initiatives being largely concerned with communication may be inappropriate for task-level participation in services, but they rightly highlight limits to operational issues.

Geary suggests that task participation is best understood as 'a set of processes', so as to avoid the danger of being overly preoccupied with the labels attached to initiatives. Geary provides a general definition of task participation that tends to encompass 'consultation with and/or delegation of responsibilities and authority for decision making to its subordinates...' (1994: 637). The use of the framework of analysis discussed in Chapter 3 enables a more detailed consideration of those initiatives in which managers consult with employees, as distinct from those where employees have some degree of discretion to make decisions about the organization of work and customer service needs. The more consultative approaches are discussed in detail in Chapter 5. In this chapter we are chiefly concerned with the delegation of decision-making authority in the relationship between managers and employees.

This chapter identifies two sets of arrangements through which employees are empowered to make decisions that managers might make under traditional arrangements. The first of these considers arrangements where groups of employees are given the authority to make decisions and are collectively accountable for their actions. Under the second arrangement individual employees are granted authority to make decisions and are held accountable for the decisions made. Bearing in mind Geary's point about considering task level initiatives as being best understood as 'processes', these terms help highlight differences in arrangements, but also convey continuity in the modes through which employees can be granted the authority to make managerial decisions. In both cases, initiatives are best judged as being empowering through the experiences of the 'empowered'. Whatever the term or form introduced, they can be said to be empowering when employees experience a sense of personal efficacy as described in Chapter 2.

Work groups and empowerment

One of the forms that is often associated with empowerment is the organization of employees in autonomous work groups (also referred to as self-directed teams and semi-autonomous teams). In part the growth of these mirrors the increasing interest in employee involvement (Marchington, 1992), 'soft' forms of human resource management (Storey, 1992) and the search for greater employee commitment, and alternative ways of controlling employee performance. Like many of these initiatives, they reflect an interest in learning from (and competing with) Japanese management techniques, or at least the perceived 'group orientation' of Japanese society and management, and thereby hope to gain competitive advantage by being able to increase productivity and quality.

Under these arrangements employees work, either completely without an immediate supervisor (autonomous or 'self-directed' teams (Attaran and Nguyen, 1999)), or under the loose guidance of a supervisor (semi-autonomous). The work team decide on how work will be organized; they will allocate tasks amongst the group, discuss and suggest ways of improving quality or working methods. In some cases, employees will decide on break, shift and holiday rosters within the guidelines laid down. They may decide on revenue expenditure, say when ordering stock, or when calling up maintenance. The key point here is that employees, as a group or team, are empowered to exercise some form of responsible autonomy. Management decide on the team's 'accountabilities' and the limits within which they operate.

Using the framework developed earlier, this type of work group is participatory in Tannenbaum and Schmidt's (1973) terms, and they involve a degree of involvement which is at the point of co-determination, or limited control, on Marchington *et al.'s* (1992) 'escalator'. The form is direct because, in most cases, all employees belong to one or other work team. In the main, these groups have task level involvement with few opportunities to influence the decisions that influence them, or the limits within which they operate. Flowing from this, the range of topics over which they are empowered tends to be around issues of task organization. They rarely, if ever, involve terms and conditions of employment, salary negotiations or any other issue that might be considered a 'bread and butter' industrial relations issue. Finally, power to make decisions is still shaped and constrained by the limits placed on what the empowered group can do. They do have the power to make decisions about tasks, and managers ideally do not intervene.

In service situations, autonomous groups can respond quickly to changes in service demand – both in deciding that there are too many staff on duty or in helping each other out in times of service peaks. Groups can be an important check on both the quality and pace of individual members' outputs. Thus autonomous groups offer management a decision-making and organizing device that responds quickly to changes in demands, faults and operational needs, whilst at the same time acting as a controlling check on individual behaviour. Attaran and Nguyen (1999) provide several case studies of service organizations that claim to have improved service quality through the use of autonomous (self-directed) teams.

From the organization's point of view, these work group arrangements allow work organization to be more responsive to immediate service needs, whilst at the same time controlling the efforts of individuals through the normative pressures of group membership. Thompson and McHugh (1990) identify this as 'coercive control', because group members internalize norms transmitted via the group dynamic. They stress that group membership and the consensual processes involved in group decision-making perform an important role in getting individuals to internalize both the organization's policies and definitions of appropriate employee behaviour. Barker (1993: 408) describes self-managing teams as 'a form of control more powerful, less apparent and more difficult to resist than the former bureaucracy'.

Without necessarily dismissing the 'tyranny of teams' (Sinclair, 1992) and the depiction of autonomous groups as another form of control of individual behaviour, the experience of group working can provide a source of satisfaction to participating employees. Ray-Chaudhuri (1998) shows that groups develop dynamics that are the source of empowerment in itself. Being able to have some influence over decisions, even though restricted to tasks, is seen by some employees as an improvement on more traditional command and control structures. Similarly, group membership and developing relationships between the work group can also be satisfying through the feelings of mutuality and support for individuals. Marchington and Wilkinson (2000: 349) report that 'some analysts would regard self-managing teams as the ultimate in direct participation, a point reinforced by studies that teams outperform individuals . . . and team working is viewed as more beneficial to employees than working in isolation.'

Harvester Restaurants – empowerment via work groups

Harvester Restaurants was, at the time of the re-organization, a wholly owned brand within the Forte Restaurants Division (subsequently sold to Bass in 1995). The Harvester Restaurant brand included 78 units based round the core concept and had an annual turnover in excess of £80 million per annum. There were approximately 3000 employees, of whom 40 per cent were full-time and 60 per cent worked varying degrees of part-time hours.

The Harvester brand • • •

The core concept is of a family restaurant and pub. Decor conveys a rustic image with menus based on traditional 'English' fare. Pricing strategy pitches the offer in the mid-price range. Although menus offer a reasonable choice of dishes, preparation techniques are based on simple routine tasks and require relatively simple skill levels to complete. Restaurant service style is through waiter/waitress order taking and plated service of meals. The bar area is designed in pub style and stocked with a typical range of beers, wines, spirits, and offers bar meals.

Menus are devised and priced centrally and there is little discretion needed at unit level, as product development, preparation methods, and serving instructions are developed at head office and 'trained out' to key unit personnel (Kitchen Team Co-ordinators and Team Managers). Service standards reflect the ethos of *'treating customers as though they were guests in your own home'*. The style of service has an informal formality, which also reinforces brand values of homeliness, hospitality, tradition and naturalness. Thus the brand can be defined as being standardized in the tangibles. Customers know what to expect and how much it will cost. Whilst the brand also defines core values in customer service, the nature of the business is such that the intangible elements of the brand cannot be standardized in the same way as with tangibles and is thereby reliant on the efforts of front-line staff. Under these circumstances it is hoped that empowerment will encourage employees to accept responsibility for the service encounter, to respond appropriately to customer needs and to be committed to 'delighting the customer'. The offer to customers is typical of an organization that is offering a 'relationship dependent service' (Lashley, 2000b). That is, the brand attributes are standardized in the tangible aspects of the goods and services but seek to be more customized in the intangible aspects of service. In these circumstances employees play a crucial role in developing appropriate service relationships with customers.

Organization and management ● ● ●

Prior to the re-organization of the business, restaurants were managed in a traditional manner. Figure 4.1 provides a diagram of the organization structure from the customer (referred to as guests) through to senior management. Each unit was managed by a Restaurant Manager and two (or three) Assistant Restaurant Managers. The management team were responsible for the day to day running of the unit – ordering stock, maintaining the security of materials and money, receiving and checking goods, cashing up and banking takings, locking premises, staffing and the management of people in the unit. Externally, the eight Restaurant Managers were answerable to a Regional Manager and four of these were accountable to two Operations Managers, who in turn answered to the Managing Director. Under this structure there were, therefore, five layers between the guest and the Managing Director.

Hospitality, Leisure & Tourism Series

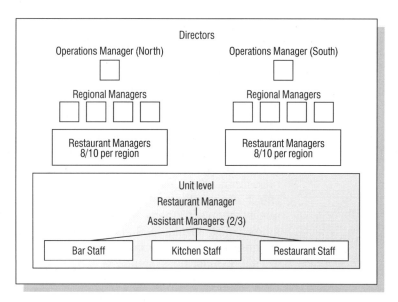

Figure 4.1 Harvester Restaurant organization prior to re-organization

Recession in the British economy in the early 1990s coupled with a desire to improve on guest satisfaction, led the senior management team to reassess the way the business was run. Unusually for a firm in the sector, management adopted a quality leadership strategy as way of coping with recession. The 'old' structure was criticized because it seemed to act as a barrier to the management of the brand. In particular the management structure itself was thought to be an impediment to creating the commitment necessary to improve service quality and business performance. Employees were not trusted and their ideas not considered. Consequently, there something of an 'us and them' atmosphere and a lack of 'ownership' at all levels of the organization.

Given this analysis, the company decided to restructure the organization. In effect two levels of management were removed, but this was more than simply delayering. It involved a major rethink of the way the business was run. This strategic approach to restructuring was based round a model that involved the consideration of **Culture – Organization – People – Systems**.

The company described its focus on these four themes in the following way.

> '*Culture* – the culture is proactively managed to be focused on the guest. In order to truly empower individuals the organization must be value-driven to

ensure that staff can make the right decisions and do the right things. The value becomes the guiding principle for every person as opposed to policy and procedure manuals. *Organization* – to truly empower the front line the traditional hierarchy must be removed. If you have the right structure, quality people will shine through and poor quality will get found out. In order to create the structure accountabilities must be defined. *People* – people need massive input, when the new structure was briefed out a tremendous amount of time was spent on philosophy as well as skills. In order to empower the front line it is essential that the organization is made up of quality people properly trained and with the right atti-tudes at all levels. *System* – the systems must be supportive to the programme. A communication system is vital. It must be systemized. Other key systems are induction – rewards – recognition and appraisal.'

Considerations of these four key issues resulted in a major re-structuring of the company. Senior managers considered every aspect of guest service and what the organization needed to do to ensure customer satisfaction. The re-definition of roles and responsibilities, and improvements to communications processes were two fundamental issues. Implementation took place 'over-night' after a substantial programme of training and re-orientation.

Some of the details of the changes will be discussed more fully later, but the revised organization structure is shown in Figure 4.2. Under this structure there are now only three layers of personnel between the guest and the Managing Director. Staff within the restaurants are organized into autonomous work teams and are now referred to as team members. Each team has its 'team responsibilities' and some team members take on additional duties as Shift Co-ordinators and Appointed Persons. Restaurant management consists of just two roles – Team Manager and Coach.

At restaurant level, the Team Manager and Team Coach were no longer 'managing' the staff but were responsible for enabling and facilitating staff to be more self-managing and empowered. Each restaurant is organized round three teams which reflect the key operational areas – bars, restaurant and kitchen. Each team has its own *Team Responsibilities,* i.e. those aspects of business performance for which it will be accountable. In the restaurant, for example, the team will be responsible for guest service, guest complaints, sales targets, ordering cutlery and glassware, cashing up after service, and team member training. In the more

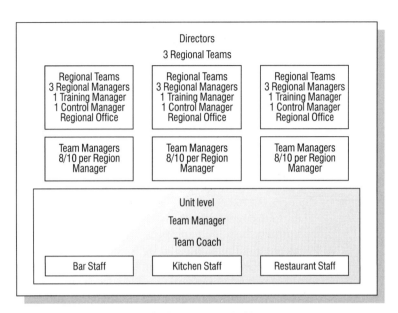

Figure 4.2 The revised organization structure in Harvester

advanced cases, teams take part in the selection and recruitment of new team members.

A Shift Co-ordinator helps co-ordinate the activities of the team. This person is a team member, serving on table, cooking the grills, or serving in the bar, but assumes additional responsibilities during the shift. In the restaurant the Shift Co-ordinator would take on the team responsibility for cashing up at the end of service and ensuring table layout was compatible with prior bookings. Several different team members would take on the role of Shift Co-ordinator during the week. Arrangements for organizing this seem to vary. In some cases, the first person on duty assumes the role, in others, the Team Manager rotas these responsibilities through the week. Interestingly, Shift Co-ordinators do not receive extra hourly rates of pay to compensate for these responsibilities.

In addition to these roles, one of the staff members operates as the Appointed Person during each shift. This person would again be a member of one of the teams working in the restaurant, bar or kitchen during the shift but would accept responsibility for securing the building, putting the shift's takings in the safe and handing over keys to the next Appointed Person. As with the Shift Co-ordinator, Appointed Persons receive no extra responsibility allowances, though in practice they get more pay by being on duty for longer hours. Given that these are often seen as core tasks in a traditional manager's job, it is interesting to note that there were no increases in security problems as a result of this initiative.

Apart from these changes to role and structure, changes to team member training and communication processes are fundamental to the Harvester restructuring exercise. At unit level, training is organized and co-ordinated by the Team Coach, it his/her responsibility to ensure that new employees are given the training needed for effective performance and that the unit training profile increases. Team member (operative) training is organized in three phases within the company. The first phase concerns effective work performance in the tasks related to the job, and covers job knowledge, skills and work pace. When an employee is judged competent in all aspects of the job they can be entered for their 'Silver Badge', which if successful, will earn an additional 20p per hour for the individual. Following on from this, team members may work towards their 'Technical Skills Badge' which entails detailed competence and the ability to train others in at least eight team accountabilities. Again this would attract an additional 20p per hour. Finally, a person may become a 'Team Expert' by taking on additional competences which 'add value to the team', say as in becoming the Coach to the team. Again, an extra 20p per hour is paid to these persons. Typically, it is expected that the majority of staff in a unit would hold the Silver Badge whilst one team member would have the Technical Skills Badge and one team member would be the Team Expert.

Communication systems include weekly team meetings to which all team members are invited, though in practice only core members attend. Either the Coach or Team Manager attends each team meeting. These meetings act as a medium for both sharing information about operational performance and identifying goals or problems. An example given by one team member related to an incident where the unit was losing customers because it was entering a quiet period. The restaurant team suggested that they consider ways of increasing the average spend per head. They subsequently met as a whole team and decided on courses of action. Average spend per head improved by 50 pence.

Interviews with all team members in the sample confirmed the communications aspect as a positive outcome of the re-organization. Team members liked to know 'how we are doing'. They seemed to take a personal interest and pride in the unit's performance, and could quote figures about sales growth, profits, and average spend per head. A key issue here is that much of the loyalty and pride was directed at the unit, rather than company level. The Team Managers seemed important in acting as a conduit which both builds company objectives into the team's objectives and generates the necessary local loyalty. In addition, the most effective autonomous groups were based on fairly stable groups within the workforce. In some cases, employees had been working in the establishment for five or six years, in some, over ten years. Strong group bonds and stability had been established before the introduction of work groups.

Senior executives reported difficulties in establishing groups where there was a stubborn labour turnover problem, or where key members of the work team left and 'pulse turnover' resulted. Some unit managers and coaches also found difficulties in adjusting to the different approach needed. That said, senior managers believed that overall organizational performance has improved since the introduction of the flat structure. There had been a sales increase of 7 per cent, team member turnover had fallen by 19 per cent and liquor stocks had been reduced by almost £250,000. Wages cost were marginally reduced, from 24 per cent to 23.2 per cent, and administration costs had fallen by 41 per cent. There has been an increase in understanding and commitment to the business objectives throughout the organization and communications were now more clearly directed to the appropriate people. People were now allowed to develop their talents and empowered to resolve issues. The organization could now respond more quickly to change by being more focused on the important issues and through processes of constant progress.

At unit level, Coaches and Team Managers in these units reported a great deal of satisfaction with the approach. They felt that it had generated much more commitment from team members and had freed them up to concentrate on business development and customer care. Labour turnover in the wider organization is low by the standards of this type of business, but high when set within a wider industrial context. Within these units, labour turnover was particularly low at about 10 per cent. This is undoubtedly an important ingredient to success and one that is likely to produce a 'virtuous cycle'. Low labour turnover enables the development of strong teams, which in turn reduces labour turnover.

Unit management also reported a low level of guest complaints. One unit registered no formal complaints for three full quarters. This was due to the front line teams being able to resolve problems as they arose. So even if a customer received a meal that was not satisfactory, or was kept waiting too long, the immediate team member could resolve the situation to the customer's satisfaction. In a few cases, complainants wanted to see 'the manager' and didn't understand the flat structure. This could be a problem, though most dealt with it by bringing in a person from another department.

Problems were resolved more quickly without recourse to the manager. One member of the unit management team said, 'A few years ago, if the freezer broke and I was away for a couple of days, it stayed broken. Now we say to everyone in the kitchen, if the freezer breaks down what do we do . . . get it fixed. OK how do we get it fixed? . . . now we get it fixed, there is no alternative, even if it costs £1,000.'

The case study of Harvester Restaurants shows that forms of empowerment based on autonomous work groups can be made to work within retail service organizations. The approach required total commitment from senior mangers. The whole structure of the organization, the distribution of responsibilities and authority, the definition of key roles, job descriptions, training and information systems were all redesigned round a consistent approach. As with many other examples of empowerment, the initiative was designed as a coherent whole, empowerment was not just grafted on to an existing traditional structure. It is also important to remember that its successful application needed stable employment and a group dynamic within the workforce upon which group working practices built. Though attractive and appealing in many ways, this approach cannot be easily transplanted from one organization to another, and requires both the appropriate social conditions and management commitment to be established before implementation. Bearing in mind the points made in Chapter 2, the organization had put in place many of the ingredients needed to produce the psychological state of empowerment in employees. They had addressed training, culture and communication needs so that employees felt competent to make choices about how they met customer needs, and feedback systems enabled them to track customer satisfaction and other measures of business performance.

Job enrichment and empowerment

Bearing in mind Geary's (1994) point that task participation is best understood as a process, our attempts to understand arrangements that empower employees by giving them authority to make decisions are best understood as processes in which there are a limited number of possibilities. Where autonomous work groups empower employees as a group, this form of empowerment is aimed at empowering the individual. The extension of their authority to make decisions has much in common with initiatives that were labelled 'enrichment' in earlier times. Important ingredients to the approach are detailed training in customer service needs – 'whatever it takes training' – and the establishment of a service culture that guides employees as they identify, and interpret, service needs. This approach usually involves individuals having the authority and responsibility for solving customer problems on the spot. Thus unusual requests for services or products that are not normally offered, or responses to complaints, can be met by front line employees. Arrangements are also sometimes linked to self-monitoring of service quality by the employee. Jobs are enriched so that employees are empowered to do whatever it takes to 'delight' the customer.

The key point is that empowerment is largely related to attempts to generate improved service quality by improving responsiveness of front line employees in the immediate service situation. Empowerment consists chiefly of authority to operate within prescribed boundaries. In some cases, a cash value is given to the guest as a refund for a complaint – reduction on the bill, free meal, complementary drink or bottle of wine, the replacement of a meal, etc. In some cases, the empowerment might involve the provision of products out of brand, or expenditure to provide the guest with an extra service. This might extend from the hotel doorman who left the hotel and followed a guest with a forgotten briefcase on the next flight (Bowen and Lawler, 1992), to the food service operative who can agree to provide dishes not on the menu, as long as they have the ingredients. In the main, however, this form of empowerment consists of empowering employees to provide extra service. It is particularly relevant to the intangible aspects of the customer offer. The employee taking ownership of the service encounter and providing a level of service not normally given, without reference to a supervisor or manager, is largely what the approach aims to achieve. It is interesting that most of the examples of extra service given in the Marriott advertisements (see Figure 3.1) involve employees providing the extra service in their own time.

The job enrichment form of empowerment therefore involves a detailed training programme that encourages employees to understand and empathize with customer experiences, to incorporate the company's service values to its customers, and use initiative in meeting customer service needs within the boundaries set. Antonacopoulou and Kanampully (2000) quote several US case studies that show how this more individualized form of empowerment can be achieved through support and a learning organization culture. Whilst there may be some change in managerial roles, to become more supportive and less directly controlling, this approach to empowerment does not usually change the nature of the management structure nor the distribution of power and authority within the organization. Putting this in a wider context of employment strategy Marchington and Wilkinson (2000: 348) say, 'These have celebrated more humanistic employment regimes, viewing them not so much as counter to alienation at work but as a key component in the search for competitive advantage'.

This form of involvement is participative, allowing employees discretion to meet customer service needs (Tanennbaum and Schmidt, 1973). The approach is close to co-determination with control limited to task-specific arrangements (Marchington and Wilkinson, 2000). The form of involvement is direct as all service employees are directly involved. Involvement is task based and the range of what employees are empowered to do is limited to a narrow range of issues related to the service task. There are rarely opportunities to make decisions about matters such as equipment ordering or staffing levels. Employees are able to exercise power in being able to make their decisions stick, though this is limited, and they will be expected to account for their actions after the event. Thus a person may be empowered to give dissatisfied customers a free meal or drink, but the amount and frequency of hand-outs will be monitored and excessive generosity may well be questioned.

Marriott Hotels – empowerment through job enrichment

This case study features the experiences of re-branding a group of Scott's hotels to the Marriott brand prior to their sale to the Whitbread organization in the mid 1990s. Executives, like their counterparts in Harvester Restaurants, also made a decision that a competitive strategy based around improved service quality was both an effective way of dealing with the recession in demand in the early 1990s and of improving the profile of the group. Like the earlier cases, Marriotts were making an offer to customers that standardized the tangible aspects of the products and services, but was aiming to gain competitive advantage in the intangible aspects of the service, particularly through the quality of the guest experience when in contact with staff. Chapter 12 expands further on the link between service types and the performance of service staff.

A company-wide training programme including all 2000 employees was undertaken with the specific theme of customer service quality. At the same time the organization attempted to establish a culture of total quality management. An important strand in developing the quality of the service offer to customers was the empowerment of employees. This was defined as 'giving staff confidence to make decisions, large or small, that impact on the guest's stay' (Hubrecht and Teare, 1993: iii). This 'confidence' was primarily developed through the 'Whatever It Takes' training programme, which took up to 40–60 hours per employee. The programme intended to develop a sense of empathy to customer experiences in the staff. Each employee was encouraged to look at things from the guest's point of view.

Contents of the programme helped employees to consider who is the customer, what it is they are buying from the company, and the importance of employees in both creating impressions and in delivering customer satisfaction. The programme took employees through guest experiences using role plays. It included the following rules for employees:

1 Please acknowledge that you have seen me and know that I am waiting to be served.
2 Please make me feel important and like a real individual.
3 Please find out what my needs are.
4 Please look as though you enjoy working here.
5 Please know what you are doing and do it promptly.
6 Please don't bring any more hassle into my life.

Also included in the WIT programme, employees developed skills in team dynamics, sales, rooms merchandising, assertiveness, product and service knowledge, creative thinking and risk taking, and problem solving.

In addition to the training directly aimed at improvements in customer service through a focused approach, the company introduced a scheme of employee development through a non-vocational training scheme. All employees are eligible to apply for sponsorship to develop a new skill. The key is that this is not specifically related to work related skills or improving job performance. It allows the learning of skills not directly related to work. Taking lessons from 'learning organizations', the assumption is that as employees personally grow and develop, they become more enthusiastic and confident, and this improves their contribution to the organization.

Although chiefly developing individual skills and commitment to the service encounter amongst employees, this was further supported by forms of employee involvement that encouraged employees to be self-assessing, self-monitoring, adopt practices which 'get it right first time', and get involved with quality circles and 'task forces'. These latter activities did not involve all employees, and, by definition, are representative in nature as employees usually volunteer to represent the group or sectional interest.

Communication processes were improved so that employees were given updates on progress through regular briefings, quality newsletters, quarterly staff meetings, and performance indicators. The aim of these procedures was to ensure employees were given the necessary information to do their work and feedback on their efforts thus far. Finally, recognition and rewards included individual bonuses, non-financial rewards such as personal recognition for efforts and achievements, employee of the month schemes and hotel of the year competitions. In this latter case winning hotels shared prizes with employees.

The company reported that benefits were gained in both employee and customer dimensions. Employee retention rates improved, as did employee attitude surveys, and the outcomes from employee involvement through quality circles. For customers, more customer retention was reported and consequently repeat business was increased, the company increased its approval rating in customer surveys, there were fewer complaints, and market share improved.

Although the approach taken within the Marriott chain was largely driven by a form of employee empowerment through restricted participation in management decisions, the ability of the employees to make decisions about customer needs at the point of service, appeared to engage employees in the objectives set by the organization. Psychologically it allowed them choice in the way they dealt with customers, and through this made service tasks meaningful and valued. The company also underpinned this with training programmes that were both directly aimed at immediate training needs, and supported personal development as a way of generating a sense of personal power, competence and confidence. These initiatives were further supported by improved employee communications systems as well as systems of recognition and reward which further strengthened the impression that the employee is important to the delivery of good service.

Empowerment beyond the task

Bearing in mind a wider definition of empowerment which involves employees in making decisions that might traditionally be the domain of management, it is necessary to briefly consider initiatives that include both co-determination and workers' control. Co-determination is best defined as a number of arrangements that involve some form of joint decision making with managers at establishment or organizational level. In continental Europe, initiatives that include works councils and employee directors are largely rooted in a pluralistic view of organizations and are mechanisms for governing enterprise through co-determination. Workers' control is again an approach more prevalent in Europe, but which involves employees controlling the ownership of the organization through some form of workers' co-operatives. Both approaches reflect a stakeholder view of capitalism (Keep and Rainbird, 2000).

Employees are empowered through their participation in decisions at a level beyond the task. In most cases there is also a corresponding growth in a representative form and employees are empowered as a collective interest set rather than as individuals. Although most individuals do not normally attend works council meetings or sit on supervisory boards, their interests as employees are represented at these meetings, and no matter how limited, they do have opportunities to influence, or have a say, about decisions which affect them.

Forms of employee participation that involve co-determination incorporate some process whereby employees join with managers and/or owners to make decisions, or at least hold decision makers to account for their decisions. These mechanisms are usually at the level of the enterprise, though in the German situation works councils can be established at unit level. Given this enterprise focus, it is not surprising that they become more representative in nature. The practical organizational difficulties are usually cited as arrangements that require elected representatives to participate on behalf of the work force as a whole. The range of issues discussed varies in different legislative contexts and forums. The degree of power that employees have to make decisions stick also varies, but in the main power is constrained by the balance of interests in the decision-making process. Where managers/owners form the majority of the committee, council or board, it is less likely that employees will be able to make decisions stick. From an empowerment perspective, employees are empowered to participate in some decisions that in more traditional organization structures would exclude them, and there may be some sense of personal efficacy felt by employees. The representative nature of the participation may well limit impacts for the workforce as a whole.

Works councils ▪ ▪ ▪

Although there are few examples in the UK and USA, works councils have a long established tradition on mainland Europe, and the European Union passed a Directive in 1994 requiring all companies operating in more than one European country to set up Union wide councils. Though the UK was not a signatory to the Social Charter, and opted out of the Social Chapter of the Maastricht agreement, many British companies with operations on the Continent are establishing works council. In many cases these include representatives from their British establishments.

The works councils set up under European provisions are largely consultative requiring employers to inform employees about planned developments. The system in Germany extends the legal rights of works councils beyond consultation, and could be a model for an organization wanting to take empowerment of its employees to another level. Works councils play an important role in German industrial relations. All employees in establishments employing five or more workers have a legal right to establish a works council. The provisions relate to establishment and thereby encompass most service sector organizations. Jacobi *et al.* (1992) estimate that some 33,000 councils exist involving 180,000 workers and include between 70–80 per cent of the eligible work force.

The Works Constitution Act requires that the works council is elected from all employees. The councils have several legal rights; works council members, as the formal representatives of the workforce, have the right to information covering the employer's plans on manpower planning, and the general economic development of the organization. They have the right to be consulted over issues such as training provision, job structures, alterations to working methods, plans for new technology, and mass redundancies. Works councils also have the right jointly to decide, through negotiation with the employer, a whole host of general employment issues, some of which relate to the implementation of national agreements, other issues relating to training and recruitment, through to the transfer of operations and mass lay-offs. Many of these issues enable employees to be involved, via their representatives, in management decisions beyond the operational issues, which include most task level forms of empowerment.

As stated above, works councils play an important role in German industrial relations, in that they perform many of the roles and responsibilities that might be fulfilled by a trade union in British organizations, and it is a mistake to think that individual arrangements can be plucked from one industrial relations environment and transplanted in another. Royle's (1996) research does show, however, that works councils could achieve some benefits for employees, particularly in developing a wider sense of employee empowerment in relation to the employer. He reports that works councils established in German McDonald's Restaurants had stopped unfair dismissal, acted as a check on employment practice, and 'created a better working environment where management no longer ruled by fear' (p. 92). It is an interesting commentary on the restricted nature of employer

Hospitality, Leisure & Tourism Series

definitions of empowerment that the company in question actively worked against the establishment of works councils, and ultimately paid out substantial sums in buying off employees who were actively involved in the works councils (Royle, 1996: 93).

Employee directors • • •

Employee directors represent another initiative that has more of a history on mainland Europe than in the UK. Notably, two organizations – British Steel and The Post Office – did introduce employee directors in the 1970s and both were public sector organizations at the time. In addition the Bullock Committee (1977) on Industrial Democracy also featured proposals for employees to be represented at board level. The Committee's proposals were greeted with a howl of opposition from UK employers, and the subsequent watered-down proposals that were written in the Labour Government's White Paper were dropped when the Conservative Government came to office in 1979.

The European Union has a draft directive on employee directors underway, but at the time of writing this has not yet produced a workable set of proposals through which to establish a Europe-wide approach. If the Vredeling proposals of the mid-1970s are anything to go by, there are considerable international and employer barriers to overcome. The Japanese employers in particular played a key role in political opposition to the European Commission's plan to require companies to institute some form of employee representation on the board. As might be expected, the Conservative Government in Britain was firmly opposed to such ideas and, given its opt-out of the social legislation, attempted to prevent legislation introduced by the other member countries from having effect in the UK. However, as with European works councils, there may be companies who will introduce these arrangements to their British operations, just for organizational consistency. As Cotton (1993: 113) shows, a significant number of EU member countries already have these arrangements in their company legislation, and it is likely that some form of directive on employer directors will eventually emerge.

Cotton (1993: 120) indicates that research on the impact of employee directors in terms of organizational performance is mixed. Opponents of the initiative generally point to the risk borne by owners as not being matched by employee directors, and state that employees should not be allowed to interfere with commercial decisions. Supporters, on the other hand, point to the benefits of winning support for strategic decision by involving employees and argue that the involvement of employee representatives may improve the quality of decisions. Again, these views often reflect different concepts of the nature of capitalism – shareholder or stakeholder models – using the Keep and Rainbird (2000) phrase.

From an empowerment perspective, employees individually have little involvement in the decisions, though the knowledge that their views have a voice at the most senior levels could be an important element in the creation of a culture of empowerment. Ultimately, the precise nature of the arrangements will determine whether employee directors have any real power to influence decisions. The experiences in German companies show that the balance of numbers on the board can be crucial (Jacobi *et al.*, 1992: 227). The German system is based on two-tier boards. A small management board, including one employee director, is appointed by the owners and is responsible for the day-to-day running of the company. The supervisory board, including employee and owner directors, oversees the running of the company and makes all strategic decisions. There are different arrangements for the balance of numbers of employee and owner directors. In organizations employing less than 2000 employees the balance is one-third employee to two-thirds owner directors. In the organizations employing more than 2000 employees, the Co-determination Act (1976) creates an apparent equal balance between owner and employee representatives (Jacobi *et al.*, 1992: 228), though the composition of the 'employee' representation includes middle managers and ultimately this means the balance is stacked in favour of owners. The Montan industries (coal and steel industries) is equally balanced, though Jacobi *et al.* (1992) estimated that this later type of arrangement covers approximately thirty establishments (p. 228). Clearly, the ability to shape senior level decisions will be largely influenced by the balance of numbers. Where employee directors are in the minority, their role is likely to be more consultative than based on co-determination.

Considering the psychological aspect of empowerment, the representative nature of these arrangements, the potential remoteness of the bodies to shop-floor workers and the ultimate balance of power in the hands of owners are less likely of themselves to create a sense of empowerment. But used as part of a wider strategy that genuinely recognizes the importance of the employee contribution to organization success, they could provide a valued device in establishing a trust culture and a sense of mutuality of interest amongst all organization members.

Participation through ownership

On the Marchington *et al.* (1992) escalator (Figure 3.4), control by workers represents the highest degree of participation, and initiatives advocated by employees have, in some contexts, advocated workers' ownership of industry. Here the assumption has been that ownership of the enterprise will assist employees in shaping decisions and this will empower employees in their workplace. Through ownership they will be able to resist, or at least ameliorate the effects of commercial pressures and exploitation by owners. Again it is possible to see a range of arrangements, some instituted by managers/owners and others which have been advocated by workers.

The John Lewis Partnership is one of Britain's most successful retailers (Rawnsley, 1996). It is a long established example of employee ownership in a service industry. For over seventy years it has been owned by its employees (partners). All profits of the enterprise, after payments of loans, etc., are distributed amongst the employees. On average this can be 15 per cent of the final pay packet. In addition a system of committees involve, to varying degrees, representatives of employees who have rights to be involved in some decisions. One recent spokesperson for the company said that a recent decision to open stores half an hour early and close half an hour later 'took hours of meetings to get approval' (Basset, 1996). It is a system avowedly democratic, yet it is a form in which democracy should not 'influence business decisions at the cost of efficient management' (Flanders *et al.*, 1968: 182). Furthermore, 'the effect of the system on management is paradoxically to reinforce its authority so it is stronger and commands greater power than is usual. . .' (Flanders *et al.*, 1968: 183). The John Lewis Partnership confirms that ownership of shares in the enterprise, even where these represent a majority holding, do not automatically produce control over managerial decision-making.

For most employees this form of participation is indirect because it is representatives who participate within the decision-making process. The level of participation is beyond the task, and employees have some valuable communication links to the most senior managers who can be held to account by the partners. That said, partners have no real sanctions against managers – they cannot dismiss a manager, and the house magazine does reveal controversy amongst partners about the levels of senior managers' pay (Tredre, 1996). The range of issues to be considered is constrained, and employees' power to make decisions that stick is limited. The extent to which these arrangements develop a sense of personal efficacy is an issue that requires further study;

the Flanders *et al.* (1968) study did show that there were generally high levels of job satisfaction, labour stability and general support for the system.

The Mondragon network of worker co-operatives in the Basque region of Spain is an example of a more worker-driven attempt at empowerment. Here the arrangements were established as a device to provide a work and economic activity from within the community without reliance on traditional commercial and exploitative structures. In this case it is argued that employees empowered themselves by avoiding situations which disempower them. 'The Mondragon experiment has shown, above all, how workers can create and extend a system of self management in an environment which is changing rapidly and becoming more and more competitive' (Thomas and Logan, 1982: 1). The network of co-operatives spans manufacturing and service industry contexts including colleges, banks, and retail outlets. Moreover, 'their growth record of sales, exports and employment, under favourable and adverse economic conditions, has been superior to that of capitalist enterprise' (Thomas and Logan, 1982: 127).

Almost 100,000 people are involved in the co-operatives, though most are not bigger than 500 members. Each person employed in the co-operative has the opportunity to take a financial stake in the shares of the enterprise – this cannot be sold on, and there is a maximum holding. Dividends paid on the basis of share holding. Those who work in the enterprise elect individuals to represent their interests on various committees and boards. They have the power to both hold managers to account, and appoint as well as dismiss managers. Employees are involved directly and indirectly in making long-term decisions, though day-to-day decision-making is in the hands of managers.

In this case employees are in control of the enterprise, its direction and policy. They share in its profits and losses. Individuals are directly, indirectly and financially involved at the level of the enterprise, which is restricted in size. The range of issues are largely of a more strategic level, and employees have the power to make decisions stick. That said, there are constitutional constraints on participants that limit complete freedom of action. Employees are empowered as owners of an enterprise in a location where there is a strong cultural acceptance of co-operation. The size of the venture seems to be an important factor, because early co-operatives were allowed to grow in size and a long bitter strike took place in one of the largest. This may show that the sense of involvement in the co-operative becomes diffused when enterprises grow too large. It is also confirmation of how fragile the state of empowerment can be and that immediate work experience, relations with managers and supervisors, communications and training have a powerful influence even when the employees are the owners.

Conclusion

This chapter has discussed a number of different forms of empowerment that involve employees, to varying degrees, making decisions which would traditionally be made by managers. In autonomous work groups, employees as a group are empowered to make task decisions about how they execute tasks and how they are organized. The Harvester Restaurant example showed that employees can take on responsibilities for organizational goals to achieve various service, sales and cost management targets. It was felt by managers that the employees were best placed to interpret and deliver greater customer satisfaction, generate increased sales and manage labour costs. In addition to providing mutual support and producing more ideas, the group also provided an important mechanism for generating employee compliance to the objectives of the organization.

Interestingly, Sosteric (1996) provides an example of a case where the process was reversed. New managers came into a Canadian night-club restaurant and imposed strict controls over how staff interacted with customers. The result was a loss of autonomy over the way employees dealt with customers and customers' dissatisfaction grew alongside employee dissatisfaction. The example provides another confirmation of the link between the management of service employees and the impact on their social interactions with customers.

The second form of empowerment was more restricted in scope and aimed directly at individuals. It was based on detailed training in customer service, and aimed at empowering employees to take decisions relating to the guests' service needs. Feelings of personal confidence and being prepared to take risks, say by crossing departmental boundaries or providing services not normally offered, were encouraged directly through training programmes. Also the creation of a risk-taking culture, improved communication, and recognition and rewards were important. Another element in establishing both the desired culture, and recognition, for excellent service was the use of 'war stories'. That is, the use of role models of individuals who did that little bit extra. The set of Marriott Hotels' advertisements are typical of devices used to both external customers and employees that demonstrate what desirable behaviour is like.

Finally, the chapter examined some examples of forms of employee involvement which extended beyond task level considerations. Here employees have an opportunity to comment on, and in some cases, shape the subsequent policies that the company operates at the most senior levels. By their nature these forms of empowerment are representative – not all employees are directly involved – but the knowledge that employees' collective interests are being progressed may engender feelings of empowerment.

Forms of empowerment through involvement

- **Quality circles and empowerment**
- **Team briefings and empowerment**
- **Job enlargement and empowerment**

Some forms of empowerment aim to involve employees in aspects of service operations without necessarily sharing decision-making. Rafiq and Ahmed (1998a) argue that the level and type of empowerment depends on the complexity of the service offer being delivered. These contextual considerations are discussed more fully in Chapter 12, but in this case employee perform-ance is considered to be even more important than in 'typical' operations, say where employees are deliver-ing some form of 'mass customized' service. TGI Fridays provides a useful example of such a situation (Lashley, 2000a). TGI Fridays will be discussed more fully later, but at this stage it is sufficient to note that employee performance is required to interpret and deliver the type of service required by the customer, but not at the same level of customized service as delivered in professional services, say by the doctor or dentist.

In other situations, employee involvement is required as a means of improving organizational, and particularly operational, performance. The service employees' proximity to the customer best equips them to make suggestions for new products and services, detect and correct service faults, and improve operating systems (Koberg et al., 1999). Here the key requirement is to involve employees in some form of consultation whereby they can make suggestions upon which managers can act. Unlike the examples given in Chapter 4, where employees were taking on some form of decision making role, under these arrangements managers continue to make decisions but informed by suggestions and advice from employees. Smith and Moulay (1998: 70) define empowerment in a way that is consistent with this concept of empowerment. 'This definition does not view empowerment as a "transfer of power" from the employers to the employees. Rather it is seen as "enabling" employees to make use of the power they already possess.'

Empowerment through involvement aims to engage employees at an emotional level, but without sharing decision-making. The forms of empowerment are largely concerned with developing a sense of 'ownership' in employees so that those directly concerned with customer service will provide the appropriate service to customers and will look to ways of improving customer service through the benefit of their own experience. Even in a production context, Ahanotou (1998) shows that employees involved in innovation processes were more committed and empowered. In particular, this research stresses the importance of developing personal knowledge as a means of becoming empowered.

Though there are variations amongst forms, it is true to say the most of these initiatives are consultative, using the Tannenbaum and Schmidt (1973) categories. They involve information giving and some consultation in the Marchington et al. (1992) dimensions, they can be both representative and direct, largely concerned with task level issues, and restricted to an agenda of items that is restricted to work organization, productivity and quality improvement, and problem-solving customer satisfaction issues. They allow employees limited power, because in all cases, managers make final decisions. Employees have opportunities to make suggestions and identify issues for improvement, but decisions remain the domain of managers.

Like the forms of empowerment via participation, it is possible to draw distinctions between initiatives that are focused at individuals and those that involve some form of group, or collective involvement. Thus suggestions schemes, in British organizations, are often an individualized form of involvement, whilst quality circles and team briefing sessions are more collective in nature.

Quality circles and empowerment

Over recent years there has been increasing use of quality circles, quality improvement groups, or focus groups as a means of increasing employee involvement and gaining improvements in service quality. Unlike autonomous work groups that involve a redesigned organization structure, quality circles represent a parallel structure (Lawler and Mohran, 1987) within the organization. This parallel feature of quality circle and the formal organizational structures suggests both strengths and weaknesses to the efficacy of quality circles.

Though quality circles were first developed in the United States in the 1940s, their use was most widely introduced in Japan in the 1960s and then 'rediscovered' with the tide of Japonification in the 1970s and 1980s. Initially, and most usually, quality circles were applied in manufacturing operations and improvements in product quality. Certainly their adoption by a large number of Japanese manufacturing firms has to be seen against a background in which Japanese products had an international reputation for unreliable quality. Western interest in quality circles was largely congruent with the growth in interest in Japanese management techniques as many Western consumer durable markets became dominated by Japanese products.

At an operational level, quality circles involve groups of employees who meet regularly to discuss common operational issues. Usually, these meetings are weekly and involve volunteers meeting for about one hour. In the majority of cases the quality circle's activities are co-ordinated by a trained facilitator. Typically, the facilitator is a management appointment, either a supervisor or manager. In some cases the facilitator is a manager from another department. The facilitator acts as the channel of communication with the organization. Typically, quality circles are created in a climate of problem resolution relating to either service quality or productivity (Lawler and Mohran, 1987), but if they are to continue to exist over the initial phase of enthusiasm, quality circles need to be established in an organizational climate which provides an unequivocal long term role and which demonstrates the support of senior managers.

Typically, quality circles are established to match organizational arrangements. These may be in departments or units. So in a hotel organization, quality circles may be established to cover the kitchen, restaurant, accommodation, and leisure operations in each hotel, or they may match just the unit structure, that is, one for each hotel. Comen (1989: 24) reports that a study of US hotels revealed that the number of quality circles varied from two in a 50 bedroom hotel to twenty in a 1500 bedroom hotel. The key point is that they match the parallel formal organization in a way that creates an ongoing opportunity for a contribution from the quality circles. Where they are successfully introduced, an organization-wide steering committee is established to co-ordinate and support the network of quality circles in the organization. This committee will consist of management, trade union and circle representatives, and will issue guidelines, set objectives and goals, and train facilitators (Dale and Lees, 1986).

Service organizations' motives for introducing quality circles have identified as being concerned with a desire to improve communications, staff morale, and commitment to service quality (Dale and Lees, 1986). In their study of twenty-seven service organizations, Dale and Lees (1986) show that the most popular projects undertaken by quality circles were service quality improvement.

That quality circles can be a valuable device for capturing employee experiences and gaining suggestions about changes in customer service needs has been identified (Barbee and Bott, 1991). From an empowerment perspective, quality circles can be seen as a means for establishing employee involvement in the service encounter. Quality circles can both provide a rhetoric that establishes employees as important to service quality, whilst at the same time minimizing the loss of managerial control, and generate genuine improvements to service delivery.

Lawler and Mohran (1987) suggest that quality circles are valuable when dealing with issues not usually considered within the organization, because there is insufficient time under normal operational constraints. In other cases, quality circles are beneficial where managers have insufficient detailed information to make an informed decision, or where front-line staff have more understanding of the practical details of operations. Quality circles can be more flexible and responsive to changes occurring in customer service needs, or operational realities. In addition, quality circles are advisory and offer no direct challenge to managerial authority.

The Dale and Lees (1986) study also highlighted the perceived benefits to organization members in service organizations. It is worth pointing out that perceived benefits in the employment relationship are bound to be muted by the representative nature of quality circles. Thus participants may feel empowered because of the opportunity to be more involved in the organization, and have an increased sense of belonging, etc., but non-participants will have no opportunity to experience these benefits. That said, there may be a general improvement in the sense of involvement because quality circles do provide a mechanism for gathering suggestions from employees, and at the very least, they do recognize the important contribution employees can make. Bearing in mind the qualification that quality circles are a representative form of employee involvement, the declared benefits seem to be somewhat evangelical. The study lists increased opportunities for involvement, better team work and increased job satisfaction as key declared benefits of quality circles.

The matching of the perceived aspirations for, and benefits of, quality circles is an important issue in experiences of quality circles within organizations. Lawler and Mohran (1987) suggest that the introduction of quality circles typically goes through three periods. The first is the **honeymoon period** in which there is a high level of enthusiasm from management and participants. There are few circles and those in operation benefit from both their unusual status and the added attention received. Suggestions generated are implemented because ideas generated are perceived to be good and lead to improvements. The **second phase** witnesses rapid expansion as managers assume that more circles will lead to a greater number of improvements. This reveals the difficulty of sustaining the early success, as more, and perhaps less committed, managers are required to implement the system. The **third phase** represents a 'backlash' when middle management resistance can lead to consistent failure to implement suggestions and a consequent loss of interest by participants. In some cases, circles are ineffectual and managers begin to count the extra costs of operating the parallel system. Benefits may be difficult to calculate – a particular problem for service industries where benefits are in the intangibles, or do not prove so beneficial as predicted. Senior managers, who were early promoters of quality circles, move on to other responsibilities, or become absorbed by another initiative or management fad. In these circumstances, organizations either disband the initiative, look to ways of overcoming the difficulties, or move on to the alternative forms of employee participation.

Lawler and Mohran point to several weaknesses inherent in quality circles. At root, their location in a parallel structure does mean that decisions and suggestions have little formal impact on the organization. Their status may be sidelined, and suggestions are vulnerable to the 'grace and favour' of managerial decision makers. Marchington and Wilkinson (2000: 347) confirm this; 'it is recognized that there are problems sustaining circles or problem-solving groups beyond 18 months to two years', once the immediate issues have been dealt with and managers begin to question their value. As stated earlier, they are representative in nature, and tensions may be caused between those who belong to the quality circles and those employees who are not members. Even amongst members, there may be hard to handle tensions, because employees are given high status whilst at circle meetings, but are treated as ordinary employees when back at the workplace.

If these difficulties are to be overcome, an organization that introduces quality circles, as with other forms of employee involvement, needs to ensure that the organizational context supports their operation. Senior managers need to be openly supportive and committed to picking up on the suggestions made. Junior and middle managers have to be both trained in their use and accountable for their successful operation. Circle members must be trained and supported with an appropriate facilitator. The range of human resource management practices needs to be compatible with quality circles – recruitment and selection, rewards and recognition, training and staff appraisal should match quality circle requirements. Reward structures should enable employees to share in gains from suggestions, and must be focused at work groups. Hence if all employees partake of the gains from quality circles, even non-participants will perceive the benefits.

The use of quality circles in service quality enhancement is somewhat problematic because of the intangible nature of elements of the guest offer. Improvements in product quality and productivity gains in product output are more easily quantified. However, advances in customer satisfaction are difficult to pin to particular suggestions. Similarly, service quality productivity is notoriously fraught with difficulty, particularly when customer complaints and customer satisfaction are brought into the equation (Merricks and Jones, 1986). Consequently, the use of quality circles have not had such a wide appeal as in manufacturing, but as the previous section shows, there can be some major benefits to the use of quality circles in service organizations.

As a form of employee involvement, quality circles are essentially consultative where managers pose problems, receive suggestions from employees, and make decisions informed by employee suggestions. Quality circles are typically task orientated with an agenda of service quality, operational, and productivity improvement. They are representative forms of involvement, with volunteers actively participating. The majority of employees are only indirectly involved. Though some quality circles may deal with health and safety issues, quality circles rarely deal with employment matters or general issues related to employee relations. Outputs from quality circles are largely advisory, and circle members have limited power to make their suggestions happen.

These consultative and representative aspects of quality circles also raise problems in that they have limited impact on individual employees, and thereby it is difficult to see how quality circles of themselves can create the necessary state of empowerment. Obviously as an element of a strategy that sets employee performance at the centre of service quality, they will add to a sense of meaning and worth, but used without other management policies to build up the sense of competence and choice, quality circles may have a limited impact on the workforce as a whole.

The Accor Group

The use of quality circles has been applied in some of the group's hotels to good effect. The approach involves a more fluid status to quality circles than is typical. In this case the circles are formed to address a specific problem and they are 'dissolved when the problem is solved' (Barbee and Bott, 1991). This fluid arrangement involving different employees may overcome some of the problems mentioned above. First circles were introduced in the company's Mercure Paris Nord/St Witz Hotel. Four circles were established to cover the four key aspects of guest service – kitchen, restaurant, accommodation, reception. In each case, the brief requires that the circle focus on an improvement to guest service, and that problem must be capable of being resolved by circle members themselves without major expenditure.

Participants are volunteers and unpaid for their contributions, though publicity of good ideas in the company's quality circles newsletter, together with the implicit knowledge that quality circles provide formal recognition of the contribution employees can make, helps to generate interest in the programme. Managers report few problems in gaining volunteers for membership of the circles. A manager from another hotel acts as facilitator. This is said to assist employees and facilitator in taking a fresh look at the problem uncluttered by past history and ego-defensive arguments.

Circle members deal with every aspect of the problem – identification, defining criteria for the solutions to the problem, suggested solutions, testing solutions against the criteria, measuring results and then 'rolling out the solution'. Speeding up customer breakfast service and guest check-out times are examples of issues which have been addressed by quality circles.

Apart from the immediate benefits arising from the circle improvements, managers report that the most important gains come from improvements in employee morale. Employees are more likely to support changes introduced as a result of quality circles, and they gain an increased sense of worth as managers treat their problems and suggestions seriously. Communications between managers and employees have improved, and there has been a general increase in employee/manager contact.

Team briefings and empowerment

If quality circles represent a parallel organization structure, team briefing sessions might be described as overlaying the organization's structure. In effect, they provide a mechanism for managers and employees to meet on a regular basis to discuss operational issues. In some cases they are used as a means of communicating 'top-down' decisions and organizational issues – shifts in demand, new product lines, successes/failures, etc. In other cases they may be used as vehicles for consultation and suggestion making from employees. Thus in Tannenbaum and Schmidt's (1973) model, team briefings are essentially consultative, but cover different degrees of involvement from 'tell and sell', through 'tell and test' to 'seek'. Like quality circles, the key difference with more participative forms is that managers make the decisions informed by comments from employees.

The frequency of these briefing meetings varies. At their most integrated with operational management, they are conducted before or after each shift. Clearly, the timing of the briefings means that they perform different roles. In the first case, they assist in briefing the team about the specific requirements of the shift – up-coming orders, stock situations, likely demand levels, priority sales targets, possible sources of operational difficulty – and they can be used to enthuse the group. Post shift sessions can be useful as learning devices for operational successes and difficulties. They are used to flag up issues to be addressed in subsequent shifts – correcting individual and group performance, praising performance, role modelling, identifying and sharing best practice. In both cases, they are used to gather suggestions and feedback from team members. Almost by definition these shift-focused meetings are task driven and operational in concerns.

In other cases, team briefing sessions may be less frequent; they may be weekly or monthly. These meetings are often used as a means of communicating progress to employees. Thus managers target issues for action and outline actions and policies being introduced. They may be used to report on unit performance or organizational developments. These meetings can be used for seeking suggestions and advice from employees, but are mostly used for passing on information to employees.

Team briefing sessions are concerned with a degree of involvement which ranges between information passing, or 'downward communicating' (Marchington and Wilkinson, 2000) through communicating to consulting or 'upward problem solving'. The key point is that managers continue to make decisions and involve employees in either merely receiving information, or at best passing comment on, or making suggestions to inform management decisions. Team briefings are a direct form of involvement, because all employees are involved in the process. They are chiefly concerned with operational issues, though may involve reporting organizational progress and policies. The range of items discussed is typically restricted to operational tasks, output, performance, quality, sales, perhaps even unit operating profits. Employees have limited power to make decisions or suggestions stick because managers exercise control over the nature of the decision.

From an empowerment perspective, the intention is that these initiatives involve employees by developing a sense of ownership through communication processes which provide targets and feedback. Those forms that involve suggestion making and consultation also aim to create a sense of ownership. In these cases, it is hoped that employees making suggestions, and having their suggestions introduced, will develop pride in their work, feel empowered to detect and correct service faults, constantly improve services, and be permanently involved in delighting customers. In addition to these intrinsic benefits to employees, which potentially improve service quality, the organization can benefit from suggestions that come from the experiences of front line staff. Thus shifts in customer preferences and choices, and service expectations can be quickly detected because team briefings provide a means of capturing them.

Team briefings at TGI Fridays

In the UK, TGI Fridays is an American restaurant and bar concept that trades under licence through the Whitbreads Restaurants and Leisure Division. The company have been operating a small chain of these (35–40 in spring 2001). Most units operate at high volume sales – typically between £30,000 and £100,000 per week. The offer to customers involves an extensive menu of both food and drink items – over 100 products on each menu. Food is typical of American/Mexican fare and drinks largely feature American cocktails and imported beers, though wines and spirits are also available. Pricing is pitched at the upper end for this type of menu. Average spend per head is around £12–£15. Decor is standardized in all restaurants round a centralized American bar with a surrounding restaurant area.

In the intangibles, the offer to guests combines quick service – there are specific service times for starters (7 minutes from receipt of the order) and main courses (12 minutes) – with service which to some degree is personalized to their needs. Thus if customers wish to linger over their meal, or celebrate a special occasion (birthday, or anniversary), employees alter the pace or create a celebratory atmosphere accordingly.

As will be shown later, much of the approach to managing employees is concerned with an individualized approach with potentially competitive relationships between employees, particularly in bar and restaurant situations. Whilst a personal and individualized reward system drives much of the motivational package, the organization cannot allow individualism to become overly dominant because it could produce a level of competition between employees which might prove harmful both to sales volumes and levels of customer satisfaction. Team briefings prior to each shift perform a useful role in managing the tension between healthy competition and harmful conflict.

Team briefings occur immediately before the two key shift periods – morning and evening. Usually two teams meet in each unit, the restaurant and bar team meet as one group, and the kitchen and back of house team meet as another. These sessions, therefore, involve all employees and are a standard feature of the working arrangement. The style of the sessions is informal and managers do not take a formal lead as chair or co-ordinator. They do however, work through a senior member of the team, communicating organizational arrangements, items to be sold up or potential difficulties. Sessions are also used to create a fun atmosphere, with jokes being told by team members. On other occasions they are used to highlight best practice and to share experiences of success and difficulties. Training and shadowing new employees with more experienced employees are all communicated. Team briefing sessions in TGI Fridays seem to last about 20–30 minutes.

Each session is largely directed at communication processes and at operational matters, but they are also used to generate a collective enthusiasm amongst the team and partly to ameliorate conflicts between individual employees that might occur as a result of the individualized reward system. They bring a collective dimension to the employment relationship. Employees are encouraged to identify primarily with the team with whom they work and with the branch. Both managers and employees repeat the organization's **'canoe theory'** which stresses the benefits of members rowing together rather than against each other. During interviews, many employees talked with pride about the position of their unit – its growth, the volume of sales, or levels of customer satisfaction. Others spoke with enthusiasm of the benefits of working for the organization as being largely associated with their relationship with fellow employees. The following comment was typical of employee views of the benefits of the briefing sessions: 'From when we start we have a meeting, well all the waiters, they try and give us a little "pep talk". At first you think it is a little sad, but it is very good, it sort of motivates you. There are jokes and everyone is out from the cold, we are all laughing away. You come in, you are laughing and your friends are round you, making jokes at the table just having a good time while you are working.'

As we have seen, the key benefits to the organization are in communicating with employees, and providing a collective dimension to the employment relationship. The sessions can also provide a valuable source of feedback from employees and they can keep managers in touch with employee suggestions and experiences of customer service needs.

Job enlargement and empowerment

Some service organizations require employees to be involved in making judgements about the nature of customer service needs but within a predictable range of options. Services that might be termed mass customization, or are referred to by Schmenner (1995) as the 'service shop' or by Heskett *et al.* (1990) as 'the technological service' require employees to exercise technological expertise in meeting the customers' individual needs. They have a technician level competence in their knowledge of the customer requirement. Consequently, they suggest that employees need more technical skill than human skills. Heskett *et al.* (1990) refer to organizations that provide a technical service with limited contact between customers and employees. They see the key employment strategies as being directed at the selection and recruitment of prior trained personnel with strong technical skills. Training programmes within the organization will further develop employees' job knowledge to cope with the technical demands of the service provided. Work will be allocated to individuals who exercise some judgement within narrow confines. Examples provided by Hesket *et al.* (1990) are based in electronic services.

Schmenner (1995) also identifies technical skills as being important, while allowing that there may be issues related to customer relationship skills also. Hence, Schmenner provides examples of motor repair services, hospital services and general service repair operations where employee technical knowledge and skills will be important to the execution of the service. The key point missed by both Schmenner and Heskett *et al.* relates to the amount of discretion needed to execute the service task. As customer needs are individualized, service delivery has to be increasingly customized and employees will be required to exercise more judgement. That said, these services require less of employees than professional services because, to varying degrees, it is possible to predict or formalize service needs and thereby predict and train employees in a variety of predictable customer requirements.

A second issue missed by both sets of writers is that it is possible to detect this approach to both the service offer and the organization of service delivery in other, less technical services. A discussion of the approach taken at TGI Fridays will be provided later. In all these examples, the work of employees involves some degree of interpretation of the individual customer's needs. Job design boundaries set parameters which involve decision-making but these are typically the sort of decisions made by technicians. Employment policies are concerned with employing people with the 'right sort' of qualities – whether that be technical or interpersonal skills, or a combination of both. In some cases, recruitment and selection criteria require people with good technical skills, and in Schmenner's auto repair example (1995: 267) also possessed 'a rich family heritage of working on mechanical things'. In other cases, where employees are required to give a performance, recruitment and selection criteria involves elaborate processes of employing people with appropriate personality traits and social skills. Training is limited to the range of job skills needed and there are some processes for updating skills whether it be to match changes in services, new technology, or revised organizational policy.

Given the key importance of employee abilities and skills, it is not surprising that employers prioritize employee retention; at the very least employers want to see sufficient stability from individual employees to provide a 'pay back' on training invested. Schmenner's technicians in a car repair unit were paid in a way that both reflected personal skills and gave individuals financial incentives to maximize high quality service. Technicians were paid according to a standard time allowance for the job. If they completed the job more quickly than the standard time, they could earn more money. If they completed it more slowly, there was no extra money and they could complete fewer jobs, earnings were consequently down. All reworking of a job was done by the technician with no extra income. This approach is consistent with an approach where there can be limited direct control of what an employee does in detail and the incentive scheme aims to provide the necessary financial rewards and penalties to ensure the desired level and quality of output.

Empowerment in these circumstances is both an integral part of the job and at the same time limited to task related and processual matters inherent in the work of technicians. In Schmenner's example Service Advisors dealt with customers and identified the items to be repaired and serviced, the technicians (mechanics) acted on the orders received. They could, though, exercise skill and ability in how they acted on these instructions. They could develop a sense of ownership with each job, because each service job was allocated to them individually. The financial reward structure gave them a calculative incentive to maximize high quality outputs. Indeed the nature of the reward structure created a situation where 'technicians are almost like independent operators rather than employees of the company' (1995: 277).

Any sense of empowerment therefore comes from the nature of the work itself, pride in being able to the job well and the discrete nature of jobs in which individuals can develop a personal sense of ownership. In addition, to these intrinsic sources of reward, individual employees are calculatively involved through the system of financial rewards which encourages an almost independent entrepreneurial approach from employees. That said, typically involvement tends to be directive, financial in form, limited to the task level and concerned with a range of exclusively job-related issues. Employees' power to change decisions and impose their own requirements are limited.

The psychological aspects of empowerment will come from being appropriately trained, and through the choice exercised when interpreting the customer's needs. Financial incentives provide a form of communication of achievement; the nature of the work and extent of real choices might be limiting factors.

TGI Fridays

There is much about TGI Fridays which resembles Ritzer's (1993) McDonaldization of society thesis. In many ways the customer offer involves attributes of efficiency, calculability, predictability and control. Customers are encouraged to expect certain service standards which allow for an efficient service. Service standards require that starters are served within set time limits. Information technology is used to ensure that these service targets are met. Like McDonald's, menus are fixed and determined centrally, as are prices and production methods. Menus are standardized throughout the country so customers visiting different restaurants know what to expect. The layout of the restaurants, staff uniforms, type of employees, decor, are also standardized. Through the various tangible and supporting intangible standards to the service, customers optimize their control of the meal experience. They can calculate how long the meal will take, the approximate cost and the style of service which they will receive. Standardization enables predictability and control.

Though there are clearly similarities with McDonald's, the nature and degree of standardization is different. For all its standardized approach, TGI Fridays does allow customers more opportunities to customize their eating and drinking experiences. The food menu, for example, contains over 100 items, and the cocktail menu is similarly extensive. This allows customers a wider range of choices over how they construct the experience. Similarly, in the intangibles, employees are encouraged, whilst operating to the service standards, to provide customers with a service experience that is special to them. If the McDonald's offer is best typified as being about mass production, the TGI Fridays experience is best typified as being about mass customization.

In these circumstances, employee involvement and 'ownership' of the service encounter become paramount. The ability to advise and interpret customer wants within the range of service scenarios offered are key skills. Thus front loaded employee training involves employees learning, and being examined on, the recipes of dishes and drinks on the menu. Employees are also trained to respond to guests' special occasions as a team. Thus a guest birthday celebration will be greeted by a large group of 'dub-dubs' (waiters/waitresses) singing 'happy birthday', or hanging balloons on their chair. Employees, particularly front line staff, play a crucial role in creating the party/fun atmosphere of contained spontaneity. For employees working behind the scenes, standardized recipes, trained production methods and dish presentation formulas limit the opportunity for spontaneity, though they are sometimes brought in to front-of-house 'party' activities. In addition to employee commitment to the organization's service offer to its customers, employee commitment to sales generation is also an important consideration.

TGI Friday's approach to generating the appropriate level of commitment required is multi-faceted. First, selection and recruitment is conducted by Restaurant Managers to procedures created by head office. Candidates undertake psychometric tests, perform role-plays and may have anything from two to four interviews before being accepted. In the UK, recruits have an above average qualification, a good clutch of GCSEs is a minimum requirement and many are graduates. Prior hospitality industry experience is not necessary. Managers report that getting the 'right personality' is crucial. The ideal 'dub-dub' is 'extroverted, but not too much'. Once selected, all employees undergo an assessed training programme prior to being put to work in their designated position. Waiting staff have an initial product knowledge training programme prior to shadowing an experienced dub-dub, and being given a couple of tables in a quiet section of the restaurant. For kitchen staff, training focuses on the designated section and involves an intensive programme of recipe knowledge and practice prior to being given that section to run. The rigidly applied pre-training requirement is an impressive aspect of the approach. Thus no employee is 'let loose' on a customer until they have satisfactorily completed the training.

The majority of employees (80 per cent) are full-time. Part-time employees are restricted to acting as 'bussers' – tray carriers and table-clearers during busy periods. Interestingly, this role can be another device for assessing a potential employee's performance prior to employment. For front-line staff in the restaurant and bar, salaries are based on three elements – a low basic pay (the legal minimum rate in the UK), a commission on sales, and tips from customers. For kitchen staff, salaries involve the same basic but the kitchen team share commission on total food sales. Front-line staff report that earnings can be as high as £20,000–£25,000 per year, but a strict hierarchy operates within the restaurant so only the top ten (of thirty or so) dub-dubs have the chance to control their shift patterns and table locations, and thereby earnings potential.

Managerial appraisal of employees and selection of the top ten occurs on a quarterly basis and includes issues related to service speed, sales generated and customer satisfaction/complaints. Obviously the hierarchy gives managers a considerable degree of control over employee performance and provides a major calculative source of commitment. Indeed many employees reported that the 'good money' was a major reason for continuing to work with the firm. However, the party atmosphere and some freedom to express themselves were also identified as sources of employee satisfaction.

In the main, employee discretion is limited, employees have few opportunities to make decisions. Serious complaints are usually handled by managers, particularly if these require some form of compensation to the customer. Pre-service team meetings do provide an opportunity to share information with employees, gain suggestions and instil some kind of group bonds. In many ways the organization structure is traditional with managers making most decisions, in an essentially control orientated organization. 'One best way' underpins much of the standardized elements of the offer, but employment practices aim to involve employees in the organization's offer of mass customization to its customers.

Psychologically, a sense of competence is developed through pre-work training and the progression through the hierarchy of performance. The roles are made meaningful and staff do exercise some choice. That said, the potential competition between staff for the areas of the restaurant that will yield the highest incomes, together with limited ability to influence decisions may act as barriers to feelings of empowerment.

Conclusions

Forms of empowerment that are described as empowerment through involvement of employees aim to develop a sense of personal efficacy in employees through closer proximity with management via various consultative processes. It is hoped that employees will feel more committed to service quality improvement and giving the performance needed to meet customer service requirements. That said, the benefits to employers are not just associated with motivational factors and winning greater employee commitment, employees can provide some valuable inputs into problem solving and service quality improvement.

Empowerment through involvement encompasses a number of forms that are largely consultative in form, though can be associated with the enlargement of service jobs to cover a range of tasks that incorporate a technician role for the service worker. Formal consultative arrangements were discussed in relation to quality circles and team briefings. Both can involve mechanisms for gathering employee suggestions for fault detection, problem solving and service quality improvement. However, there are important differences in that quality circles are representative in form and frequently have a focus on specified issues. Team briefings on the other hand tend to be direct in that all employees attend the briefing sessions, and are often concerned with improved communication processes. Whilst team briefings form part of the formal organization structure and represent a device built into management/employee relations, quality circles are in effect a parallel structure to the official management hierarchy. This can produce some tensions in the relationship between circle members and other organization members. In both cases, employees have limited opportunities to make decisions stick, because managers continue to make decisions, albeit informed by employee views.

In the second basic type, employee performance is essential to the successful service encounter and it is necessary to develop a sense of ownership and personal efficacy which will enable employees as consultants to give the performance needed by different customers. Organizations that provide 'mass customized' services involve service standards and processes that are highly standardized, yet elements of the service require some form of customization. Strategies for the management of service deliverers involves a package of selection, induction, training, and appraisal processes, designed to deliver an offer to customers which is both 'McDonaldized' (Ritzer, 1993), yet which allows customer choice within a limited framework.

In all three of the variations of employee empowerment through involvement, the key issues as to their success, or failure, is the extent to which they produce feelings of personal efficacy in the workforce. Employees used to traditional command and control structures may well regard any move that signifies their importance in the service delivery process as an improvement. That said, each of the forms outlined in the chapter are varied in the extent to which employees are involved in the initiative; they range from being directive to being consultative in style. They tend to be largely concerned with task level issues and are restricted to an agenda of issues set by management. In all cases, employees are limited in their impact on decisions, because managers continue to make decisions. As a consequence employees may not have the opportunity to develop the sense of empowerment, because taken on their own consultative and representative forms of involvement do not develop the elements that build to the state of empowerment. However, taken as an element of a strategy for managing people in an empowered environment, they can help to build a culture that recognizes the key value of employees in delivering quality service experiences for customers.

CHAPTER 6

Forms of empowerment through commitment

- **Employee commitment and empowerment**
- **Employee commitment**
- **Calculative commitment**
- **Non-calculative commitment**

The empowerment of employees occurs at a number of different levels and meets different managerial needs and meanings. The definitions provided in Chapter 1 suggested that there were differences of emphasis between those definitions that stressed that employee empowerment was chiefly concerned with sharing decision-making power such as those highlighted in Chapter 4, and those definitions that see empowerment as being concerned with employees accepting responsibility for the service encounter. This chapter focuses on forms of empowerment that operate at this level. In other words they are initiatives that involve little by way of decision-making, or even in making suggestions which better inform managerial decisions. They aim to develop to empower employees by developing commitment to the service encounter and creating customer satisfaction.

Wyer and Mason (1999) suggest that empowerment in service firms means encouraging employees to act 'beyond contract'. In these circumstances, delighting the customer by exceeding customer expectations is a concept that can be applied in any context, because the different levels and types of service discussed by Rafiq and Ahmed (1998a), and in Chapter 12, involve different levels of customer expectations. Thus in a highly 'uniform dependent' (Lashley, 2000b) service, like the one supplied by McDonald's Restaurants, employees can act beyond the expectation of customers by providing that balloon for the restive child or by not responding angrily to the insulting customer.

Employee commitment and empowerment

The notion that initiatives which claim to be empowering may vary in levels of intensity and variety in what individuals can do as a result of being empowered has also been noted by Bowen and Lawler (1992) and Lockwood (1996) as well as Rafiq and Ahmed (1998a) mentioned above. Bowen and Lawler interweave the language of involvement and empowerment in their piece. The article is entitled 'The Empowerment of Service Workers: why, how and when?' yet their model outlines several levels of employee involvement. Their notion of suggestion involvement equates to this model. Their model suggests a shift away from traditional control models. Employee ideas are generated through formal suggestion schemes. The essential ingredient, however, is that managers still retain control of the decision-making and directing role. In other words the organization structure distributes power and control in a 'traditional' top down manner. Bowen and Lawler suggest that this form of involvement 'can produce empowerment without altering the production line approach' (p. 36).

Bowen and Lawler also provide a contextual explanation of this in that they look to business contextual factors that might explain the different forms and levels that empowerment might take. In particular they point to basic business strategy – tie to the customer, technology, business environment, and types of people – as factors likely to influence the form of empowerment introduced. The decision to introduce a form of empowerment is typically taken by management in response to their perception of the business context. Clearly, different service organizations are in different positions regarding their customers; the marketing offer and business strategies, and the decision to introduce a

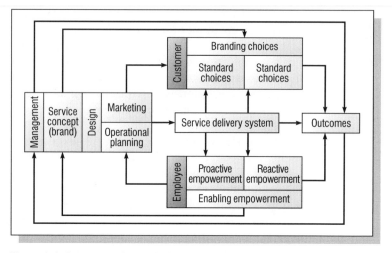

Figure 6.1 A conceptual model of empowerment in the operations process. *Source:* Lockwood (1996)

particular initiative may well be shaped by these. The normative model suggests that there should be appropriate links between human resource management and wider business strategies.

Lockwood (1996) also builds a model of forms of empowerment that allows for different levels of employee involvement in the interpretation and delivery of service encounters. Figure 6.1 provides a diagrammatic model that indicates how different levels of empowerment might interface with customer service choices.

Lockwood envisages *enabling empowerment* as equating to this concept of empowerment through commitment. He suggests that this provides an essential 'base level of commitment to the organization's goals and the service concept to be delivered' (1996: 217) from which no further initiative could succeed. Building from this base Lockwood suggests that *proactive empowerment* and *reactive empowerment* are developed. Without enabling empowerment providing employee commitment to the service encounter and customer satisfaction more involving and participating forms of empowerment cannot be applied. Proactive empowerment is 'where employees are required to make a creative input into their work performance' (p. 217). TGI Fridays and other organizations looking to improve organizational performance through some form of quality circle or team briefing process, given in Chapter 5, are examples. Reactive empowerment on the other hand may enable employees to make decisions and 'act beyond script' (p. 227) in both meeting customer service needs and correcting faults in service. This is reflected in the

Harvester Restaurants and the Marriott Hotels examples given in Chapter 4. In effect, this is similar to the psychological; dimension to empowerment mentioned in Chapter 2 and Conger and Kanungo's (1988) motivational dimension. Through these concepts it is possible to recognize that the psychological/motivational/enabling aspect of empowerment is essential for the relational forms of empowerment to succeed, but people may feel empowered even though the relational aspects remain traditional.

Both Bowen and Lawler, and Lockwood's models are interesting in that they both suggest variability in the meanings, intentions and forms of empowerment. Both also suggest that the nature of the customer service offer and managerial perceptions of business strategy are likely to be powerful influences on the experiences of being empowered in different organizations. A common criticism of both, however, is that they fail to recognize that some organizations attempt to empower employees in situations where neither creative powers nor their decision-making capacities are needed because the customer offer largely revolves round a highly standardized experience and operational management requires tight monitoring of employees within standardized systems designed to deliver the standardized customer experiences.

Bowen and Lawler, in particular, fail to recognize that different forms of empowerment involve different 'political' dimensions to the relationship between employees and managers. The models outlined in Chapter 3 show that some relationships are largely directive (Tannebaum and Schmidt, 1973) and involve different degree, forms, levels and ranges of subjects (Marchington *et al.*, 1992) and power to make decisions stick. Yet in some cases (McDonald's Restaurants will be given as an example) employers are attempting to empower employees in a way that encourages them to 'accept responsibility for the service encounter'. Empowerment acts as a rhetoric to encourage greater commitment and enthusiasm, to learn to love the job in Hochschild's (1983) terms. And most importantly, to accept the boundaries that have been set by the organization and its service offer to customers. These latter two points cause some potential tensions and difficulties because individuals vary in their preparedness in accepting the boundaries and willingness to love the job.

Often these tensions are described as representing the difference between the rhetoric of empowerment and the reality of making limited decisions over meaningless tasks. Indeed advertising material for Wilson's (1996) text entitled *The Empowerment Manual* asks 'Is your empowerment rhetoric or reality?'. These issues will be discussed more fully in Chapter 9 because the feelings created in different individuals by initiatives which claim to be empowering are fundamental to achieving the desired effect. The key issue is that individuals vary, and some people feel comfortable in highly structured environments. Others may find these same experiences stifling. Sweeping generalizations about the unacceptability of some limited forms of empowerment are therefore unhelpful because they fail to acknowledge these important differences. In addition the creation of this dichotomy between the rhetoric of empowerment and a reality of drudgery also fails to recognize that rhetoric and reality are both social constructs and that a powerfully espoused rhetoric of empowerment can have at least a short term, if not long term, impact on individual definitions of reality.

Lockwood's (1996) model showing the enabling (commitment orientated) empowerment is also useful in establishing the notion of the 'bedrock' on which other forms of empowerment can be built because it hints at the symbiotic relationship between empowerment and commitment. The successful introduction requires an appropriate context. It cannot not be developed in circumstances where mutual trust between managers and employees does not exist (Sternberg, 1992), and a base level of employee commitment is required. That said, one of the aspirations for empowerment is that it creates and enhances employee commitment. Thus empowered employees are supposed, as we have seen, to be just waiting to be empowered and most of the claimed benefits of empowering employees is said to be due to the increase in employee commitment that ensues. Empowerment and employee commitment are therefore interwoven. Committed employees are required to develop empowerment and empowerment develops and extends employee commitment.

The distinguishing feature of forms of empowerment through commitment is that they involve little influence over decisions or actual decision-making. Communication styles and involvement between managers and employees are located towards the left hand side of the Tannebaum and Schmidt (1973) continuum for the majority of employees. They are largely directive and chiefly concern a command style of communication in that managers either tell (or tell and sell) employees what to do. In the Marchington *et al.* model (1992) the degree of involvement is largely located at the information stage of the escalator of involvement (Figure 3.4). Employees are involved in receiving and acting upon instructions. The form of involvement is direct because it includes all employees, though as we shall see later, it may include indirect forms through the operation of suggestion schemes. Involvement is almost exclusively at the task level. The range of issues are related to the execution of the tangible and intangible aspects of the task. Power to see decisions through is constrained by the highly prescribed nature of the task. This type of operation uses prescriptive training procedures that limit the amount of discretion and authority to be exercised by employees.

Though choice might be limited for employees, the provision of effective training together with a genuine recognition that employees make a crucial contribution to service quality and business success, can produce the sense of meaningfulness, effectiveness and value as essential elements in building the psychological state of being empowered.

Employee commitment

In situations where employees have limited opportunities to make decisions about the organization of their work, or are not regularly consulted in any meaningful or on-going manner, claims to be empowering employees are likely to be judged against the extent that they engender feelings of personal efficacy (Houtagers, 1999). The extent that these initiatives are empty rhetoric will be dependent of the degree that a range of practices engender feelings of personal commitment to, and pride in, the organization's policies and service offer to its customers. Most importantly, according to the normative model, these initiatives must result in the empowered feeling that they personally affect the outcome, and they accept the responsibility for successful service encounters. So as to best understand the means by which employees might come to develop this sense of empowerment it is necessary to discuss the development of employee commitment.

Concern for employee commitment is not in itself a new concern for managers, but recent debates about the nature of human resource management have given the concerns about the importance of generating employee commitment, as expressed by both academics and practitioners, a new spin. Though a somewhat slippery and ill-used term, human resource management describes a supposedly new approach to the management of people at work that is intrinsically concerned with employee commitment. Many of the definitions of HRM that support the claim that it represents a different set of work practices for managing employees suggest that techniques to gain greater employee commitment are central to this supposedly new way of managing people (Guest, 1987). For others, Storey (1992) is concerned with the 'soft' version of HRM. In this case, a concern for employee commitment becomes a distinguishing feature between the 'hard' and 'soft' notions of HRM.

The assumption in many of the pronouncements about committed employees is that they will be more satisfied, more productive and more flexible (Legge, 1995). In the service sector, committed employees will be less likely to leave the organization (generally a problem), they will produce better quality goods, they will deliver improved service encounters with customers. Furthermore, commitment is described as developing an internalized set of beliefs and concerns with their work that encourages behaviour that is over and above normal requirements. All these aspirations are shared with aspirations for empowering employees. Indeed employee empowerment is an essential element of the HRM-commitment-seeking organization (Sissons, 1994).

The problem with the more evangelical claims in both the literature and the pronouncements of practitioners of empowerment and commitment is that rarely do they make explicit 'empowerment to do what?' or 'commitment to what?'. Some of the issues about the contradictions in empowerment have been discussed earlier, but the 'what' to which employees are committed requires further discussion. In the main, the aspirations for the power of employee commitment tend to be located in a unitary perspective where the commentator expects that the practices introduced will result in greater commitment to the organization and its policies. In the service context this means being committed to the organization's commitment to its customers and shareholders. Again there is rarely an expressed concern that these groups might have contradictory needs. 'Satisfied customers mean more repeat calls, which in turn results in increased turnover, more profits and increased market share', is the oft expressed mantra. The fact that customers may want services that are out of brand, or want to use the service in a way which is inconvenient to sales maximization is rarely recognized in the simplistic rhetoric of the 'service driven' organization. The tension between customer service needs and sales maximization can be seen in busy restaurants when customers may want to linger over their meal whilst restaurant management may want to re-use the table for another set of customers.

When we add service employees to this situation there are some interesting contradictions in the service encounter, particularly where tips from customers are an important element of the employee's total income package. Many organizations in the restaurant service sector pay employees a low basic wage, which is then supplemented with tips, or service charges from customers. In effect the employee has two employers who may have contradictory requirements and present the employee with a tension to manage. The organization may have objectives about the style and attentiveness of service to be given to customers together with sales targets or promotions which the employee has to match. TGI Fridays give this further spin by paying employees a commission on the food and drink that they sell. In these circumstances the employee has to make a judgement between strategies that maximize sales – pushing maximum sales per customer and/or guiding customers quickly through the process so as to maximize customer throughput – and strategies that maximize the tip from customers – giving extra attention, spending time to talk, providing extra services (perhaps providing out-of-brand items).

It is possible to identify, therefore, that the employee may be committed to both customer and employer. Employer policies that advise the employee to 'delight the customer; but not too much' create tensions that the employee has to manage. Under a more pluralistic perspective, it can be seen that employees may be committed to a number of different organizational members. Many service organizations consist of small dispersed units. Thus an organization like McDonald's Restaurants employs (spring 2001) about 50,000 employees in the UK within almost 1100 restaurants – an average of 40–50 employees per unit. In service organizations therefore, it may be that employees are committed to the unit, the unit manager or fellow employees within the unit. Certainly interviews with people in both Harvester Restaurants and TGI Fridays Restaurants suggested that their commitments were firstly to their fellow employees in the units, then the unit and its mangers. So many employees reported enjoying their work because 'its a good laugh' or 'we have worked together for years' (Ashness and Lashley, 1995), and then made favourable comments about the unit or the unit manager.

Employees may also have commitments to trade union, department, occupation, profession within the workplace and a whole host of potential sources of commitment outside. An issue frequently missed by the advocates of empowerment and commitment is that employees vary in both their reasons for working and the foci of their lives. For some people, the reason for working is quite instrumental and there is little interest in the precise nature of the work, beyond certain base level expectations. For other people the field of employment is an important source of self-definition. It helps them to identify and define who they are. Thus orientations to be committed may vary between individuals.

Attempts to define and thereby identify those factors that are likely to influence its growth tend to reflect a number of debates about the nature of organizations and people. On one level, commitment and organization culture are bound together. Hence the work of Peters and Waterman (1982) assumes that successful organizations are based round strong cultures which reinforce and reproduce shared beliefs, attitudes and values. In particular it is assumed by some that commitment represents a psychological bond to the organization (Cooper and Hartley, 1991). It is assumed that this psychological bond is developed through the congruence of a set of beliefs, attitudes and values that match with the organization. Others, writing in a more behavioural perspective, see commitment as being the result of a set of material benefits which the individual gains by remaining in the organization.

On another level some commentators on commitment assume a calculative or instrumental (Etzioni, 1961) approach to commitment. That is, committed employees join an organization and continue with it because of their calculations of the benefits of membership and calculations of the losses associated with joining other organizations. Etzioni also identifies moral commitment which is associated with an emotional attachment to the organization. Moral commitment occurs when the individual identifies strongly with the aims, values and purpose of the organization.

Schein (1988) referring to employee motivation makes an apt point, 'One of the situational factors that determines patterns of motivation is the organizational context of behaviour' (1988: 44). Later Schein typifies organizations that have a 'utilitarian' system as being based on 'rational legal principles' and that include a range of leader titles that stress their formal role in the organization. Subordinates feelings often include caution, suspicion, a concern for independence and equity, and organizational leaders are frequently confronted by the dilemma of how to generate employee involvement. 'Normative' organizations on the other hand, are more charismatic and exercise moral authority. Leadership roles tend to stress expertise and qualities that generate subordinate commitment and enthusiasm. Employee feelings tend to include a sense of involvement, commitment and a shared sense of goals. The dilemma for these organizations is concerned with the maintenance of employee involvement and the management of leadership succession (Schein, 1988: 108).

Aspirations for employee empowerment can be seen to engage both these dimensions of commitment. In some cases, managers are attempting to gain the employee's commitment and thereby generate a sense of empowerment through material benefits of organizational membership – better than average rates of pay for the labour market, good chances of promotion for loyal employees, appropriate training programmes, performance related pay reflecting both output and behavioural aspects. In other cases, empowered employees are being engaged on an emotional level. The application of more participatory or involving techniques have, as we have seen, important organizational benefits in service organizations, but also at the level of commitment it is hoped they are generating employee commitment by developing a sense of ownership in the decision-making process (even this is limited to making recommendations) and thereby in the organization. An array of techniques discussed in earlier chapters are either systematically learning from employee experiences or giving service workers the necessary decision-making power to meet customer service needs. In both cases, it is hoped that empowerment wins greater commitment to delighting the customer in the way the company defines it.

Research evidence that attempts to measure the benefits in organizational performance flowing from this array of techniques are inconclusive. The work of Cotton (1993) (which surveys a large number of US studies covering the full range of calculative and moral sources of commitment – gainsharing and employee share ownership schemes through to quality of work life and autonomous work groups) identifies mixed results. In some cases results are hampered by dubious research design and the difficulties associated with proving improved organizational performance in a dynamic business environment. In other cases, situational factors, and fit with the organization, make the benefits difficult to generalize to all contexts and organizations. The work of Kelly and Kelly (1990), in their survey of a host of different techniques, suggests that improved attitudes to the organization of work do not necessarily translate into improved attitudes and commitment to the work organization. Their work was discussed more fully in Chapter 2. Suffice it to say at this stage, that there are likely to be some management practices that, though not directly causing improved commitment, may not harm it and may meet employees' base levels of expectation.

Calculative commitment

Given that the firms who aspire to empowerment via commitment are, in the main, organizations that make their customers a highly standardized offer, with largely tangible sources of customer satisfaction. Typically, interactions between employees and customers are brief and simple, and though customer service is important it plays a less significant role than in some other service operations. Hence management of the operation is largely concerned with delivering standardized experiences to customers. There is little scope to vary the operation or to allow employees to interpret the service because this would distort the brand offer and create customer confusion if services varied in different units. Opportunities to engage employees via more participatory and involving processes are limited. These types of organizations, known by some writers (Schmenner, 1995) as 'the service factory', may have to rely on more calculative forms of commitment because there are limits to the amount of discretion an employee may be allowed to exercise.

- **Pay**: to be consistent with the aspirations to generate employee commitment, firms have to pay rates at the leading edge of rates for that segment of the labour market. The simple and routine nature of job design means that these firms are frequently recruiting employees who are at the lower end of the qualifications and attainments spectrum. But within this context, they pitch wages at a point that pays more than the potential recruit could get elsewhere. When McDonald's Restaurants in Germany had some public relations difficulties in the 1980s, the company wanted to raise its wages to crew, but was constrained by the national wage negotiating frame-work for the hotel and catering industry. It withdrew from the industry body and set up a new national wage board just for the fast food sector which it dominated, and then pitched the wage at a level higher than the other hotel and catering industry body. The aim of pitching wages at these levels is clearly related to the issues mentioned above in creating a calculative attraction to the firm and an incentive to stay. In the UK the company aims generally to pay above the legal minimum rate of pay.

- **Performance related pay:** many organizations in the service sector have payment structures that allow employees to add to their earning through both organizational incentives and/or income from customers (in the form of tips or service charges). Arrangements for organizational performance related pay vary, but the underlying principle is that the financial incentive is directed at those behaviours that the organizations wish to reinforce.

  The McDonald's performance related pay for crew members is achieved by crew members working closely to the prescribed training programmes. Observation check lists are used to ensure that employees are performing each task as defined and extra pay (up to a maximum of 15p per hour) is awarded if the crew member performs the full array of jobs as defined. Harvester Restaurants had a performance related pay system that rewarded the achievement of training grades. Thus an employee could gain 20p per hour if he/she achieved 'silver badge' – the job competence badge. Further increases could be achieved if an employee took on extra training (up to a maximum of a further 40p per hour). TGI Fridays on the other hand has a performance related pay structure that is based on a commission on sales (for restaurant and bar staff) and on kitchen production (for kitchen staff).

In addition to these formal organizational mechanisms of reproducing and reinforcing desired behaviour, many service employees work in situations where customers also reward employees for service. Tips direct from the customer, or structured arrangements via service charges, are important parts of the reward package in some sectors of the service industry. As was shown earlier, tips in particular present some interesting dilemmas for employees to manage, because of the dual employer status. In addition, tips can be the subject of much confusion for customers because the expectations about tipping and the contexts in which they are appropriate, or not, is unclear and a source of anxiety for some customers. There is no shared understanding of the size of the tip, or when to tip. Is it for extra service, or is the tip expected on every occasion? Why are tips expected in some service situations (restaurants/ taxis) but not in others (fast food/bus conductors)? In addition the arrangements as to what happens to the tip is unclear to the customer. Is it given personally to the receiver, or is it shared amongst the staff? Even where there has been an attempt to regularize these situations by the addition of a service charge to bills (a fixed percentage added), arrangements as to what happens to the money collected are unclear and are the source of some employee resentment. In some cases the service charge is shared amongst employees as a sort of commission on sales, in other cases it is used to pay wages.

All these variations and confusions provide problems for the role of extra customer payments in developing employee commitment through the total reward package. Employees cannot guarantee that they will receive them, nor that they will achieve a fixed amount related to effort. That said, food service employees in Harvester Restaurants reported that tips from customers added considerably to their total pay. Most experienced employees reported that they could double or treble their wages through tips.

- **Performance review:** associated with formal mechanisms for rewarding performance are arrangements for reviewing performance. These vary, but for the performance review to be effective in contributing to employee commitment it must meet certain requirements. It must be regular, recognized as important, the basis for future action and developmental in style. In McDonald's Restaurants performance review is undertaken for crew via a systematic series (22 typically) of observations over a given period (6 months). Each observation is scored against the appropriate observation check list and the aggregate scores are used in the performance review meetings. In other situations, such as TGI Fridays, regular performance reviews are conducted by managers and they decide, on the basis of service and sales criteria, a ranking of all employees in the restaurant. Those ranked highest are able to choose preferred shifts and positions in the restaurant so as to be able to structure their working patterns to meet their own objectives. Performance review in Harvester Restaurants is team based, and the team had responsibility for individual performance.

Regular performance review can play an important part in creating employee commitment because at the very least it can be a vehicle for informing employees about what is expected of them and for providing feedback on performance. However, these can be a source of dissatisfaction and employee frustration where employees feel that the manner in which they are conducted and the outcomes are unfair, or where they are not regarded as important by managers.

- **Training and employee development:** the narrow and prescriptive nature of job design to a cluster of simple and routine tasks leads to training programmes that are limited in scope and focused in a 'one best way' approach. Training is largely employer specific and focused on immediate job needs. Depending on the organization and its offer to customers, training will probably be focused on tasks and customer care issues. Thus supermarket, fast food and financial service organizations all train employees in core elements in the customer interaction – smiling, making and maintaining eye contact – creating the feeling that the welcome is genuine. In the past, many of these organizations have scripted the interaction so that training would have included the precise words that were to be used when answering the telephone, greeting the customer or closing the encounter. During the early to middle 1990s many organizations became aware that these somewhat mechanistic approaches to controlling the standardized service encounter could be counter-productive because customers became aware of the forced nature of the employee's relationship with them. The key point is that training in these organizations does provide individuals with the skills they need to complete their tasks, though the tasks are narrow and constrained. For many employees the nature of the work is a barrier to commitment, but for others, the tightness of the focus assists in creating a system that is unambiguous in its expectations of employee performance and the restrictions rejected by many are found to be comforting by others.

Another feature of these organizations has been their meritocratic openness to individuals who wanted to stay with them. Most of these branded and 'McDonaldized' service organizations have witnessed rapid growth over the last three decades. Many have developed employees and managers from within and it is possible to provide role models of senior managers who have risen from within the company. In the UK, approximately one-third of McDonald's Restaurant Managers have been promoted from within the organization, and all senior line managers have been promoted through the company. This use of an internal labour market, to which entry is either at employee, or graduate trainee level, has several benefits in creating the 'pull factors' of commitment. For some the prospect of rapid promotion, or for others the realization that they would not be able to achieve a similar position elsewhere, creates some considerable material reasons to stay with an organization and be committed to its success.

Non-calculative commitment

Most of the 'service factory' organizations (Schmenner, 1995) operate reward systems that rely on calculative motives as sources of commitment, and the nature of the job design restricts the use of 'soft HRM' techniques. I have argued that some firms are not able to involve employees in the array of consultative and participative techniques, because the brand attributes are dependent on a predictable and standardized set of experiences. The offer to customers is 'uniformity dependent' (Lashley, 2000b). Many organizations, however, attempt to develop a sort of moral commitment in the Etzioni (1961) mould through a series of techniques that are based on information sharing. Using the Marchington et al. (1992) framework these are at the lowest stage on the escalator of degrees of involvement (Figure 3.4). They do have an intent that attempts to establish a collective interest between managers and employees. The famous quotation from Peter Wickens at Nissan is a good example of these aspirations; the collectivist struggles of the past have been replaced by a new collective struggle between the organizational membership and the 'competition' is an image that dominates many of these forms of involvement. In Kelly and Kelly's (1990) article, the selection of a mutual enemy – 'the competition' – can be a means of building common goals and purposes that ultimately change attitudes.

- **Newsletters:** newsletters or company magazines are widely used by management as a way of communicating with all employees. Typically the content is determined by management and distributed to all employees. Distribution is all inclusive and editorial content is usually managerial, few allow employees to have uncensored inputs. As a form of involvement they are potentially direct, though the extent that employees read the outputs might question just how many employees receive the messages sent. They generally involve several levels of topics covering organizational performance, though they may have issues related to tasks, particularly if in relation to quality and productivity issues. The range of topics is potentially quite broad, though they frequently avoid 'political' issues – directors' salaries and reward packages are not usually deemed to be suitable topics for inclusion in newsletters, for example. Clearly, the limits placed on employee inputs reflect the limits that employees face in the power to influence this form of involvement.

  As a means of generating employee commitment and thereby developing a sense of being empowered, newsletters are limited; the content of the communication, its source and tone are likely to present considerable barriers to the receipt of the messages even amongst those who bother to read them. That said, they can perform a role in keeping employees informed about organizational matters, as defined by management.

- **Suggestion schemes:** again there are a number of different arrangements for suggestion schemes in different companies. Typically they are passive instruments for gathering suggestions from employees when the mood takes them. Usually there is some formal process for registering the suggestion, but there are few proactive process introduced by management to generate suggestions. Some Japanese companies require work teams to produce at least one suggestion a month. It is unusual for Western companies to be that prescriptive. Individuals may or may not participate if they choose, though some form of financial incentive programme is usually in place. That is, some means by which suggestions made are rewarded.

  As a means of involvement, suggestion schemes represent a low level of involvement somewhere between information and consultation. They are direct in that all employees may be involved in making suggestions, but their proactive nature limits the extent that all employees are involved. In the main suggestions will be task level, though in principle they could involve other issues. A famous outcome of the McDonald's suggestion scheme was the 'Egg McMuffin', and company executives report that several worthy ideas have been generated by the suggestion scheme. Range issues would typically be limited to output, quality, productivity type issues. Again suggestions about reduction in directors' reward packages would not be deemed serious or suitable topics. Power to make decisions about both the agenda – what are legitimate and illegitimate topics – and how individual suggestions are handled, rests typically with managers.

As a means of generating employee commitment, suggestion schemes can provide individual employees with an avenue for directing and building upon commitment. An individual probably needs to feel some sense of commitment to make the suggestion in the first place, but if the suggestion is acted upon individuals are likely to feel involved and committed. The key flaws with suggestions schemes are in their limited scope amongst the workforce as a whole, and in the levels of reward that are usually paid to employees.

Barriers to the creation of employee commitment

Within the normative assumptions about employees and their employers, which suggest that employee commitment is natural to the employment relationship, there are some inconsistencies that need to be explored. On a more fundamental level, a pluralist analysis of organization life may suggest that attempts to gain employee commitment are unlikely to succeed because the relationship between employees and employer is one in which the interests of employees and employers are rarely congruent.

- **Low discretion job design:** many organizations who operate in the 'service factory' mode design jobs is such a way as to ensure standardized experience for customers by limiting the amount of discretion needed by the individual employee. Personal idiosyncrasies have been limited in this service production process. A consequence of that is that organizations deliver, for many people, a mixed message. On the one hand the process is designed to remove the impact of the individual, who can always be replaced by another individual with minimal impact on the service process. On the other hand, employees are individuals and their commitment is needed.

Though, as was stated earlier, some individuals are content to work within the certainties of this system, many others have difficulty in adapting to it and a high labour turnover is typical for these organizations.

- **Labour turnover:** this can be a difficulty for organizations, because it is difficult to establish the necessary 'investment' if individuals rarely stay long enough. Similarly, training costs, recruitment costs and the effects on customers and other employees can have adverse effects. For an organization that is trying to improve employee commitment, the reduction of labour turnover represents both a goal and a part of the process. Thus labour turnover represents both an indication of limited employee commitment and it has to be reduced so as to establish more committed employees.

- **Numerical flexibility:** many service sector firms operate in an environment where demand fluctuates, both predictably and unpredictably. Thus it may be recognized that at different times of the day/week/year varying numbers of employees will be required. Similarly, changes in weather or events beyond the management's control may mean that more or fewer customers use the business. In these circumstances mangers may need to have a flexible pool of labour who can be called in or left idle as business demand requires. Many organizations have attempted to cope with these fluctuations by employing a large pool of part-time, or temporary staff. These arrangements have, in the past, caused difficulties because the level of commitment by the employee tends to reflect the somewhat limited commitment to the employee from the organization. Currently some firms are attempting to overcome this with 'zero hours' contracts, where an employee is registered as an employee but to whom there is no commitment to provide work.

At a more fundamental level, the unitary perspective that is implicit in some of the pronouncements about employee commitment can be criticized because it fails to recognize that organizations are likely to comprise of a variety of sets of interests that may have quite different aims and objectives from others. Employees and managers may have organizational survival as a common objective, and all are ultimately employees of the organization, but there are a number of fundamental differences that create a potential for conflict – whether openly expressed or not. Managers' role as agents or owners gives them a different role in the organization with different access to organizational power and authority. The wages for one represent costs to another, issues about effort and productivity, numerical flexibility and tenure are just some examples of how employees and managers have different expectations and needs from managers. Given these potential issues over which managers and employees can have conflicting needs, increased employee commitment and feelings of empowerment may be something that occur exceptionally, and when the labour market together with organizational conditions are right.

McDonald's Restaurants Limited: managing the service factory through command and control

McDonald's Restaurants typify an approach to managing service encounters, which according to Ritzer (1993) is extending beyond fast food operations to business throughout the service sector. Ritzer describes the 'McDonaldization of society' as being 'the process by which the principles of the fast-food restaurant are coming to dominate more and more sectors of American society as well as the rest of the world' (1993: 1).

In particular, Ritzer identifies four dimensions in this approach to managing the service process. These dimensions cover both the sources of customer satisfaction – what people are buying into, and the way the employees are managed. The first dimension is that McDonald's offers *efficiency* in that 'McDonald's offers the best way from getting from the state of being hungry to the state of being full' (p. 9). Work is designed to maximize the use of labour most efficiently via the application of technology and simplified job design. The second dimension is that McDonald's offers services which can be easily *quantified* and *calculated*. Hence customers can quantify what they are going to get and the time it will take. Tight job design and productivity levels allow managers to be more certain as to the level of outputs from a given level of labour inputs. Customers are able to *predict* products, services and prices. Customers know what they will be offered in different McDonald's Restaurants and even the prices to be charged. From an employment perspective, employee performance and the need for labour hour by hour can be predicted with reasonable accuracy. Finally, customers, through the impact of these other dimensions, can experience a sense of personal *control*, though according to Ritzer, it is they who are being controlled (p. 11). Certainly from an employment perspective the design of jobs and management hierarchy aim to ensure maximum external control of employee performance.

As Ritzer (1993) shows, standardization and the accompanying psychological benefits are important features of the offer made by

Hospitality, Leisure & Tourism Series

the company to its customers, and this shapes much of its management of human resources. Its brand values are tightly drawn and closely managed. The uniformity dependent (Lashley, 2000b) offer to customers requires standardization across all units. Even franchise businesses are bound by the disciplines of the brand. Indeed a story frequently retold by company executives relates to an early experience where a franchisee 'let the company image down by not keeping to the brand'. That said, Ritzer is correct in stressing that these approaches were not created by the company; the service dimension is largely shaped by concepts and practices developed in manufacturing industry. The approach draws on principles and techniques such as the intensification of the division of labour (Braverman, 1974), scientific management (Taylor, 1947) and the use of technology to minimize the need for much employee discretion.

Using Schmenner's term, McDonald's is typical of the service factory (1995). Production and service operations are centrally designed and individuals are trained to produce and serve dishes according to the standards laid down. The menu of products on offer, the contents of dishes, their appearance to the customer, the manner of their production, pricing and promotion are substantially planned and executed at national head office in the UK (Lashley, 1995b). Traditionally, Restaurant Managers have little control over any of these issues, and even more senior operations managers would have limited powers to alter the nature of the offer to customers. In the UK some restaurants sell salads in addition to the 'national menu'. There are some aspects of the 'brand offer' that not even the most senior officials could alter. Thus any attempt to remove the 'Big Mac' from the menu, or to allow customers to have vinegar for their chips, would be seen as a major contravention of the brand.

Consistent with the tightly defined brand, the management of employees tends to focus on the delivery of a consistent standardized service. Training is task related round 'one best way' of doing things. The use of work study, work measurement and ergonomic techniques design minimal employee discretion into the manner in which tasks are completed. Until recently, even the language used in the service interaction used by counter staff was scripted. Observation check lists are used by managers to ensure that trained employees continue to use the one best way in the production and service of the menu. Typically an employee would be evaluated through the OCLs 22 times over a six month period. Results are scored, and employees who achieve average scores above 95 per cent receive an additional 15p per hour. Scores below 75 per cent would be seen as providing cause for concern.

For those employees who are prepared to stay with the organization, McDonald's does have a good record of promoting from within. Approximately one-half of their UK management at unit level, and a substantial number of senior managers, started their careers with the company as *crew* members. These are held out as role models for both crew and more junior managers. Over 90 per cent of crew (operatives) work varying amounts of part-time hours. Pay rates are reasonable for this segment of the labour market and the company has ambitions to be seen as an employer of first choice within the segment. The provision of a reasonable pay rate, together with training and chances for promotion, are seen as key elements in the employment package. These calculative considerations are further embellished for crew through schemes that reward long service and excellent performance.

Employee involvement is largely task centred and includes 'rap sessions', 'crew meetings', 'suggestion schemes' and 'crew-trainer meetings' (Royle, 1996). As Royle says, 'this form of participation is not about giving decision making power to the workforce' (p. 85). Given the perceived need to retain tight control over the output of employee performance, it is not surprising that forms of employee involvement provide limited scope for employees to make decisions, or to empower employees.

The customer offer and the role of management systems that maximize standardization exemplify the findings of Poole and Mansfield (1992) as being unitary in approach. Language of team membership and pulling together through good communication are important elements. If crew members have problems they are exhorted to take them to their line manager, rather than to external sources such as a trade union or a works council (Royle, 1996). *Crew meetings* occur, in most units, about once a month. These are used to convey information from management. They fit well with the Marchington *et al.* (1992) information giving form of involvement, and Tannebaum and Schmidt's (1973) directive styles which involve 'tell' and 'tell and sell'. They perform the role of keeping people informed about company and, most importantly, unit performance.

Rap sessions are another device for communicating with crew, and these do have a more consultative role. These sessions do allow individuals to raise complaints and problems with managers. Usually they are chaired by a senior manager from outside the restaurant. All crew are eligible to attend these meetings, which are usually held outside of normal working hours (after 5 p.m.). In some cases managers select individuals to attend. Though all directly managed units are required to hold rap sessions on a regular (quarterly) basis, the timing of these is left in management's hands. In some cases, they are used as quality circles, where problems of store performance have arisen. In other cases, mangers see them as providing a *'forum for trouble-makers'* and consequently avoid organizing them. Franchise operators are not formally required to hold them. One manager reported, *'They are quite a good idea as long as they don't get out of hand, crew can let off steam but sometimes they turn into bitching sessions'*. These sessions are formally minuted and company information systems monitor the frequency at which they are held.

Suggestion schemes allow employees some mechanism for making improvements to the organization, though these do tend to be related to task matters. The company identifies some important benefits form suggestion schemes. Several new product innovations have been made from crew member suggestions. That said, suggestions schemes are limited to those who choose to participate. They are therefore dependent on the enthusiasm of unit managers and crew in the volume and usefulness of suggestions generated. There are no targets set for either individual employees or units to produce suggestions.

Such empowerment as does take place is empowerment through commitment (Lashley, 1995a), and is largely focused at gaining commitment to the company's definitions of service quality through the detection and replacement of service faults and customer complaints. Managerial roles are largely concerned with checking the performance of subordinates. There is, typically, a narrow span of control and consequently a fairly tall organization structure. There are eleven tiers of personnel between the customer and the Senior Vice President in the UK (Lashley, 1995b).

In summary, the McDonald's organization manages the service process in a way typical of Schmenner's service factory via the management of employees that mirrors the command and control approach outlined above. Over recent years, however, business strategies aimed at both improving service quality, and business performance, have required some changes to the management of employees and the organization structure (Lashley, 1995b). Employees have been given some limited empowerment to deal with customer complaints and restaurant mangers have been encouraged to be more entrepreneurial. The key business offer based on a highly standardized, tightly defined brand, does limit the scope of these initiatives.

At crew level, commitment is largely calculatively driven, though there are some devices for gaining non-calculative commitment through crew meetings, rap sessions and suggestion schemes, and promotion prospects. Through the provision of better-than-market rates for wage rates, systematic training in operational tasks together with matching performance payment, and a career structure that can demonstrate many successes, it is hoped that employees will identify the company as their preferred employer. It is also hoped that these feelings will be further reinforced by the provision of some devices to capture employee experiences and suggestions, and thereby encourage employees to develop a sense of ownership and identification with the company's objectives.

Conclusions

This chapter has argued that there is symbiotic relationship between employee commitment and employee empowerment. On the one hand employees need to be committed to experience empowerment and empowered employees are likely to be more committed. In addition, the chapter has shown that several writers have acknowledged that empowerment has a variety of forms and meets a number of manager intentions and meanings. One meaning is that employees become empowered by taking on responsibility for their actions, in this case for delighting the customer and making the service encounter a success.

A key issue for the consideration of employee commitment is 'commitment to what'. This has some major difficulties for firms that are attempting to enhance the service quality as a competitive strategy, whilst at the same time maximizing sales revenue. Employees may be put under added pressure as they have to manage the tensions inherent in the company's offer to its customers. These tensions are given added intensity where employees supplement their wages with tips from customers. They have to match different demands from employers and customers.

Some organizations, delivering highly standardized service and very tangibly orientated in the customer offers, have service operations management processes that have been described as 'service factories' (Schmenner, 1995). These service factories offer few opportunities for deviation from 'one best way' job design and thereby few opportunities to participate or be systematically consulted at their workplace. Consequently, attempts to develop feelings of empowerment in employees are mostly restricted to developing feelings of commitment through calculative commitment. To be effective packages of incentives need to be consistent and carried through carefully. Organizations have to be concerned with developing a sense of personal efficacy through the removal of barriers to these feelings. That said, it is possible for the state of empowerment to be developed, even in organizations where the relationship between employees and managers are still traditional. Appropriate levels of training and communication systems that build a sense of meaningfulness and worth, together with a culture that celebrates the employees' contribution to customer satisfaction, are ingredients that must be in place.

CHAPTER 7

Forms of empowerment and delayering

- **Beyond bureaucracy**
- **Empowered managers**
- **Barriers to managerial empowerment through delayering**
- **Empowered franchisees?**

Whilst the managerial intentions and forms of empowerment in the preceding chapters have been concerned with the empowerment of employees, particularly front line service personnel, some initiatives that claim to be empowering are aimed at the management structure or with organizational forms like franchising (Lashley and Morrison, 2000). That is, by removing some of the tiers of management, junior managers are empowered to take on some of the responsibilities and authority of their former senior colleagues. The result is that the organization is 'delayered', 'flattened in structure', or 're-engineered'; the key point is that there are fewer levels of manager within the organization's structure.

During the early years of the 1990s, many service organizations went through this process. Often the motives were associated with creating a more 'service driven' or 'customer orientated' organization, the thinking that was given popular prominence by Peters and Waterman (1982). Organizations need to be close to the customer, and large organizations with tall hierarchies create barriers between customers and senior executives. Thus a 'flatter' structure with fewer tiers of managers is thought to be more responsive to customers and changes in customer wants. This has found particular resonance with service organizations, where the development of multi-unit, branded businesses had resulted in organization structures with many levels of managers. Interestingly, and contradicting Peters and Waterman's own pronouncements, McDonald's Restaurants was hailed as an 'excellent' company but displayed many of these supposedly harmful hierarchical tendencies. As we shall see in more detail later, McDonald's Restaurants Limited (UK) had eleven levels of personnel between customer and the Senior Vice President. The structure in McDonald's case was a result of the narrow span of control associated with the ensuring that 'one best way' was being applied. As the organization grows in size the consequences of a narrow span of control result in more tiers of managers.

Beyond bureaucracy

Many of the current nostrums for organizations in the twenty-first century have a much longer tradition than updated terminology allows. There has been a strand of criticism of organizations designed on principles of 'scientific management' and legal rational authority stretching back to the beginning of the twentieth century and the growth of large 'industrial bureaucracies and monopoly capital' (Braverman, 1974). In recent decades, responses to industrial unrest featured an analysis which said that these formal and mechanistic organizations were alienating and created too much distance between decision makers and operatives. Foy's (1994) comments about the need to participate in the 1970s reflects this strand of concern. At the time, initiatives relating to job rotation, job enlargement, and job enrichment were designed to overcome task level job design and supervision problems which had applied 'Taylorist' and 'Weberian' principles to the exclusion of employee discretion. Joint consultative committees, works councils and employee directors were devices for ensuring that organizational governance was sensitive to employee concerns and ideas.

By the 1990s the focus of managerial concern had shifted from employee relations and the reduction of industrial conflict to globalization and international competition. Again a key concern was the organization structure. The very strengths of the formal and mechanistic organization structure were now seen as its weakness in allowing firms to compete in the fast changing competitive international market. There has been a recognition that the down-side of economies of scale adopted by massive commercial organizations which dominate production and distribution in many Western economies is the growth of inflexibility and a sense of powerlessness among managers. The diseconomies of scale resulting from the growth of bureaucracy, longer lines of communications, a lack of customer orientation, and organizational atrophy can limit the benefits enjoyed by large organizations. Empowering managers can be a 'direct assault on the bureaucratic methods and mind-set that characterize life in most organizations (Block, 1987: 1).

In response, many large firms have adopted a range of organizational strategies which are designed to 'maximize flexibility and minimize costs' (Goffee and Scase, 1995: xiii). Subcontracting out activities which were previously done in-house, management buy-outs of none-core activities, the establishment of shell corporations co-ordinating the activities of complex networks of small suppliers, and the encouragement of 'intrapreneurialism', are all examples of responses to a perception that greater competitive advantage can be gained from removing the restrictions of bureaucratic structures. The initiatives under discussion in this chapter involve the removal of layers of managers in an organization as a means of creating a more flexible and responsive organization. The aim being that senior managers are better able to understand customer needs, and empowered line managers are given the autonomy to build the business in a way that is relevant to their customer base.

Another motive for the removal of levels of managers, associated with the above, is the impact on communications flows. As more levels of managers are put in place, the communication flows between the front line and senior managers become more distorted because there are more intervening stages that can distort or divert 'inconvenient' messages. This is particularly relevant when senior managers are attempting to gauge some sense of operational performance across units and managers. As one executive from Harvester Restaurants commented, 'There are more places to hide. Middle managers can cover up problems in their group'. Thus it is hoped that a 'flatter' structure will not only make the organization more responsive to its customers, but it will also assist senior mangers in gaining

Hospitality, Leisure & Tourism Series

better information about operational performance at unit level. Clearly, the advent of ever more sophisticated information technology has been an influential enabling force in this respect. Managers can call up sales figures, unit profit and loss accounts, together with up-to-date consumer reports, unit by unit across the whole organization.

The removal of layers of managers can also reduce operating costs, as there are fewer overheads on any given level of output. In some cases, it may be that cost reduction is a primary consideration in the decision to remove, or merge, particular grades of managers within the organization. This can be problematic, because the organizational need may be counter to this cost-saving initiative and as a consequence service quality or operational effectiveness suffer. In addition, any cost saving may be off-set by the increased need to train subordinate managers in their new tasks.

The removal of layers of middle management is also motivated by a desire to encourage unit or junior managers to be more intra/entrepreneurial. Managers closest to their markets are best able to develop those markets and run the business in a flexible way to meet business demands. Many organizations feel that managers at local level will be better able to spot opportunities, develop relationships with key market segments, reflect customer tastes and needs, and manage costs more effectively. The case study included later in this chapter was largely motivated by an analysis that suggested that McDonald's franchises out performed the units directly managed by the company through MCOPCO – the management company for restaurants directly managed by group.

Whilst the above provide some positive attractions for the introduction of more empowerment amongst junior management, some organizations look to their own control structures and the tendencies towards bureaucracy. The problem over control of organizational activities can be overcome with a more empowered approach to managing the hierarchy. Many organizations develop 'go no go' control systems through which approval must be sought for actions. Whilst this creates the appearance of increased and control, it can be difficult to manage because there are tensions over what is to be controlled. Hence decision-making may require people who are not close to a problem making decisions about the problem. One possible consequence is decisions become stalled or put-off, or the wrong decisions are made. As organizations grow there is a particular need to adjust to the new situation and locate decision-making authority at different levels. In fact, 'as the organization develops, appropriate levels are rarely adjusted to keep in step' (Mitchell,

Hospitality, Leisure & Tourism Series

Table 7.1 The purpose of control

Problems	Answers
1. Failure to recognize the real reasons for success, drifting into unprofitable ventures.	1. Focus analysis and attention on strategic questions and control to stay in chosen segments.
2. Approval is frequently required of people who have no way of knowing the facts.	2. Ensure approval is only required from people in a position to make a contribution.
3. Innovation is often stifled by over-administration and monitoring details.	3. Give innovators clear objectives, tight time and money budgets and a free hand.
4. People like to exercise authority and frequently do it by over-controlling downwards.	4. Focus attention and accountability on strategic questions.
5. Uniform solutions are applied across non-uniform situations causing complexity.	5. Put responsibility for the solution close to the problem; segment and separate the real differences; act strategically.
6. The desire to get control by direct means often leads to losing it.	6. Ensure that there is alignment of your objectives with those of the elements controlled.

Source: Mitchell, 1979

1979: 3). Empowerment can provide both a rhetoric and a technique for getting senior managers to 'overcome their reluctance to let go' (Mitchell, 1979: 3). By adopting a more 'directional' approach to control, senior managers can concentrate on the strategic direction of the organization. Mitchell suggests the problems and responses outlined in Table 7.1 are needed to overcome these bureaucratic tendencies.

There are, therefore, several perceived benefits of delayering organizations in the service sector. It is held that organizations become more responsive to customer needs, because senior managers are closer to customers and the communications links are more direct with the front line. Decision-making can be located closer to the points of the problem and senior managers can concentrate on the strategic direction of the company. Operating costs can be reduced as overheads are lowered through the removal of middle managers, without directly influencing production capacity. Flatter structures encourage more entrepreneurial behaviour among junior managers and enables large organizations to capture the flexibility and responsiveness of smaller organizations (Senge, 1999).

Empowered managers

The removal of layers of managers results in a wider span of control in which the direct supervision of subordinate managers is less possible. The remaining senior managers have more units or junior managers to manage and can consequently spend less time with each. 'Reducing bureaucracy requires more than removing jobs and becoming more lean. It requires an attitude shift on the part of people in the middle to become more empowered to do what is best for themselves and for the business' (Block, 1987: 1). In these situations the relationship changes, unit or junior managers have to operate with more responsible autonomy. In other words they are left to manage their responsibilities without close and ongoing supervision. They require less direction over their actions and are more likely to be empowered to act within guidelines and account for their action after the event.

The measure of degrees of empowerment as experienced by managers are similar to those experienced by subordinates. The question that attempts to establish 'what can you do now that you could not do before?' is essential in defining the objective nature of the changes in working practice. Here changes to the boundaries of authority are interesting, because they can help in establishing the degree to which junior managers are taking on decision-making tasks that had formerly been the domain of more senior managers. As with employees' empowerment it is possible to note a number of positions. For some managers, there is a genuine, planned and co-ordinated change in the decisions that he/she can make. They are given more latitude to spend money on new equipment, staffing or advertising without reference to their more senior colleagues. Typically this might be fixed through some cash sum, so the empowered manager can spend amounts up to a given figure. In other cases, particularly in tightly branded businesses, the manager may not be able to make many more decisions than they could make in the past, but they are allowed to manage their unit/section without direct instruction. They have what Freidman (1977) calls 'responsible autonomy' in that they are allowed autonomy to operate within boundaries set.

In these circumstances, the relationship between the more senior manager and their empowered subordinate managers becomes more of coach and counsellor in these circumstances. In part this is a consequence of the wider span of control, the individual is unlikely to have the detailed understanding of each unit/section and will need to rely on the immediate manager. In part this approach is required if the empowered manger is to be encouraged to take 'ownership' of the unit/section. Empowered managers need to be convinced that their empowerment is meaningful and that they have some degree of control over the things that they regard as important. Managers, like other empowered individuals, soon recognize the inconsistencies if they are told that they are empowered, but senior managers retain all the important decisions, or 'steam in' with instructions and a directive style when problems arise.

The form of empowerment of managers can be based round the individual managers, or through teams in semi-autonomous groups. The case study outlined at the end of the chapter was based round individual managers. Unit Managers were empowered via responsible autonomy, and the redesigned role for the two General Area Supervisors were both individually orientated in the McDonald's case. The introduction of empowerment in Harvester Restaurants on the other hand, started with the removal of two Regional Manager posts and the creation of teams of Area Managers, each with a support network of administration, personnel, etc. In this latter case, a member of the senior management team was allocated to each group, so that the group was linked into the senior management structure. Another interesting aspect of the Harvester model was that the empowerment of Area Managers (middle management) occurred prior to any attempt to roll out employee empowerment to the wider organization. Whilst individual approaches to the empowerment of managers might be more consistent with aspirations to create a more entrepreneurial management culture, team based approaches have benefits in creating internal support and monitoring of performance. The team monitors individual members and is capable of providing the appropriate support where needed.

The level at which empowerment is focused needs to consider two issues, where in the organization structure is the focus for empowering managers, and what opportunity is there for managers to influence the policies and decisions which impact upon them? The positioning of the empowering initiative is important because it establishes the extent of empowerment within the organization. Again there are a range of possibilities from a fully integrated approach which extends from senior management down to operatives with managers at all levels involved and empowered. Harvester Restaurants provides a

Hospitality, Leisure & Tourism Series

good example of a service organisation that had this approach. Other organizations may locate the empowerment at particular roles. It may be unit management as in the case of Jones and Davies (1991) study of empowerment amongst hotel managers. In other cases, the key focus may be Area Managers, with unit managers experiencing some empowerment, but the Area Manager is encouraged to run the units in the area as though they were her/his own venture. Where the initiative is targeted at a particular job or couple of jobs, as in the following case study, there is a potential difficulty for empowered managers experiencing the inconsistency with the wider organization culture. It is difficult, in these circumstances for organizations to graft empowerment on to a traditional culture and structure (Sternberg, 1992).

In addition to the level in the organization structure in which managerial empowerment occurs, it is necessary to consider the level of the decisions that the manager is empowered to make. Chiefly these are concerned with the extent to which empowerment involves the manager's day-to-day tasks, or the extent to which they are now able to participate in the decisions that affect them. Like operative empowerment, to what extent is empowerment task orientated or strategic? The Whitbread's leased and tenanted property division employs consultants to advise and develop lessees and tenants who operate Whitbread licensed properties. These consultants have both a high degree of task-oriented empowerment and have involvement in the strategic planning process that sets the division's budget and objectives for the forthcoming year. In other cases, managerial empowerment involves some decision-making that might be typically undertaken at the level above the post. The General Area Supervisor's role outlined in the case study is an example of this. They were given the authority to run the five or eight restaurants in their area and were allowed to make decisions about expenditure within predetermined limits.

In many branded service operations there is a tension between empowering the manager to respond to market needs and the need to maintain a consistent brand across all units of the business. Under the current orthodoxy, standardization is seen to be key and the strength in what the branded service operator offers. Variation between what customers can buy in different branches and in different parts of the country are thought to be confusing and potentially frustrating to customers. It is possible to detect an alternative view that defined the service brand, either in terms of intangible benefits, or in a way that celebrated and embraced regional/unit variations. The Campanile Hotel and Grill chain in France, for example, has highly standardized accommodation and menu, but each restaurant is encouraged to add a small number of local dishes, which add interest. This could be a model for UK branded services. Whilst this may be a reality for the future, empowered managers in many UK branded business have to manage the brand to ensure uniformity and consistency and this frequently limits the issues that the manager has any discretion to alter. Typically, therefore, the menu in branded restaurants is determined and priced at head office. Production and serving methods are designed centrally, as are procurement sources, ordering systems, and employee training programmes. National promotional and advertising campaigns limit the promotional decisions that managers can make to links with local businesses, community or social groups. Managers may well be responsible for recruiting, scheduling, supervising and disciplining staff, but pay rates, grades and reward packages are typically systematized, which again limits the range of empowered manager's tasks.

Empowered managers have much in common with empowered employees in that their empowerment frequently fixes boundaries in which they have the power to affect decisions, but may present some inconsistencies and tensions that either nullify or meliorate the beneficial effects intended by those introducing the initiative. Thus the relationship between the objective description of what a manager can do now compared with past working arrangements, and the manager's subjective responses to these changes is crucial. Depending on how new empowered posts are filled, and by whom, individual managers' reactions may vary. Figure 7.1 provides a diagram depicting three possible positions comparing objective analysis of changes introduced and subjective responses to them.

In the first position, the individual's work has changed little, they are not substantially doing anything different in their tasks than they did prior to the being 'empowered'. The likely reaction is that the individual reacts cynically and sees empowerment as either empty rhetoric, or as just another fad. The second position involves the individual doing essentially the same work, though their relationship with *their* manager changes so that they have more freedom to take action without asking permission. Here the likely reaction may well be supportive as experienced managers, in particular, feel trusted to do the job without someone immediately vetting and monitoring their actions. The third position is where managers are given some decision making over issues that would previously have been undertaken by more senior managers. Here the manager is likely to see the initiative as providing an opportunity for growth and personal development.

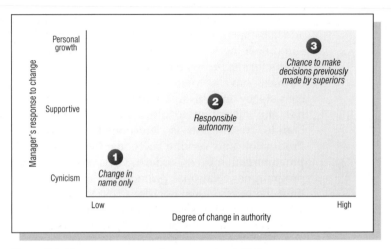

Figure 7.1 Manager responses to empowering initiatives

Again it is worth remembering that the individual managers may respond differently because of their own experiences and expectations, and personalities. Most organizations who go through the process of delayering report that some managers find it difficult to work under these new arrangements. In some cases, the approach requires different skills, which are not available to all managers within the management team. In other cases, the change in role cuts across the role expectations with which they have been socialized. In the pilot study, which is provided as the case study, McDonald's Restaurant Managers were 'empowered' in a manner consistent with position two in Figure 7.1. Reactions to their changed relationship with the 'General Area Superviser' were chiefly related to the experience of the Restaurant Manager. More experienced managers welcomed the opportunity to 'get on with it', whilst newer managers were concerned about the reduced contact with their supervisor, and reported a sense of isolation.

Barriers to managerial empowerment through delayering

At root, aspirations for the empowerment of managers have many similarities with the empowerment of operatives. In part the aspirations are directed at improving operational perform-ance by locating decision-making at points in the organization which enable quicker response times and greater flexibility in meeting change to customer demands and operational con-straints. These aspirations are concerned with developing an intensified sense of ownership and commitment. It is hoped that the empowerment of managers through the removal of layers of the hierarchy will unleash the necessary confidence to make decisions and feelings of commitment, which will then produce the desired effects.

The cornerstone of the success of any initiative will be the response to the experiences of being empowered. If managers feel that changes in working procedures, processes and relationships genuinely give them power to affect outcomes, through the exercise of personal skills, in a way that is meaningful and valued, they are more likely to view the experience of being empowered in a positive light. Whilst there are clearly important individual differences that will further mediate the response to initiatives in a way that cannot guarantee given behaviours from given responses, however, there are likely to be a series of factors that produce negative influences on the ability to generate the positive feelings from being empowered.

As was discussed above, the tight definition of the brand offer to customers and the need to control the standardized service offer to the market, the need to take advantage of economies of scale in purchasing, advertising and promotion, and finance create situations where the organization's control procedures limit the ability of managers to exercise a wide range of judgements. Manager empowerment brought about by delayering therefore may restrict what the manager is empowered to do to a narrow range of operational decisions. This may represent an improvement from past practices where even operational decisions were tightly managed and junior managers were subjected to command and control management. However, it may also present barriers to the managers that in effect mean that initiatives which claim to be empowering allow little scope for the manager to make any significant impact with this new found 'power'.

The impact on the management hierarchy and management progression is another issue that organizations who have introduced delayering report can cause problems. One of the consequences of removing one or more tiers of management and flattening the structure is that there are fewer senior management jobs to which junior managers can aspire. Not surprisingly, this can have a counter-productive impact on the commitment and motivation of the very managers whose improved commitment is the objective of the initiative. One of the comments oft voiced by managers in the pilot study (discussed later) is that the more experienced unit managers, who might have been in line for promotion under the traditional structure, now had no immediate progression route. Several said that they did not want to be running a restaurant all their lives. In part these managers' concerns are about material rewards, promotion and status, but in part, they are also about expectations and past practice. Rapidly expanding branded service businesses have, in many cases, grown in such a way as to provide managers with rapid promotion prospects. Managers have learnt to live in an organization culture where colleagues were promoted quickly and most senior executives have grown with the company. Managers in these organizations grow to expect rapid promotion. A flatter structure changes that and there are some shocks to manager expectations that can represent negative effects of empowerment.

The issue of who benefits from empowerment is something that impacts on the effectiveness of all employees. For managers, the perceived gains from delayering and 'empowering' them are no different. If managers perceive empowerment to mean that they are now undertaking their former manager's job with no additional reward, they are unlikely to develop the positive feelings upon which the supposed benefits of the initiative are to build. Even allowing for the possible developmental benefits of individuals taking on more responsibilities, the issue of perceived rewards is an important one because each manager is concerned with the personal outcomes from changed working relationships. At root, the question of 'what's in it for me?' has to produce a positive response if the experience of being empowered is to be beneficial to both the individual and the organization.

Resistance to empowerment often occurs in situations where managers can see others in the organization gaining more from a change in working relationships which extend their responsibilities and work load without a corresponding increase in either material and/or psychological rewards. The pilot study, which forms the basis of the case study, provides an example where the restaurant management group felt that they were not gaining sufficiently from the changes, and that the General Area Supervisors and senior management were the key beneficiaries.

Pilot study at McDonald's Restaurants Limited (UK)

The McDonald's Restaurant Corporation requires little introduction to readers. The company's growth and size are well documented (Love, 1986; Walsh, 1992; Gordan, 1993; Ritzer, 1993). As a background to the initiative described in this section, two important factors influence concerns of the company's management in Britain. Unlike the dominant pattern in all other countries in the Corporation's businesses, approximately 80 per cent of the British restaurants were managed directly by the company via MCOPCO, and local management were clearly under pressure from the US parent company to bring the UK operation in to line so that more restaurants would be run by franchisees. A second and related factor concerns the company's return on capital employed. The 1992 accounts show that the company was returning 13.54p in the £. This was not a favourable return compared with international performance within the Corporation. Subsequently the British company set and achieved targets to increase the proportion of franchisees to 30 per cent by the year 2000, and to increase return on capital to 25 per cent. The UK company was therefore being told that it had to lift profitability and this could be done by having more franchise restaurants – which were seen by the Corporation as out-performing the company-managed units.

Both these factors lead to an increased focus on individual restaurants as centres of profit so as to improve the financial performance of each unit (restaurant), and to adopt an organization structure that would empower individuals in a way that encouraged entrepreneurism and a sense of 'ownership' amongst managers. The aim being that increased profitability would either make the units more attractive to franchisees, or bring unit profitability into line with company targets. The initiative described here was applied amongst a group of restaurants in Wales, but these were clearly being used as a pilot for potential application elsewhere.

The MCOPCO organization structure in Britain tends to be based on a narrow span of control and 'tall' organization structure. There are eleven levels of personnel between the customer and senior board members, and the ultimate aim is to make MCOPCO a 'flatter' organization. Figure 7.2 shows the levels between customer and the senior operations executive.

Figure 7.3 highlights the MCOPCO structure within the restaurants in Wales. Originally there had been twelve restaurants, each with a manager who was answerable to one of four Area Supervisors, who in turn answered to an Operations Manager.

As a result of promotions and transfers of two of the Area Supervisors, the company decided to take the opportunity to reorganize the management of these restaurant into two areas, with a General Area Supervisor being responsible for restaurant performance in each. These two individuals were given three-year contracts with a general brief to improve the profitability of their 'businesses'. By removing one of the levels of management (delayering) it was hoped that both General Area Supervisors and Restaurant Managers would be empowered and thereby be more entrepreneurial in their respective roles.

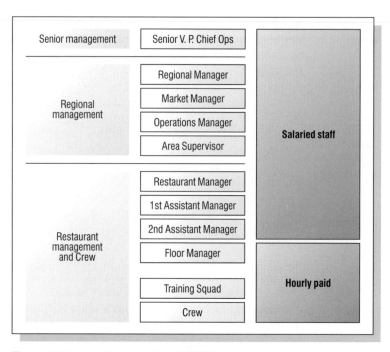

Figure 7.2 Levels of personnel in MCOPCO

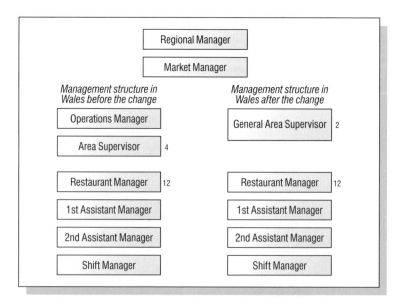

Figure 7.3 Organizational structure of restaurants in the study – before and after the change

Interviews with the participants revealed changes which had largely focused on the General Area Supervisor as the chief instrument with which to fashion a more entrepreneurial approach. The reward package gave them considerable personal benefits, they were encouraged to develop a sense of ownership of their area, and were charged with the responsibility to improve restaurant performance. In both cases, empowerment could be typified as being largely concerned with responsible autonomy. That is, it involved job holders being given autonomy to get on with their jobs without on-going close supervision, but ultimately they were accountable for their actions and performance.

A shared view of Restaurant Managers and General Area Supervisors was that there had been a lack of clarity as to the precise boundaries of responsibilities and authority and that managers at all levels were still 'feeling their way' round the possibilities and options.

Restaurant Managers   •   •   •

Most Restaurant Managers spoke favourably about their relationship with their General Area Supervisor. Due to the extended span of control, this tended to be more consultative and negotiated. Meetings between them would be more along the lines of general target setting than in giving and receiving detailed instructions. In some cases, particularly amongst less experienced managers, there was a perception of isolation and lack of support. The more experienced managers tended to see little difference in the new working arrangements. In many cases Area Supervisors had tended to leave experienced managers to 'get on with it'. Detailed questioning confirmed this view. Tightly defined brand attributes and highly standardized control systems meant that there was little scope for discretion in restaurant management. Product mix, advertising, pricing and promotional activities were largely decided nationally. There was some authority to agree minor contracts, say for window cleaning or landscaping, and low cost local promotions at unit level, but these were highly constrained.

Restaurant Managers had more discretion in staffing their restaurants, though again operational targets set limits within which they had to work. Manager experience appeared to be an important factor. Prior to the changes experienced managers would have been allowed to fix staffing levels without recourse to the Area Supervisor, whilst some of their colleagues would have been given a figure to work towards. Little had changed after the reorganization. Restaurant Managers were not formally involved in the selection of their junior management. This was typically the responsibility of Operations Managers in the past, and now the General Area Supervisors. Having said that, managers in west Wales were participating in junior management development and several managers reported that this gave them a better sense of involvement. Empowerment, such as it was, for these managers was restricted to task power. They had few opportunities to influence the objectives that affect them. Managers in both areas met on a monthly basis and this provided an opportunity to expand this feature of their work in the future. One of the recommendations to the company was that these meetings might promote more team working amongst managers.

Whilst most managers liked the change in style in the relationship with their General Area Supervisor, several commented on *'feeling more in charge'* and *'more responsible'*, there were some important qualifications. These may well have a bearing on the extent to which these feelings influence personal performance in the long run. Most of the experienced managers expressed some disquiet, with varying degrees of intensity, about their long-term future. The key problem was the removal of the post of Area Supervisor, the next promotional post for them. Several managers specifically said, *'What's in it for me?'* Others did not want to work for a franchisee and many specifically said that they did not want to be *'running a restaurant for the rest of their lives'*. The newer managers were not always in a good position to appreciate the change in style and approach. Several wanted more contact with their General Area Supervisor, as they developed confidence in their operational management skills. These variations in perception confirm the need to be sensitive to individual differences in empowerment.

In the main, managers enjoyed their work. Unit management does provide opportunities for a sense of personal achievement, with a degree of territorial control and immediacy of outcomes. However, this not to say that managers were completely happy with their experiences over the first few months. There were some important barriers present in the current arrangements. Feelings of insecurity about the future, together with a perception of inequity in the outcomes and a lack of institutional support did seem to blunt the ability of these changes to gain the moral commitment which would stimulate managers' creativity and entrepreneurial skills.

At a fundamental level, there were potential tensions between the detail and extent of empowerment given to managers. These are tensions which are bound to exist when an organization is attempting to run a tightly defined brand with a recognizable product mix across a multi-unit distribution system, and at the same time encourage enough freedom to interpret local needs and opportunities. The key issue is the extent to which these tensions inhibit or enable managers in a way that they perceive to be significant. In this case, experienced managers did seem to welcome the looser controls that allowed them to do their work without direct supervision and instruction. These differences are consistent with feelings of competence, essential for feelings of empowerment to develop. Less experienced managers were yet to feel competent in their role, whilst the more experienced managers did feel competent.

General Area Supervisors ● ● ●

The two General Area Supervisors approached their new role from different experiences and background strengths. Bearing in mind my earlier comments about the importance of individual perceptions in empowerment, it is not surprising that the shift from Area Supervisor to General Area Supervisor was seen by the post-holder as involving considerable development. Concerns with wider business performance, direct contact with senior managers, more autonomy and a significant bonus package all contributed to the post-holder's enthusiasm for the changes and high levels of job satisfaction were reported. Nor is it surprising that for the former Operations Manager, changes represented less of a shift into more strategic issues, many of the tasks and issues in the new role were part of his former post. Hence the post-holder was bound to feel less newly empowered to do things he had always wanted do. He was, however, committed to making these new arrangements work and saw the possibilities of the wider application of this model to MCOPCO.

Both General Area Supervisors felt that their jobs were essentially very similar to previous posts, though obviously in different aspects. Paradoxically, both post-holders felt that they also had considerable re-adjustments to make in the early stages of the job. For one, this meant learning to adopt a more hands-off, consultative approach to Restaurant Managers, for the other it meant re-examining the restaurants in the group in detail. They felt that the company had not defined the detail of what they were empowered to do and there were some resulting tensions. It is also true to say that the company had not identified the sorts of skills that would be needed in the new roles and had not provided a detailed staff development programme for them.

Detailed questioning revealed that there was some discretion in the tasks, though this was constrained within overall organiza-tional control. Again there was a degree of freedom over promotional and marketing matters, though only in so far as these were contained within the local market and did not go against national policy. Major campaigns and promotions were organized and imposed from the centre. Product mix issues were largely decided centrally. Pricing decisions were determined centrally, except where it involved a local promotional offer. There was some degree of discretion in capital expenditure though this was limited to £2500–£3000. Expenditure above this amount would be sanctioned by the next tier of management. Similarly, both had some responsibility for recommending new sites, though the decision to invest was taken at a more senior level.

Although both General Area Supervisors would have been involved in the appointment of 1st and 2nd Assistants in restaurants, the appointment of Restaurant Managers was taken by the Market Manager or a more senior manager. This proved to be a matter of some tension, because there was a feeling that this represented undue interference, which would not occur with a franchisee. One area, in particular, required several new managers and the General Area Supervisor was frustrated by the decision of senior regional managers to retain this decision. He thought that as the 'empowered' manager he should be able to make these appointments himself.

Like the Restaurant Managers, it is possible to conclude that this form of empowerment is more about responsible autonomy, with power being largely limited to operational management issues. Hence they were free to decide on priorities with Restaurant Managers, but on many issues were limited to consultation and recommendation making. Many decisions were taken at more senior levels. In different ways, both post-holders accepted this as to be expected, though felt in some aspects the boundaries between themselves and senior managers needed to be more clearly drawn so as to avoid the tensions mentioned above.

The two General Area Supervisors reflected intrinsic and extrinsic sources of satisfaction with the new arrangement. They appeared to have a sense of ownership of their area and a drive to achieve the objectives set. In both cases there was an awareness that there were not inconsiderable material rewards for making their areas successful. They key issue here was the extent to which the tensions between their desire to run their areas in an autonomous way and the organization's desire to control the significant aspects of their activities were resolved in future. During the pilot stage, there was a sense of personal efficacy and autonomy, but some degree of frustration with some decisions made by senior managers.

Hospitality, Leisure & Tourism Series

Subsequent changes to the structure ● ● ●

As a response to the pilot study, and a report produced on arrangements in the USA, the subsequent revised organization structure focused more on unit managers. Using the arrangements for managing the franchised business the company has produced a structure where a new General Manager role replaces the Restaurant Manager's role. This new role allows each manager more freedom to run the restaurant as an 'independent' business in the same way that it might be run by a franchisee. These managers, therefore, run the restaurant with 'responsible autonomy'. Budgets are largely focused at profit and operational targets. How the individual achieves the targets, is up to the judgement of the individual, within limits. Bonus schemes for the General Managers come into effect only when the business is achieving good grades in the company's customer satisfaction assessment levels, which measure quality, service and cleanliness over a twelve-month period. These service quality measures were said to establish 'green fees' which attracted a bonus after which further bonuses were calculated on profits growth. Given these bonuses, it is possible for General Managers to earn a further £10,000 over and above the basic salary of £20,000 per annum (1995 figures). Under these arrangements, the General Manager may be responsible for one large unit, or several smaller units.

General Managers themselves report to an 'Operations Consultant', whose role and style is similar to the 'Field Consultant' in the franchisee structure. As the job titles suggest, consultants in both cases act in a more negotiated and supportive role. The General Managers are left to run the business and Operations Consultant visits them on a less frequent basis than would a Supervisor in the traditional structure. As the General Managers have more delegated authority, the consultant provides advice and guidance as and when required. The agenda of issues to be discussed between the manager and consultant becomes more business rather than operationally focused. Thus issues related to marketing, and profitability are more likely to be discussed under these circumstances than in the traditional relationship between unit manager and Area Supervisor.

Figure 7.4 provides an organizational structure for the company under these new arrangements. Interestingly, the company decided to keep both the traditional structure and the new structure in place at the same time, the view being that new managers needed closer supervision until they had enough experience to operate as General Managers. Ultimately, the company envisaged that the new structure would become the dominant model for the organization in the long term.

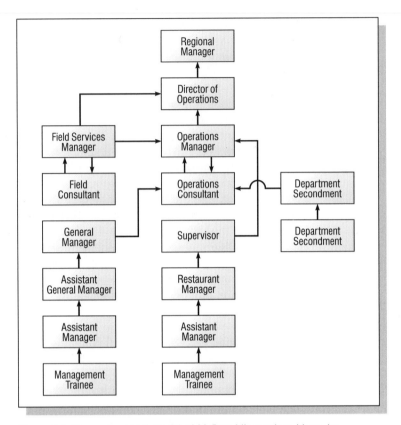

Figure 7.4 The restructured model of McDonald's services hierarchy

This form of empowerment did allow managers more freedom to make immediate decisions about the restaurant as a business and did encourage the participants to develop a sense of ownership which was reinforced by a reward package which gave managers a considerable material incentive to achieve both quality and profit targets. That said, the McDonald's system retains tight control even within franchise businesses. Early experiences of allowing franchisees too much freedom resulted in relationships with franchisees where there is a great deal of attention paid to ensuring that all franchisees run their units in the way prescribed by the company. Most franchisees are either ex-McDonald's managers (as Area Managers or above), or they undertake a long training period during which they spend a minimum of 2000 hours working in a restaurant prior to taking on the franchise (Lashley, 2000c). The relationship with franchisees is instructive in that it reveals much about the potential limits placed on the 'empowered' General Managers.

Hospitality, Leisure & Tourism Series

The General Managers were empowered to operate the restaurant as a business, but would not be allowed to let service standards slip in the name of increasing profits. The inter-relationship of labour costs and customer service targets is an interesting case in point. Reducing the amount of labour on duty has the effect of reducing labour costs, and thereby increasing profitability, but customer waiting times increase and service quality decreases. Similarly, the reduction of buffer stocks of pre-cooked product, or using pre-cooked product beyond its shelf life, reduces food waste but also damages customer service and product quality. In all these situations, the managers (and franchisees) are expected to manage the business in the 'McDonald's way'. That is in a way that does not compromise the company's service quality standards. Similarly, empowered managers cannot change the product range, or national advertising and promotion strategies. As stated earlier, General Managers have to manage the business within the constraints of the brand. All these examples confirm the key consideration that managers must have internalized the company's policies and objectives, and exercise the necessary control of the business through their own personal self-control.

The new organization structure overcame some of the problems identified in the pilot study in that the focus of the initiative was the unit, and managers were encouraged to operate as though they were franchisees, that is, as though they were entrepreneurs. The amount of control which the company exercises over the brand, product range, pricing, promotional activities, service standards and processes, etc., does mean that managers have a considerable tension to manage. They do have freedom to act, but that freedom is constrained to tightly defined limits. Though managers have the authority to make decisions about the management of the business, they are ultimately required to account for their actions.

Empowered franchisees?

The main thrust of this text is about the use of empowerment in directly managed multi-unit service organizations, and it is worth commenting briefly on franchising as a means of operating these businesses, which have many similarities with delayering the organization structure. The motives for operating service business in the form of franchising are similar to those concerned with empowerment. Namely that the organization wants to be flatter, closer and more responsive to customers, and recognizes that the immediate unit management needs to be incentivized to manage the operation in a way that is flexible and concerned with customer service experiences (Lashley, 2000c). Franchising services is supposed to provide a nominally independent smaller firm the right to run the service operation within a particular location. Here the entrepreneurism hinted at in the delayered unit management example given earlier in this chapter is more central to the approach.

Franchisor companies hope that these 'independent' small firms operating the business unit level under licence will bring an enthusiasm and attention to detail that will enable successful operation of the business at minimum cost and risk to themselves. From the franchisee's perspective the small firm owner gets access to a 'proven' business formula, and the resources of the big firm at minimum risk. In this they are more 'intrapreneurs' than entrepreneurs (Morrison, 2000) because they are risk minimizing and have to be prepared to work within the confines of the big firms' operating systems. A franchisor like McDonald's runs a very tight franchise ship. Franchisees, new to the company, have to work for the company for a year without wages. During this time they go through all the crew and management training and have successfully to manage a unit to the company's standards before they are allowed to take on a franchise. Once installed in the restaurant they have to meet the company's service quality audits and may not vary the offer to customers without company permission (Lashley, 2000d). In these circumstances, it could be said that franchisees operate more like 'empowered managers', rather than independent businesses.

Conclusion

Service organizations, particularly those offering high-volume consumer services, have developed distribution networks that are delivered through multi-unit organizations where the units are located close to their customers. Fast food, themed restaurants and public house businesses have limited opportunities to gain from economies of scale because units need to be within easy reach of customers. The consequence has been that this type of organization runs large numbers of establishments and there has been a corresponding growth in organization structures – narrow span of control and multi-tiered bureaucracies.

Over recent years many of these have gone through at least two phases. In the first phases, organizations increased control over the organization's activities, and in the second they have attempted to maintain that control whilst looking for ways to give unit managers more freedom to develop the business at local level. One senior executive of a major brewery chain explained, *'In the 1970s and 1980s we looked for ways of increasing our control of what went on in the pubs. Now we realise that we have reached the limit. Future profit growth will only come from tapping the talents and abilities of those closest to the business and its customers'.*

This has resulted in organizational managers looking to the redesign of the traditional structure to what Goffee and Scase (1995) call 'adhocracies'. Organizations that attempt to be both large and small, centralized in strategic direction but decentralized in tactical operation, global and local. Whilst there are many different terms to describe these organizations and many different forms that the redesign can take, the empowerment of unit managers to make more business related decisions is a common feature within service firms.

Empowered managers are encouraged to act as 'independent' entrepreneurs, making the necessary 'nips and tucks' to the service offer to match local conditions. Through this it is hoped that managers' experiences and immediate unit knowledge will assist the organization to respond more quickly to both current and future service needs. Like other initiatives aimed at employees, empowered managers within service organizations have to manage a tension which is constrained within a framework determined at more senior levels. The nature of the brand being offered to customers may also limit the individual's freedom to meet customer requirements. The response of the individual to these tensions is likely to be a key factor in determining whether empowered managers see the new arrangements as a benefit or liability. To be successful empowered managers, like empowered workers, need to develop a sense of personal efficacy and be convinced that they can make a difference to the performance of the business.

The pilot study at McDonald's provides a useful example of the motives behind changes to organizational structure that are taking place in many service firms. It also shows some of the difficulties involved in taking out layers of managers where there has not been a clear analysis of decision making processes and conscious attempt to reconsider the boundaries within which the empowered manager needs to operate. The case study is also instructive in that it shows that multi-unit branded service organizations are often caught within a tension that is inherent in the nature of the operation. Organizations that are attempting to manage branded offers to customers have to deliver consistent products and services across all units. The Pierre Victoire case (Morrison, 2000) is instructive in showing what happens to a business that is not consistent. At the same time the organization is operating hundreds and thousands of units that are close to their markets, they need to be flexible enough to respond to local needs. McDonald's, like many similar companies, is constantly searching for the 'right formula' and policies frequently fluctuate between control and flexibility.

Changes in working arrangements

- The task dimension
- The task allocation dimension
- The power dimension
- The commitment dimension
- The culture dimension

The preceding chapters have identified variations in managerial intentions for empowerment and variations in the form that initiatives claiming to be empowering can take. It has also been stated that the study of empowerment needs to recognize the distinction between the objective changes to working arrangements and the subjective experiences of those who are empowered. Even those writing from a more normative perspective make this distinction (Johnson and Redmond, 1998), though do not provide any framework for analysing the nature of the changes, and how these are to build to empowerment. Bowen and Lawler (1992) do provide some insights into possible variations in the degree of empowerment, and the match between these and the organizational context. Their model has particular relevance to a discussion about the contextual influences on approaches to empowerment and these are discussed further in Chapter 12, however they do provide an interesting model for comparing empowered organizations and production line organizations. Although somewhat simplistic in creating two dichotomous types of service organization, this model is a useful one because it does provide the basis for Table 8.1 that suggests a five-dimensional model for analysing the objective changes to working arrangements. In other words, it assists in comparing these dimensions between a 'production-line' service organization and the aspirations for an empowering organization. The Bowen and Lawler model can be criticized because it fails to recognize that empowerment can be generated even in 'production line' organizations. They fail to deal with empowerment as a psychological state, however, their model is useful as a tool for analysing initiatives the claim to be empowering because it enables us to study the changes introduced and comment on their likelihood of generating feelings of competence, meaningfulness, choice and impact on the 'empowered'.

This chapter starts from the assumption that any serious study of empowerment needs to make a distinction between initiatives that are called empowerment and those that produce feelings of being empowered in the 'empowered' – that create the psychological state of empowerment. It also recognizes the need to construct a picture of the objective changes in working arrangements by exploring five dimensions in the new arrangements which assist in developing answers to the fundamental question, 'What can you do now that you could not do before?'

Table 8.1 therefore suggest a five-dimensional framework for analysing empowerment in service industries. Using Bowen and Lawler's dichotomous model of the production line approach and the empowered approach it is possible to produce a description of the nature and range of the changes which have taken place. This model (Lashley and McGoldrick, 1994) has been used in the investigation into empowerment with the different cases studies outlined in this text. It is necessary to recognize that there are a number of dimensions to empowerment and that service organizations are likely to **choose** forms of empowerment based on their perceptions of organizational needs, the benefits of employee involvement and different definitions of empowerment. Table 8.1 attempts to show how considerations of these themes might further develop an understanding of Bowen and Lawler's contextual considerations and forms of empowerment.

Hospitality, Leisure & Tourism Series

Table 8.1 Dimensions of empowerment and contingencies

Dimensions	Employee involvement – production-line organization (high volume, standardized, short time, simple technology, theory X organization)	Employee involvement – empowered organization (personalized service, long time period, complex technology, unpredictable, theory Y organization)
Task dimension	Low discretion	High discretion
Task allocation	Seeks permission	Responsible autonomy
Power	Limited to task	Influences the direction of policy
Commitment	Calculative	Moral
Culture	Control oriented	Trust oriented

The task dimension

The task dimension involves consideration of the amount of discretion that an employee is allowed in performing the tasks for which he/she is employed. It is possible to identify two elements to the performance of service tasks. For those who are employed in 'front-line' departments with direct contact with customers there has to be consideration of the **tangible** and **intangible** aspects of both **goods** and **services**. To what extent are the physical, tangible aspects of the customer's purchase standardized or open to customization? For example, hotel guests may request more towels, courtesy packs or milk in their room. Customers in a restaurant may ask for both ice-cream and cream with their dessert, or larger portions, or dishes not on the menu. What degree of discretion does the room attendant or waiter/ waitress have in meeting these requests, and at what costs?

Similarly, the intangible elements in the customer purchase, particularly in relation to the service provided by employees may be open to varying amounts of interpretation in different service operations. Given the view that intangibles become more important in the upper price band of service markets, giving individuals the freedom to 'delight the customer' (Hubrecht and Teare, 1993: iii) may be fundamental to the organization's competitive strategy. The following is another example from the Scotts/Marriott stories and highlights the idealized behaviour required of the customer delighting empowered employee. 'A guest at the same hotel asked Marlene Abbott, a guest room attendant, to arrange for items of clothing to be laundered. The

Hospitality, Leisure & Tourism Series

timing of the request meant that it would be difficult to fulfil, so rather than telling the guest this, she took the guest's laundry home and did it herself' (Hubrecht and Tear, 1993: iv).

Setting aside the 'political' aspect to this example where the employee is being 'empowered' to give up their own free time, soap powder and electricity, the quotation does provide a valuable insight into the level of employee commitment to delighting the customer which empowerment is supposed to deliver. Here the employee is so committed to meeting the company's service offer to its customers, she is prepared to give up her free time to provide the extra service which is a defining feature of 'delighting the customer'.

When analysing the tasks that empowered employees undertake, much depends on the nature of the brand being offered to customers and the attributes that are promoted with the brand identity. We have already seen three possible models of service offer in the preceding chapters. The 'production line' approach discussed by Bowen and Lawler, is totally compatible with the 'service factory' of Schmenner, the 'McDonaldized' firm of Ritzer, or 'uniformity dependent' (Lashley, 2000b). These organizations make a standardized offer to their customers and task discretion is limited. Production systems are designed to ensure that the standardized offer to customers is consistently delivered. The approach is highly influenced by the work of F.W. Taylor (1947), which informed much of the development of mass production techniques in manufacturing. Thus 'one best way' of performing operations dominates and allows limited scope for employees to interpret customer needs. Given the highly tangible driven nature of the offer, there is also limited scope for employee discretion in the intangibles, because service times are often specified. Many pub and fast food companies, for example, set target times for customers to be acknowledged when they arrive at the counter.

Indeed in some roles, employees still work to scripted interactions with customers, thus their scope for personal interpretation is further limited. However, many of these firms are attempting to gain competitive advantage through service quality and are encouraging employees to accept more responsibility for the service encounter. Thus some degree of discretion is being encouraged, albeit in a limited form.

Firms in Schmenner's 'service shop', or Heskett *et al.*'s (1990) 'technical service' operate largely in a 'McDonaldized' format, but have some requirement for employees to demonstrate either technical competence or exercise some creativity in performing the service task to customers because they are largely making an offer to customers which reflects 'mass customization', or is 'choice dependent' (Lashley, 2000). Here jobs may be highly standardized, and trained to a tight repertoire of actions, say in servicing a car, or cooking a dish. The key difference with tasks done in the service factory is that employees may have to advise and counsel customers, interpret customer needs, and provide the appropriate performance to meet customer service needs.

Firms who offer customers services which are fairly standardized, but also intangible dominant, 'mass service' organizations (Schmenner, 1995) or 'relationship dependent' (Lashley, 2000), may still have features common to Ritzer's McDonaldized organization, but because of the significance of the intangible aspects of the service have to allow front line staff a fair degree of discretion to meet customer's needs. Thus employees will be instructed, in one form or another, to do what it takes to meet customer needs. Marlene Abbott, referred to above, provides an idealized example of the behaviours required of employees empowered in this type of organization. In some cases, Gleneagles Hotel is a well publicized example, employees are allowed to spend money without reference to a supervisor to provide items and services which will 'delight the customer'.

There are, therefore, likely to be several important constraints on the introduction of task discretion. Firstly, to what extent are customers buying, and the organization supplying, a standardized product? If the organization's 'brand' represents a cluster of tangible and intangible attributes, to what extent are these consistent when different employees 'delighting customers' differently? In the example above, would Marlene Abbott's customer expect similar service from other staff in other hotels within the group? Would customers be dissatisfied if they do not receive it? Indeed to what extent does the customer identify their satisfaction with the hotel group or with Marlene Abbott?

A second problem might occur in winning commitment but in losing control. Material and labour performance appraisal are likely to be difficult where employees are given the brief to 'delight the customer'. Bowen and Lawler quote the example of a hotel doorman who took a flight to return a guest's briefcase. Whilst the guest may have been pleased, the hotel accountant may well have been far from 'delighted'.

Finally, all the above assumes that there is likely to be a best fit between the organization's service offer to its customers and the employment strategy it follows, particularly in the extent that jobs are designed to fit the appropriate degree of empowerment with the discretion needed by employees in executing their service tasks. Bearing in mind Watson's (1987) point, the employment strategies do involve managerial choices, managers do have the option to make choices in employment strategy

Hospitality, Leisure & Tourism Series

which do not fit with customer service objectives. Indeed much of this assumes that business strategy is itself rational and informed by a detailed analysis of the business environment, which in turn informs all functional strategies without any other mediating processes. None of this is absolutely guaranteed and it may be that job design and employee empowerment do not fit with customer service offers for all sorts of cultural, historical, political, status and power reasons.

The task allocation dimension

The task allocation dimension is a related aspect of the task dimension, though it requires specific attention. The arrangements made by which work is both allocated to individual employees and the sequence in which tasks are undertaken is an important consideration in the analysis of empowerment. Under 'traditional' arrangements, employees would be supervised by managers/supervisors who kept tight control over the activities of their subordinates. Traditionally such managers would make all organizational and work sequencing decisions, giving employees instructions and making decisions about what may, and may not, be done by employees. Even managers in this type of organization would receive instructions and 'check-lists' of jobs to be completed by agreed dates. Many unit managers in fast food, retail and other service organizations have been managed in this way (Lashley, 1995b).

The amount of responsible autonomy given to employees is an important feature of empowerment, because it provides some indication of the degree of personal control the empowered have over their actions. To what extent are the empowered allowed to organize and sequence their own tasks, decide on their own priorities and account later for their actions? Where are the boundaries? Are there limits to what the empowered can decide without reference upwards?

As we have seen, Harvester Restaurants present an example of an attempt to empower staff at restaurant level to take on more of the organizational tasks – many of which would be responsibilities of management in other contexts. Here staff co-ordinate the allocation of work amongst themselves, they select and train new members, draw up work rosters, monitor restaurant sales performance and can decide on their own 'shift co-ordinator.' Furthermore, 'Chefs and waitresses are accountable for ordering their own stock, conducting their own hygiene checks, sorting out their own problems, dealing with customer complaints, or cashing up' (Pickard, 1993: 28). Clearly, in this example the tasks themselves remain largely unchanged and the discretion to interpret customer needs is limited, though there is some. The key benefits are in the winning greater employee commitment through job enrichment, social control of individual contributions through peer group pressure, improved communications and suggestions from service deliverers and the reduction of a management cost through the removal of layers of unit management (Pickard, 1993: 28).

McDonald's Restaurant Managers, in the pilot study (Lashley, 1995b), were given more responsible autonomy under the new 'empowered' arrangements. In practice, their work tasks altered minimally, but they were less tightly managed than under previous arrangements. The new General Area Supervisors called on them less frequently – once every two weeks as against once per week – and acted in a more consultative way. Managers were encouraged to adopt a more entrepreneurial approach, and the supervisors gave advice, shared best practice and acted more as a co-ordinator than previously. The final reorganization of roles within the company further extended the ability of managers to work on their own with responsible autonomy.

The major limitations are in the potential tensions between empowered staff and the organization. In the case of Harvester Restaurants, the system is highly structured from the 'top down' with systems prescribed from above *'handed down and the same for each restaurant'*. Performance targets are also tightly defined, though monitored by the team. Overall standards and customer satisfaction measures are mostly monitored from the centre. Thus there is a danger of sending mixed messages. Staff are empowered to make choices about the organization of work but not about the direction of the work organization. This can be a source of conflict, particularly where performance measures and assessment criteria shape and impinge on the immediate work team. The support of senior management to the approach is crucial (Cotton, 1993).

A further limitation in the introduction of such an approach is in the attitude and support of junior and middle management. Their roles change and for some managers, the change and perceived loss of status, their own role definitions and career aspirations may all appear to be threatened. This was certainly evident from the interviews conducted with McDonald's Restaurant Managers in the pilot study. The changes introduced in the pilot were largely focused at 'General Area Supervisors' and several Restaurant Managers asked themselves, *'what's in it for me?'* A further limitation was experienced in the boundaries set for the General Area Supervisors. Whilst they were allowed to recruit and select assistant managers in the restaurants under their control, they were not allowed to select Restaurant

Hospitality, Leisure & Tourism Series

Managers. This proved to be a point of some conflict between empowered General Area Supervisors and senior management.

The power dimension

The power dimension is fundamental to understanding the concept of empowerment and variations in its form and application. As a management rhetoric operating on a number of levels, empowerment essentially implies that organizational power structures are being altered so as to allow individuals (operatives or managers) more power. This is the core story which underpins the various rhetorics. The discussion thus far shows that arrangements that are called empowering are so varied as to question the general validity of this assumption, but some arrangements may involve power redistribution. Dahl's (1957) observation about power might easily be said of empowerment. He said, '. . . a Thing which to which people attach many labels with subtly or grossly different meaning in many different cultures and times is probably not a Thing at all but many things.' (1957: 201).

Thus any attempt to understand empowerment both as a general concept and in its application in individual contexts needs to consider the extent to which organizational power has, or has not, been redistributed, and the extent to which the empowered feel that power has been redistributed. This latter point is important, because if empowerment has distinguishing features from initiatives called involvement or participation, it is in the declared need for the individual to feel in control (Conger, 1989); have a sense of personal power together with the freedom to use that power (van Oudtshoorn and Thomas, 1993); and a sense of personal efficacy and self-determination (Alpander, 1991). In his context it is important to recognize that these individual perceptual issues are important considerations in the power associated with empowerment and these may influence the development of the psychological state of empowerment.

What is it the empowered are being given the power to do? In most of the examples discussed in earlier chapters, empowerment largely operates at task level. Power to make decisions stick, such as it is, is defined and prescribed by management with few opportunities to influence decisions above the task. Thus in the Harvester Restaurants, employee teams were allowed to make organizational decisions, and as individuals in the role of Shift Co-ordinator, or Appointed Person, could make decisions that in traditional structures would be a manager's responsibility, but power was limited to interpreting the operational plan. There were no institutional arrangements for employees, or their representatives, to share in, or even be consulted about policy directions. The power to set budgets, decide on promotional targets, bonus schemes, pay rates, and general employment matters were still in the hands of the formal management structure.

Similarly, the 'whatever it takes training' approach, or the Gleneagles employee empowered to spend money, restricted participation to the task with no mechanism to influence more strategic issues. Indeed, suggestions that European style Works Councils and two-tier boards should be introduced in the UK have been stoutly resisted by British employers, many of whom advocate employee empowerment.

In other cases, in quality circles, team briefings, suggestion schemes, and the array of techniques designed to build calculative commitment, there was no significant attempt to redistribute organizational power. Even within the so-called 'flatter structures' management decisions are made by senior managers and passed down the line – albeit a shorter one. Again the Harvester case is instructive. Even though Area Managers worked in teams, each area team had a set of 'team accountabilities' and a member of senior management as a team member. Thus senior managers had a direct presence in all area teams and set the operational agenda through which the area management teams operated. Such redistribution of power that had taken place was limited to a narrow agenda of operational issues.

Within the rhetoric of the supposed benefits of empowerment, the empowered organization was to be 're-engineered'. Drucker provided us with an analogy with the orchestra. All the players were of equal importance and had to be left to play their own instrument. In other words the future organization would have much more equality of power than its traditional 'disempowering' cousin. The problem with many of these observations is that they display, at best, a naive understanding of the power and politics of organizational life. Even using Drucker's simplistic example, there is no suggestion as to who decides which music is being played, how the piece is to be interpreted, who shares in the results of the performance, nor that different pieces of music might require the specific skills of particular sections of the orchestra. These matters can be of great dispute even in classical orchestral settings. The disputes at Covent Garden in 1991 showed how even professional musicians can be driven to taking strike action when they object to managerial power being used in a manner with which they disagree.

This latter example raises some interesting omissions in discussions about empowerment. Fundamentally, the assumption is that power is held by senior managers who are charged with the responsibility to manage the organization in the best interests of the shareholders, who in turn through the hand of self-interest ensure that scarce resources are used efficiently for the greater social good (Parsons, 1995). The are some on the New Right who hold a particularly extreme version of this view and who see no role for employee participation or empowerment; for them, the risks held by the suppliers of capital are paramount and decisions should not be subject to amendment by those who bear no risk. For others, many of whom are referred to in this text, the empowerment of employees is a strategy required to build the employee commitment necessary for long-term business success.

The problem with this view is that it displays a failure to understand that the nature of organizational power and politics can result in either over-optimistic expectations for empowerment because the existing power structures are unchanged, or produce a cynical set of initiatives which are largely politically motivated, designed to overcome internal opposition, or to impress external commentators. In either case, the barriers to empowerment, or the limits placed on the empowered, can quickly create the impression that the empowered are not being empowered to do very much.

It is here that there is potentially the most fundamental contradiction in the claims for empowerment. If we take Dahl's (1957: 202) definition of power as '. . .a relation between social actors in which social actor A, can get another social actor B, to do something that B would not otherwise have done.'

The power of A over B is the amount of resistance by B that can be overcome by A (Pfeffer, 1981). Power given to employees might assist them either to change decisions that managers might otherwise have made, or at least to provide an effective resistance to managerial decisions (Poole, 1986). The contradiction, therefore, is that either the power redistributed to the empowered is sufficient to challenge the decision-making structures within capitalist organizations, or it is insufficient to generate a real sense of power in the empowered.

In these circumstances, there may be considerable barriers to the application of empowerment. As we have seen, operational practices and the detailed nature of the brand offer to customers may restrict the power to act for the supposedly empowered. The traditional production-line service organization, as typified by fast food operations, do seem to provide limited scope for feelings of autonomy and control and frequently experience very high levels of labour turnover. Even in other organizations, where the potential to adopt more participative approaches might assist the organization to meet its service offer to its customers, the restrictions placed on employees and the boundaries within which they have to work can be limiting to such an extent as to negate the sense of being empowered.

On another level, there may be problems in the introduction of empowerment because of differences amongst the workforce. Not all employees have the same levels of need for power (Kizilos, 1990). Employees who have years of experience of being powerless may have major difficulties in accepting the new responsibilities placed upon them. Or there may be different orientations to work amongst employees, some of whom may relish extra responsibilities and power, whilst for others, work occupies a less central position in their lives and consequently their need for a sense of power at work is lower. Interviews with both Appointed Persons in Harvester Restaurants, and with Unit Managers at McDonald's Restaurants showed these differences amongst the empowered. Whilst most of the Appointed Persons reported satisfaction with the extra responsibilities in the role, others were less certain and just wanted to do their operational job. The managers in the McDonald's case were more or less likely to accept the new role depending on their experience as Restaurant Managers. The more experienced managers chiefly responded positively to the absence of more direct control over their work, whilst the newer managers were concerned with their ability to cope with less close supervision.

Finally, the expectations of managers may well create a major barrier to empowerment. Several writers have commented on the training needs of managers in an empowered organization (Barry, 1993; Ripley and Ripley, 1993; Sternberg, 1992) and the crucial need for the commitment of senior management (Lawler and Mohran, 1987; Barbee and Bott, 1991; Ripley and Ripley 1993). In part this is due to role conflict, prior training and professional culture. In part it is also due to the power of middle managers to resist changes that may well challenge their status and position. Kizilos says, 'Empowerment is something that sounds real good if you're out of power; it's an ambiguous and perhaps unattractive thing if you have power' (Kizilos, 1990: 51).

The power dimension, therefore, needs to be examined in any analysis of initiatives that claim to be empowering. At a fundamental level, it may be that the notion of the boundaries set within which the empowered operate creates such tensions as to either threaten existing power structures of the organization, or limit the amount of power which the empowered can exercise to such an extent as to make the initiative meaningless. Few writers address this potentially fundamental flaw in the aspirations for empowerment. Even accepting the model as outlined by many advocates, the potential variations in the need for power amongst the empowered and the internal resistance to empowerment by key stakeholders can provide some major difficulties for the introduction of empowerment into an organization.

The commitment dimension

The commitment dimension is, as we have seen, another important theme in the many claims for the benefits of an empowered workforce. Through greater commitment to the organization's goals employees take more responsibility for their own performance and its improvement (Barry, 1993); inherent skills and talents within the employees can be realized and put to work for the benefit of the organization (Ripley and Ripley, 1993) so as to produce more satisfied customers (Hubrecht and Teare, 1993; Johns 1993); and greater profits (Plunkett and Fournier, 1991). They will be more adaptable to change (Barry, 1993) and perhaps even accepting of organizational down-sizing and redundancies (Shirley, 1993).

Empowered employees are supposed to be more committed and have improved motivation through meeting people's power needs (Alpander, 1991); social needs (Plunkett and Fournier, 1991); and improved self-esteem (Barbee and Bott, 1991; Johnson, 1993). As we have seen few of these aspirations consider commitment to what, or the commitment tensions that employees may have to manage. Nor do they consider the precise nature of the commitment being generated by various forms of empowerment. It is, therefore, necessary to investigate the variety of sources of commitment that might be at play when particular forms of empowerment are introduced.

Again there are likely to be a variety of options and combinations, but they can be analysed through a model informed by Etzioni's (1961) notions of calculative and moral commitment. In Table 8.1 these are shown as two ends of a dichotomous model. The traditional production line organization relies heavily on calculative commitment where there are attempts, with varying degrees of intensity, to create calculative reasons for joining and staying with the firm. In these cases the strategy involves a concern to pay leading edge labour market rates, and tie employees into the organization with an internal labour market in which the employee's chances of advancement are better than with competitors. Empowerment, such as it is, will be associated with accepting the responsibility for service quality and customer satisfaction and general identification with the organization's goals because the employee's calculation of personal self-interest is closely allied to the organization.

Hospitality, Leisure & Tourism Series

The empowered organization will, on the other hand, be concerned with gaining employee commitment, which matches closely with Etzioni's moral commitment. Here the empowered employee finds a close match between personal values, attitudes and needs, and organizational demands and requirements. The role of empowerment, therefore, is in providing employees with opportunities to match their needs to their work in the organization. In reality, of course, the package of changes introduced may well combine elements of both calculative and moral commitment. It is unlikely that moral commitment will be generated if individuals feel there is inequity in the benefits of empowerment (Kelly and Kelly, 1990).

Much of the literature over-simplifies the discussion of employee commitment and fails to deal with the symbiotic relationship between employee commitment and employee empowerment. Thus employee commitment is an essential requirement of empowerment, and supposedly reinforces employee commitment. An absence of committed employees in the first instance may create considerable barriers to the introduction of employee empowerment. In all the instances under investigation, it was felt that high labour turnover – a demonstration of a lack of commitment to the organization – presented a considerable difficulty for building employee empowerment. In those units within the Harvester brand where that approach had found the least success, high labour turnover was being experienced within the unit. Similarly, mangers at TGI Fridays reported that high labour turnover was a key barrier to their attempts to establish employee involvement and empowerment.

A second aspect of the relationship between empowerment and commitment that needs to be investigated is that empowered employees are more committed to the organization. Again the more evangelical claims assume an almost axiomatic relationship. From the investigations included in this text, this is no certainty. In some of the interviews with Harvester Restaurant employees, staff did claim greater job satisfaction since the introduction of the '*flatter structure*', but many reported that their commitment was to their fellow employees, and where the scheme worked best, stable employment had long been a feature of that work group. Reports from the Marriott group suggested that labour turnover did not reduce as significantly as anticipated, it changed its character. Prior to more empowered working practices, employees tended to leave the organization because they were dissatisfied with their work experiences – push factors. After the changes, employees were more confident and skilled, and were more attractive recruits to competitors who 'poached' them from the organization – pull factors (Lashley and Taylor, 1998).

Thus a series of issues emerge from in the analysis of particular forms of empowerment. At root, these need to go beyond the simplistic assumptions that empowerment will create more committed employees. For example it is necessary to explore how employees perform under these arrangements – are labour costs reduced; is productivity increased; does job satisfaction increase; is labour turnover reduced? Is there a breakdown in 'us and them' considerations? How does the overall organization perform? What circumstances, if any, are likely to influence the appropriateness of different approaches?

The cultural dimension

The cultural dimension has been at the heart of a renewed interest in employee commitment via involvement, participation and empowerment. The notion that excellent organizations are those that are 'people driven' and have 'loose and tight properties' as expounded by Peters and Waterman (1982) did create a renewed interest in organizational culture and the strategic significance of human resources and their management. Apart from providing an initial philosophical base to empowerment, organizational culture is deemed to be significant in that it creates the overall context in which different forms of empowerment are located. Many writers agree that empowerment cannot be just 'bolted on' to an organization (Ripley and Ripley, 1993). To be effective, empowered service organizations will need to move from 'control to trust oriented' cultures (Sternberg, 1992). They need to develop cultures that recognize that service is customer driven and which outline appropriate attitudes and behaviour for employees (Barbee and Bott, 1991; Bowen and Basch, 1992). The culture must be developed by top management and flow down through the organization (Bowen and Basch, 1992).

According to the expectations of the simple model of empowerment, there will be some sort of fit between the empowered organization and the organization's culture. The empowered organization will be trust orientated, it will be a high commitment culture, it will be people driven. Sternberg (1992) says for example, 'In responding to our work force, we must move from an attitude of distrust and control to one of trust and respect' (1992: 72). These observations about the culture of organizations that have empowered are not so different to those mentioned earlier when Nicholls talked about moving the organization's approach to its employees as from 'thinly disguised contempt' (TDC) to 'tender loving care' (TLC).

Harrison and Stokes (1991) take this a stage further by suggesting that there are four types of organization culture, and each is more or less suitable as a culture for empowerment. Organization cultures that are typified as 'power' or 'role' cultures are less likely to provide the context in which empowerment can be fully developed. Cultures which are 'achievement' or 'support' are more appropriate to the development of empowered employees. That said, organizations can adopt strategies to better develop empowerment in employees though its form and extent will be different in each type of culture. Power cultures will develop empowerment through identification with strong leaders. Role cultures will achieve empowerment through systems that serve the people and the task, reducing confusion and conflict. Achievement cultures achieve empowerment through identification with the values and ideals of a vision; though the application of creativity, and through the freedom to act. Support cultures empower through co-operation and trust, through providing understanding, acceptance and trust. Each of these reinforce the point that empowerment takes a range of forms and there is likely to be an appropriate fit between an organization's culture and the form of empowerment introduced.

Again the evangelical claims for empowerment need to be examined alongside the initiatives introduced, because these somewhat simplistic pronouncements on organizational culture need to be examined. Do the initiatives introduced match the current organization culture? Is there a mismatch, or are there several rhetorics at work that create an 'official' and an 'unofficial' culture (Watson, 1993). This latter point needs expansion, because the organization that Watson studied had an official culture that was typified as being 'an empowerment, skills and growth discourse' (1993: 9), whilst the unofficial culture that existed alongside and interwove with this official culture and was typified as being a 'control, jobs and costs discourse' (1993: 9). Watson goes on to say that managers in the organization switched between both discourses, but they provided more than two sets of language. 'They are two ways of looking at the world, two frames of reference, two orientations towards action. They are both ways of thinking about customers, employees, technologies, departments other than one's own and so on.' (1993: 9).

Analyses of particular initiatives that claim to be empowering need to consider the possibilities that several cultures are in operation and these in turn produce different rhetorics which may establish differences between official managerial definitions of the culture and other definitions which are held by other groups within the organization. Leading from this, the ability of senior managers to manage organization culture is not unquestioned. Many who write about these matters have a tendency to reify organizations into material beings that possess cultures, almost like office decor to be changed and redesigned at the whim of senior managers (Harrison and Stokes, 1991; Kanter, 1989; Wickens, 1987). This notion of manipulability implicit in the work of Peters and Waterman (1982) and Harrison and Stokes (1991) may well be pleasing to senior managers and may well be true at the level of the official culture, however the unofficial culture(s) which operate as the 'real' culture (Watson, 1993) may be much more difficult to manipulate, because it is fundamentally an outcome of social interaction.

Legge (1995) identifies three sources of doubt about the ability of management to change the culture of organizations. There are epistemological and conceptual problems because culture managers have limited opportunities to shape the development of culture that flows from 'social interactions and [is] socially produced' (1995: 198). In these circumstances they attempt to reshape the manifestations of culture. Second, there are important paradoxes in cultural management because 'strong culture' may already exist with organizations, which culture management may well be attempting to overwhelm. Even if it were possible to manipulate and create organizational cultures where there is a consensus between official and unofficial cultures (Watson, 1993), it is not certain that the core claims of the enthusiast for strong cultures and empowerment are correct even in their own terms. Legge quotes the work of Anthony (1990), who draws on examples in the NHS where managers were attempting to impose their own more instrumental culture on the long established and widely shared ethically based professional cultures of doctors and nurses. Finally, empirical evidence tends to question the depth and extent of cultural change beyond senior management. In some cases, employees felt confused by the ambivalence of the messages being communicated in the new culture (Proctor, *et al.*, 1999). In others, employees recognized these new cultures as being little more than a shift in emphasis, with a revised list of behaviours against which they could be judged (Collins, 1999). Service organizations, in particular, can create difficulties for management to manipulate culture across the organization, because of the multi-unit nature of most big service organizations. In these cases, each unit may have its own culture that overlays the organizational culture, and different professional groups bring to bear their own occupational cultures.

Initiatives that claim to empower service workers and create trust cultures may have several major barriers to overcome based on both the past experiences, expectations and practices of managers, and employees; and on the potential contradictions of managerial policies which espouse contradictory policies. The cultures which managers attempt to manipulate may well differ and do not present an easy subject for manipulation.

Conclusion

This chapter has sought to provide a framework against which initiatives claiming to empower service workers may be analysed. For the rhetoric of empowerment to be translated into the desired feeling of being empowered, changes in working arrangements have to be genuine and perceived as valuable and meaningful. The state of being empowered, as a psychological state, will be discussed further in Chapter 9. Here, it has been suggested that the key question relates to what employees can now do that they did not do before, and that five key dimensions relating to the changes in their tasks, how jobs are allocated, the source of their new-found commitment, the power that they now enjoy and the nature of the organization culture need further investigation.

By analysing initiatives claiming to be empowering via these five dimensions it is possible to build a picture of the degree and intensity of the initiative. According to the literature of the advocates of empowerment, an empowered organization will allow employees a fair degree of discretion when undertaking their tasks. It will involve the allocation of responsible autonomy in organizing tasks, allow some influence on decisions above the task, generate moral commitment and operate within a culture which generated trust and support for employees.

Although this is an ideal, the framework does allow a comparison of this with initiatives that are located at different positions towards it. Harvester Restaurants allowed no discretion to employees over the tangible aspects of the brand, though they encouraged a high degree of discretion over the intangibles. For those who took on key team tasks, such as Shift Co-ordinator or Appointed Person, the amount of discretion to be exercised increased. Most employees worked in a situation where they had responsible autonomy, though this was focused through the team in which they worked. There was limited power to influence decisions above the task, and no formal mechanisms for influencing decisions at the level of the organization. That said, employees were able to make suggestions at unit level and these could be passed up the line. There was some evidence of calculative commitment through the operation of tips, though there was also evidence of commitment to fellow employees and the unit which, though not classically moral commitment, did extend beyond the calculative. The organization was still largely control orientated, though some trust was built into a system which allowed employees a fair degree of responsible autonomy.

The empowerment of employees at TGI Fridays allowed no discretion in the tangible aspect of dish production and service. That said, employees were allowed to produce dishes off the menu if a guest wanted something not usually offered by the brand providing ingredients were normally stocked by the unit. Even the intangible aspects of the service included some fairly tight service time targets. However, employees were encouraged to exercise discretion when it came to customer entertainment – to create the party atmosphere. That apart, employees exercised no responsible autonomy, had little opportunity to influence decisions outside of their work, were largely calculatively committed and worked in a culture that was control orientated.

McDonald's crew work within a context where most of their tasks are constrained by job designs which are based on the completion of tasks in the 'one best way'. Discretion, such as it is, is limited to interventions in the intangible aspects of service by responding positively in unexpected situations. Commitment is largely calculative, though opportunities for promotion into the management structure do provide some non-calculative and moral forms of commitment. There are opportunities to make suggestions and bring up problems through suggestion schemes and rap sessions, but the infrequency and status limits general crew participation. Managers continue to make all decisions and employee power to influence decisions is constrained. Crew work within a highly structured formal setting where supervisors instruct their actions, and the culture is typically command and control orientated.

General Managers in the new structure do have some control over tangible aspects of the guest offer, but this is limited to composing peripheral elements of the product range – introducing salads or pizzas. They would not be allowed to alter the core range. Much of their new role involved responsible autonomy, that is they were allowed to make decisions relating to the business unit as they saw fit but would be held to account on a range of service quality and business performance indicators. General Managers who manage the business within the targets laid down were able to achieve considerable material benefits.

Calculative commitment was a strong feature of these arrangements though the sense of ownership and personal control over the unit did provide a strong moral commitment to the new arrangements. Power over decisions was limited to within the unit and there was little opportunity to influence decisions that were *'passed down from on high'*.

Feeling empowered

- Emotions at work

- Emotional service

- Emotions and empowerment

One of the rarely expressed, but clearly present aspirations for empowerment is that it will enable organizational members, whether workers or managers, to manage their emotions in a way that ultimately enhances organizational effectiveness. Service organizations specifically, require employees to engage customers in a way that builds a perception of genuine delight in meeting their service needs. For organizational members in general it is hoped that empowerment will enable employees to generate feelings of loyalty and a sense of personal worth within that organization. Empowerment is an initiative that attempts to create an emotional bond between the individual and the organization.

In fact all organizations are contexts in which members feel 'Obsession, pride, fear, anger, apathy, stress, passion, anxiety, guts, determination, commitment, grit, belief, enthusiasm, as well as hostility, greed, hatred, self-ishness. . . (Thomson, 1998). In the past these emotions have been seen as deviant and inappropriate for the serious world of making money. More recently, emotions in organizations have attracted interest because they are an element of the real world of people at work, and increasingly people are required to provide 'emotional labour' (Hochschild, 1983) in the performance of their daily work.

The nature of emotions in the workplace, plus the benefits and limitations they present to managers attempting to put emotions to work for commercial gain, is an important field of study. Some advocate that future business success is dependent on the level of 'emotional capital' (Thomson, 1998) at their disposal. In other cases, the study of emotions in the workplace is interesting and informative because emotions create the context in which management policies and approaches are shaped or distorted. The 'have a nice day' culture in particular is an important feature of much service organizational life and it is important to understand both the demands of organizations on their front-line staff, and the ways employees react to and manage the emotional dimensions of their jobs. Some cases, where emotions felt are in dissonance with emotions that have to be expressed, result in the 'have a nice day syndrome' (Mann, 1999). Added stress, absenteeism, and withdrawal are all likely consequences of having to provide emotional labour in circumstances where these are at odds with the emotions felt.

Empowerment is considered in two ways. Firstly, as Chapter 2 argued, for empowerment to take place, employees have, by definition, to feel empowered. Without feeling empowered employees or managers who are the subjects of empowerment have not been empowered, and it is useful to better understand the feelings of empowerment and the circumstances that generate them. On a second level, empowerment might be a means by which employees can be managed to create the feelings needed for their performance in the service contexts so that feelings of dissonance are dispelled.

Emotions at work

Traditionally emotions in the workplace have been seen as a bad thing, inappropriate in a rational and 'scientific' context. Classical management theorists such as Weber, and Taylor (1947), stress that organizations are efficient and rational goal seeking bodies; and the careful use of organizational resources is required of all organization members. Bureaucracies, hierarchy, experts, and 'scientific management' are rational and by implication managerialism is opposed to the 'logic of sentiment' (Karmel, 1980). It is interesting how so many commentators use the language of science and rationality when discussing organizational structures, work design and work behaviour, and dismiss emotional displays as inappropriate. *'Emotion had no place in work. Be emotional at home, on the bus, whatever. But in my office, I expect cool unemotional workers'* (Mann, 1999: 1). Ball and Johnson (2000) refer to research where, 'Only 1 per cent of 200 executives questioned believed that quips are appropriate in internal office meetings, while 39 per cent consider them inappropriate even in informal conversations with colleagues' (p. 205). As if to reinforce this mind-set Ball and Johnson's own survey about the use of humour in hospitality organizations came across, 'A director of one hospitality organization questioned the validity of our enquiries and raised concerns about the funding of our activities' (p. 205). Putnam and Munby (1993) sum-up a common view amongst practitioners and many organization theorists alike, 'Emotional reactions at work are often seen as disruptive, illogical, biased and weak' (p. 36).

Increasingly however, emotions have been seen to play an important part of organizational life with an economic value. Indeed future work organizations are predicted to account for their emotional capital in the same way they currently account for their physical assets (Thomson, 1998). Emotional capital is defined as having two core elements, **external emotional capital** and **internal emotional capital**. The external emotional capital describes the way that important external stakeholders such as customers, suppliers, communities and investors feel about an organization. This has been traditionally accounted for as being 'brand value' and goodwill. Brand value is seen as important because it results in customer loyalty and recommendations and referrals to potential customers.

Internal emotions are, according to Thomson (1998: 7), '. . .the feelings, beliefs and values held by everyone in the business. It results in behaviours that result in actions which generate products and services'. Internal emotions are held by 'internal customers' and relate to the way people operate with the organization. Clearly, these ideas bring together some of the issues discussed earlier in the book. Service quality and enthusiasm to delight the customer, employee commitment and empowerment are central issues when considering the emotional capital within service organizations. For Thomson, emotional capital provides the 'heart' that is the essential working of the 'mind' that creates the intellectual capital that is now becoming recognized as an accountable asset of the organization. Many

organizations in the financial services or management consultancy arena already recognize that their assets are primarily
knowledge assets, or that competitive advantage is gained by
having access to, and managing, knowledge. In this sense some
organizations describe themselves as a 'giant brain', but '... a
giant brain will only function if it is driven by a giant heart'
(Thomson, 1998: 12). Whilst the broad thrust of Thomson's
approach builds on the general view of organizations that
recognize that people are the 'key asset' because they aim to build
competitive advantage though quality, or uniqueness (Johnston,
1989a), or that are working towards being a 'learning organization' (Senge, 1990), Thomson does descend into evangelism in
places. 'The bottom line: emotional capital is the stuff of dream.
It is the energy, drive and commitment invested and held in the
hearts of everyone connected with the business. Emotional
capital is expressed not in terms of data, process or guides, but
such wonderful emotive words as passion and obsession'
(p. 13).

This observation aside, Thomson's work does provide a
persuasive argument that emotions are not only an essential
aspect of successful organizational life, they are an essential
element of managerial work. Ensuring satisfaction for both
external and internal customers is chiefly concerned with
developing emotions that meet business objectives through a
sense of loyalty, and identification with the 'personality' of the
brand or organization. Ball and Johnson's (2000) work exploring
the use of humour in hospitality retailing organizations reveals
much about the use of 'fun' as a specific offer to external
customers and as a way of coping with stress amongst employees. *It's a Scream*, a Bass brand, quite deliberately uses humour
because it sees its target market is 'students and like-minded
people seeking fun'. Similarly, TGI Fridays is an organization that
sells a party atmosphere in which fun and party celebration are
important ingredients in the offer to customers (Lashley,
2000a).

The F.W. Marriott quotation linking happy workers and happy
customers is another example of attempts to link the emotions of
internal and external customers. The example of the Marriott
advertisement in Figure 3.1 also appeals to emotions. For external
customers, the sense of being cared for and the 'hospitality' being
offered is being delivered by 'empowered' service workers who
are proud to serve and delight their customers. Ball and Johnson
(2000) quote several examples from other companies where the
emotion of fun is being used as a device for influencing employee
behaviour. The HR Director of Radisson SAS told the authors,
'Where managers and employees enjoy a working atmosphere of

serious FUN, stress levels are decreased as well as employee turnover. Employees enjoy less formal relationships with guests which leads to the personal touch being emphasized and encourages empowered attitudes when dealing with difficult situations' (p. 210). A senior executive at Gardner Merchant also felt that humour is important as a stress release, as a way of building a team spirit and as a way of building a shared vision of service standards.

Apart from this use of fun as a way of influencing employee performance, emotions are involved in explaining motives at work. Maslow's (1954) theory is a well-known example of a model that suggests that people have a range of needs and that these can be seen as having priorities that may differ between individuals and often go beyond mere economic rewards. People often do things that demonstrate a commitment to doing the work for its own sake, or because they are committed to work-mates or the organization. In all these examples, 'Emotions such as enthusiasm, interest and excitement become more central to the job than more tangible rewards' (Mann, 1999: 12). They represent the non-calculative source of commitment discussed in Chapter 6. In addition, forms of participation in the 1960s aimed at either job enrichment/enlargement, or at extended industrial democracy, were, like later forms of employee involvement and participation, introduced by managers in an attempt to meet employees' emotional needs. Though rarely expressed in these terms, each of the waves of initiatives introduced across the decades, discussed in Chapter 3, are attempts to tap these emotional needs, whereby employees are motivated by emotions more than by tangible rewards.

On another level the managers as leaders, at team or organization level, want to engage workers emotionally (Mann, 1999). Leadership that goes beyond material rewards as a way of getting team members to follow is often able to generate levels of commitment to the objectives whereby team members become self-directing. Emotional leadership frequently involves the use of mission statements and values, similar to the Harvester Restaurants example provided in Chapter 4. Treating the custom-ers as a personal guest is an appeal to these emotions of hospitality that a worker might use in a private context. Emotional leaders use emotional language. The use of emotional language creates an emotional response in the workforce and guides actions even in unusual situations, or when the team leader is not present. Likert's work (1961) is a classic for showing that the most effective leaders were those who were not just concerned with production but had complete confidence and trust in subordinates, allowed subordinates to make decisions, motivated by mutually agreed goals and shared ideas and opinions. In other words the most effective leaders appealed to emotional responses from subordinates.

Finally, emotion at work involves consideration of the impact of group membership on individuals. Working life typically involves individuals in a number of formal groups as a consequence of the organization of jobs, and informal groups that arise out of the social dynamic, perhaps bringing people together from several different formal groups. In addition people at work belong to primary groups in which they have a face-to-face relationship with all the members, and to secondary groups, which are larger, like the organization itself, and one individual is unlikely to know all the other members personally. Organizations try to tap emotional responses through both types of group. They understand that group membership helps to shape individual behaviour. One of the consequences of working in teams is that group membership helps to influence individual behaviour as individuals tend to conform to group norms. The Harvester Restaurants model used autonomous work groups and executives felt that individual performance improved and staff turnover fell as a result. Similarly, organizations are often attempting to appeal to emotions when they suggest a common set of interests. The quote from the head of Nissan UK mentioned in Chapter 6 refers to *us*, the shared organization interest, and *them*, the competition. In this case the aim is to both suggest a common interest and commitment to success and also suggest that internal conflicts are no longer appropriate.

Emotions are an important dimension of work organizations, and despite some denials, organizations have frequently appealed to emotions in their communications with customers, and with their employees. Empowerment, in particular, has been introduced in forms that appeal to emotional responses, through changes in the relationship with managers, or through more involvement in making decisions, or by working in teams. These links between empowerment and emotions will be discussed more fully later; before this it is necessary to discuss the links between the use of emotions and service behaviour, and deliberate attempts to use emotional labour in service organizations.

Emotional service

Branded service organizations are selling some form of standardized service to their customers. Chapter 11 shows that not all service organizations are selling the same set of experiences, but to some extent they all rely on the emotional displays of front-line employees to match the expectations of their customers. Many of them require what Mann (1999: 20) describes as the 'Have a Nice Day culture'. Although some see this approach to service interactions sweeping the world (Ritzer, 1993) other professions – such as doctors, accountants, and solicitors – need emotional displays that are seen as serious minded. In other cases, workers have to deliver 'Have a Rotten Day' emotions. Hochschild's (1983) seminal work provided case studies using debt collectors. Mann also suggests that police are another example; we could also include security guards and 'bouncers' outside pubs and clubs as also requiring emotional displays that are different though none-the-less important aspects of their labour.

That said, the 'have a nice day' approach is one shared by large numbers of people working in a service environment. In some cases, these are scripted and the employee is required to run through a pre-written dialogue to ensure that the message given to customers is consistent and that individual perform-ance conforms to an agreed standard. In many service establish-ments, those answering the telephone will use a set piece dialogue. In some cases, it is printed on a notice by the telephone. In other cases, the script is learnt by heart and then used during the service of each customer to ensure that the appropriate level of welcome or 'up-selling' is taking place. In other cases, such as TGI Fridays, the emotional display has to be fun and party-like, so it cannot be scripted in the same way. Similarly, the emotional displays at Harvester Restaurants or in Marriott Hotels do not lend themselves so readily to scripting but should still engage customers, making them feel wanted and welcome. Many service organizations suggest a strong service culture in which staff performance is seen as a key feature of the offer to customers. 'A strong service culture means that staff are happy and pleased to help, enjoy their work, like the company and will always deal pleasantly with customers' (Mann, 1999: 22). Conversely, organizations are unlikely to be tolerant of displays of the wrong emotions. Displays of temper or aggression, frustration and anger, or whatever is deemed to be inappropriate, are not tolerated. Hence employees are frequently in a position of having to display one set of emotions when they actually feel something else, say when dealing with an unreasonable customer.

The rules of the display may vary between organizations, depending on how the expectations of managers and customers define the appropriate behaviour for that service occupation. In most cases, smiling is an important aspect of the 'have a nice day' performance. Certainly in most UK and US organizations the smile is a key element of the HAND culture, as Mann calls it. That said, it is worth remembering that this is a relatively new and perhaps US exported influence. Traditional retail service, restaurants and hotel service would not have encouraged these levels of informality in the past. The Blackpool landlady of the 1940s and 1950s was not renowned for friendliness and hospitality. Indeed the notion that the customer was **never** right was a dominant impression at the time. Certainly, there has been a spread of informality that now encourages service customers to use the employee's first name and to expect a friendly exchange that verges on matey.

Whilst the service organizations are pushing front-line employees to be friendly and smile, there is potentially a difficulty both for the service deliverer and the customer. Does the stewardess really like me, or is it that she is very good at the display of appearing to like me? Do we resent the false friendliness of many of these service interactions? Certainly, the scripted cheerfulness can be insulting to some. McDonald's Restaurants in the UK have dropped the tightly defined script in their restaurants because they felt it was counter productive with British customers. In other countries too, the ubiquitous US smile can cause difficulties. Mann (1999) reminds us that when Muscovites first encountered the McDonald's smile they thought the staff were laughing at them. That said, Mann quotes research that 84 per cent of UK customers wanted 'Have a Nice Day-ness' (p. 28), even when this was acknowledged to be false. 'A substantial number of people . . . want the forced *bonhommie*, the fake smiles, the phoney grins that typify the HAND culture' (p. 29). Of the people surveyed in the UK Mann reports 57 per cent 'reported being happy if the smiles and warmth from service personnel are faked' (p. 29).

Employees have to exercise 'emotional management' in their interactions with customers, managers and other staff. Service employees in particular are required to display emotions that are appropriate to the job. In the HAND culture this involves smiling and patience with customers even when they are unpleasant and insulting. Not that this unique; emotional management in one form or another, is the stuff of everyday life because in many domestic and work contexts we have to limit the display of our emotions to those that are deemed appropriate to the situation. In varying ways we use lips and eyes, body language, facial expressions, and the tone of voice to create the display we want or think is right for the situation. In service work, staff are often trained to deal with conflict by 'neutralizing' the strong emotions of others. When dealing with angry and aggressive people the natural response is to become angry oneself, but neutralizing involves adopting a quiet and calm manner. In other cases, emotions are expressed and released 'back of house' where these displays would not be allowed 'front of house'. Many hospitality retail employees will display the 'right emotions' in front of the customer but then release their anger in the kitchen or non-public areas.

At heart, emotion management requires acting. Service workers have certain roles to act and even within these jobs there are variations. For example the performance required of TGI Friday staff is different to that of crew in McDonald's, or receptionists in a Marriott hotel. For the TGI 'dub-dub', acting needs to include the array of celebratory performances that create the party atmosphere (Lashley, 2000a). Crew on the other hand have shorter service interactions, but need to provide the appropriate 'customer care' dealing with complaints, awkward customers or bored children. The way that each organization defines service and the appropriate service performance alters the details of the 'act', but in many ways requires the same techniques so as to *'hide what they feel and fake what they don't'* (Mann, 1999). Even people who are naturally cheerful will have times when they do not feel cheerful, welcoming, hospitable, pleasant or friendly, but they will be expected to manage the emotional performance required by their employer.

Looking to the techniques used by professional actors shows that there are two main approaches. The first, the technical school, involves the actor adjusting his or her physical appearance to display the emotion(s) required. So this surface approach to displaying the emotions does not need the service worker to actually feel the emotion, they just create the impression they do. Whilst this is less demanding of the individual, it is difficult to continuously display these appearances over a prolonged period, or when the person is tired, or when the feelings felt are opposite to the one intended. The second approach requires the actor produce the feeling required, by calling on a past experience or imaging how it would feel to have these experiences. Often service workers use this approach when dealing with a client. They imagine how it would feel if they were in the customer's place. So there is an attempt to get the service worker to empathize with the customer, 'treating the customer as a guest in your own home' is an example of this technique being encouraged.

Organizations attempt to manage the emotional culture for their customers. Scripts and cultures do not just happen; managers, '... will have thought out and developed a very careful plan aimed at teaching the rules and the script to new employees from the moment they first approach the company for a job, to the moment they are promoted, months or years down the line' (Mann, 1999: 55). As we have seen in the case study organizations, more professional service organizations are adopting recruitment practices that involve appointing the 'right sort of person', and in some cases this can involve role plays and psychometric tests. Most organizations in the HAND culture have training programmes that include customer care programmes. Though this may vary in detail, a substantial element of the content, whether expressed or not, is about managing the emotional display defined by the brand. These are further managed by the organization through staff appraisal, further training and development, and reward systems that reinforce the performance required. As we have seen, McDonald's restaurants require simple customer care similar to many other retail operations, but even here they use the observation check lists to monitor 'counter skills' that include the approach to customers. In TGI Fridays the performance requires a particular set of skills that are supported by reward systems linked to sales and tips from customers. Staff with the highest earnings are further encouraged by being able to select their shifts and areas of the restaurant in which they work.

The problem that most employees face is that emotional management requires emotional labour as each person works on making the appropriate emotional display required in their work. Mann (1999: 69) reminds us that emotional labour has three components; 'It involves the faking of emotion that is not felt, and/or hiding of emotion that is felt. This emotion management is performed in order to meet social expectations – usually as part of the job role'. Emotional labour, therefore requires the faking of emotions or the hiding of emotions felt typically in work situations. Mann defines three potential situations regarding the match between emotions felt and emotional display, particularly in work roles. *Emotional harmony* is said to exist in situations where the individual actually feels the emotion required of the display rules and social expectations. In this case, no emotional labour is taking place because the individual is not having to hide or fake emotions. *Emotional dissonance* takes place when the emotions displayed for the purposes of the job role are not the emotions felt. Mann identifies a third state, *emotional deviance*, which occurs when the person displays the emotions felt, but these are not ones that are expected to be displayed. Again this does not require emotional labour because individuals are not having to display emotions that they are not feeling, though they may find that they are in a disciplinary dispute with the employer. Table 9.1 provides a simple overview of these three different situations at work.

Table 9.1 Emotional harmony, dissonance and deviance at work

	Emotional harmony	Emotional dissonance	Emotional deviance
	Displayed emotion is the same as felt emotion and expected emotion	Displayed emotion is the same as the expected emotion but different from the felt emotion	Displayed emotion is the same as felt emotion but different from expected emotion
Emotion actually displayed	**Happy**	**Happy**	**Unhappy**
Emotion really felt	**Happy**	**Unhappy**	**Unhappy**
Emotion expected by company or society (display rule)	**Happy**	**Happy**	**Happy**

Source: Mann, 1999

Emotional harmony involves the least stress because the emotions felt match those displayed and these are consistent with the displays required in the role. In the HAND culture of many retail organizations, the service worker who feels happy and helpful, and displays these emotions, is not providing emotional labour because they not having to display emotions they don't feel. Similarly, the individual who displays emotions that they feel, but which are inconsistent with displays required of the role, are not providing emotional labour because they are displaying what they feel, even though this is in conflict with the expectations of the role. The emotional display does not cause stress, though there may be some problems created through the performance being at odds with the display rules.

Emotional labour is supplied, as we have seen, when emotional dissonance occurs, that is a person acting within the confines of the expected displayed emotions, provides a display of emotions that are not felt. Here stress stemming from this emotional dissonance can lead to 'Have a nice day syndrome' (Mann, 1999: 84), that is, the psychological effects of providing emotional labour. Mann suggests that the effects of working in a situation where emotional dissonance is an almost permanent feature of the work experience are likely to produce stress related behaviour. Emotional labourers are likely to be less satisfied with their jobs, more likely to leave or be absent from work, suffer minor illnesses, complain of being 'burnt-out', and '. . . have an increased susceptibility to serious conditions like coronary heart disease' (Mann, 1999: 85). Interestingly, in an incident where a McDonald's employee working on the counter was personally insulted by a customer, whilst she remained calm and merely said, 'And will there be anything else, sir?', she made an error on the next order, giving the customer two cups of tea instead of two coffees. At root dissonance causes mental strain that cannot easily be reduced, though, it is hoped that changing the way people are managed might result in reduced dissonance. In other words, happy employees are happy to make happy customers in the Marriott mode. It is here that empowerment may have a role by creating the necessary inner psychological state that is in harmony with emotions needed in the service interaction with customers.

Emotions and empowerment

The series of advertisements by Marriott Hotels, introduced in Chapter 3, are ultimately selling employee feelings of welcome, concern for guest comfort and service, linked to empowerment. The implicit message is that employees genuinely care for their guests, because they are *empowered*. The training programme for employees in the group includes six principles that confirm the inter-relationship between employee feelings and customer feelings. Going beyond Marriott Senior's link between worker happiness and customer happiness, the list requires employees to think like customers, and thereby call on 'deep' school acting techniques. The list of requirements in the training programme advises staff to look as though they enjoy working in the organization and to want to serve customers. Positive employee feelings are an essential feature of producing positive customer feelings.

Front-line staff in Harvester Restaurants are also required to internalize an emotional relationship with customers. Here, as we have seen, they should 'Treat guests as though they are guests in your own home' (Ashness and Lashley, 1995). Homeliness, the decor, the traditional nature of the menu and the motherly character of many of the bar and restaurant staff all complemented the offer to customers. In a world of threatening change, insecurity and brash rudeness, here is an environment that recreates life as it 'used to be' – the idealized rustic home complete with an idealized mother/sister/aunty to meet your needs in an environment of continuity, security and caring informality. In a different way, staff at TGI Fridays are meeting the emotional needs of their customers. Here the party atmosphere, controlled fun, flirtatious relationships between staff and customers, supplement the American diner and bar image of the ongoing party atmosphere, providing customers with a social base where people can meet and party. Employees in this situation are required to be fun loving, friendly, a bit 'zany' and 'off the wall'. Essentially, like the other examples, they are required to manage their emotions so as to meet the organization's offer to its customers and empowerment is a common tool used by these firms to engage their employees in providing the emotions required.

Hochschild's (1983) work on the emotional contribution required of passenger airline cabin crew has much in common with these examples. The cabin crew were mostly women who were required to supply the emotional support to passengers by creating an atmosphere which reduced the anxiety of flying by reproducing the certainty of the homely living room. Hochschild suggests that to be most effective the cabin crew had to manage their emotions so as to ensure that positive feelings were communicated to passengers, and that negative feelings (anger, a desire to answer back, etc.) were not communicated. 'The rules about how to feel and express feelings are set by management, with the goal of producing passenger contentment ...' (1983: 116). Similarly work with debt collectors (Hochschild, 1983), and a host of other service employees (Fineman, 1993), shows that appropriate emotional displays were required of employees facing different types of service encounters. In each case emotional labour is required of the service deliverer. Emotional labour is 'the term used to typify the way roles and tasks exert overt control over emotional displays' (Putnam and Mumby, 1993: 37). Frequently, the employee experiences stress because of the gap between the felt emotion and that which is to be displayed to customers. This when emotional labour is most strongly felt and causes the greatest difficulties for employees (Hochschild, 1983; Putnam and Mumby, 1993).

Service organizations, therefore, increasingly require front line service personnel to manage their emotions so as to be appropriate to the given situation and to be consistent with the offer being made to be customers (Leidner, 1993). 'Through recruitment, selection, socialization and performance evaluation, organizations develop a social reality in which feelings become a commodity for achieving instrumental goals' (Putnam and Munby, 1993: 37). The use of employee empowerment might also be added to this list. Bearing in mind that empowerment takes a variety of forms, it is hoped that those initiatives that involve employees, enable them to participate in decisions and generate high levels of commitment will result in an increased sense of ownership of the service encounter and generate the required emotional display more easily. Through empowerment, employees are expected to be able to genuinely feel the warmth to customers required of the organization.

On another level, Fineman (1993) suggests that much organization theory fails to recognize the role of emotions in all, including service, organizations. Many of the writers on empowerment see organizations from a unitarist and essentially rationalistic model. Even though many imply a challenge to the Weberian bureaucracy that has dominated organization design in most Western economies, few give any credence to the role that emotions play in the realities of organization life. Fineman (1993: 9) acknowledges that, '... people with personal needs, goals, skills and preferences will collide, collaborate, resist and comply in ways that make organization life messier, but much more interesting than traditional organization theorists have led us to believe'. Peters and Waterman (1982) are generally credited with raising issues in organization management that have given importance to the management of people. Their advocacy of organization structures that are 'close to the customer' and 'people driven' has much in common with the aspirations of *empowerers*. Their work stresses upbeat emotions of fun, love, empathy, etc., but in their essentially unitarist model they do not see organizations as places where negative emotions are a natural consequence of emotional life. Yet fear, jealousy, greed, hate, etc. may be in play and have devastating effects on the intentions and policies of managers.

Traditional organization structures and the organization of work provide employees with many opportunities to develop feelings of fear through the threat of redundancy and through low security of tenure, lowliness of status through mechanisms of reward and position, of worthlessness through decision making processes, jealousy through inequalities in pay, and hate through inter-group conflict. These emotions, or the conditions that generate them, are rarely discussed. If they are mentioned, these emotions are treated as some form of deviance – a fault of the employees rather than the by-product of organizational power and politics.

If 'the play of and quest for status and power can be regarded as key dimensions of organisational social relations' (Fineman, 1993: 22), empowerment has something to offer in developing positive feelings about the organization. By introducing techniques that flatten structures, involve employees in decision making and thereby communicate employees' importance to the organization, improve the flow of information and by this reduce fear of the unknown, and meet employees' security needs by providing employee training and long-term employment, many of the negative and destructive aspects of emotions in organizations can be removed.

Having made that point, it is necessary to remember that organizations consist of individuals and groups with different needs and aspirations and empowerment can pose a threat to some people. Middle managers in particular have been seen to be a barrier to the successful introduction of empowerment. Barry (1993) reported that organizations that had introduced empowering initiatives had often found the newly empowered employees adapted to, and welcomed the changes quickly, but middle mangers took much more training and could hamper the successful introduction of empowerment. Clearly, sharing decision-making and giving more credence to front-line employees, change the management styles of a life-time and pose threats to the feelings of status and power in middle managers. Executives at Harvester Restaurants reported that the introduction of empowerment resulted in some managers leaving the company because they could not adapt to their new role and status. Fear of not being able to cope in the new role, and a loss of perceived status, were key reasons. The introduction of the new structure during the pilot study at McDonald's Restaurants also revealed that managers, particularly more experienced managers, were fearful for the future because the new post introduced above the level of Restaurant Manager removed their next promotable post (Area Supervisor), and they could not apply for a franchise unless they had experience of the Area Supervisor's role. Most were geographically tied to the area of the pilot, and so managers were in a double bind – they could not be promoted within the management structure without leaving the area, and they could not take on the franchise. Hence fear and insecurity were generated by the initiative, which was supposed to be in part liberating for them.

It has been argued here that emotion, far from being a deviant and unworthy subject of concern, is a natural part of organizational life. Empowerment has the potential to create positive emotional responses to working in an organization, though the nature of the change and the means by which it is introduced does not inevitably produce organizational benefits. Changes that fail to address the negative feelings of employees will leave these feelings unchanged, whilst initiatives which result in challenges to the status and position of other organization members, such as managers or shareholders, may well result in the development of negative feelings in them.

Several team members talked about the satisfaction that came from working in a team. In some cases this meant it you could 'have a good laugh'. One team member said, 'We have to work hard in this place. It is very busy, but we all get on well together and have a laugh.' In other cases, the team was seen as a source of support, particularly when team members were in Shift Coordinator or Appointed Person roles. Thus if a person had a problem about which they were unsure, they could call in another person for advice.

Team members who took on the role of Shift Coordinator seemed to like the responsibilities that came with it. Of the six people interviewed who performed the role at some point in the week, not one indicated dissatisfaction with the extra duties or the reward system. All seemed to relish the extra responsibilities. One kitchen Shift Coordinator summed up the feelings expressed by several. She said of the role, 'It's nice to know that ... (Team Manager and Coach) trust you and let you get on with it. To know you're in charge, well not in charge, but that you have all this stock and staff to look after and there's so much going on and its nice to be given the responsibility to get on with the job ... I don't mind the responsibility at all, I quite like it. I never used to get that much responsibility ... so yeh it's good'.

Interviews with Appointed Persons in the sample suggested that most also enjoyed 'the extra responsibility' and the feeling of 'being in charge' that the role allowed. Thus the Harvester Restaurants case showed that empowerment in the form introduced via autonomous work groups and restructuring the roles and responsibilities to correspond with these groups had the effect of developing employees' sense of personal efficacy and abilities to make an impact on the service encounter. Employees also registered positive feelings about the experiences of working under these arrangements. Feeling trusted, in control, being in charge, important, and supported by colleagues and team management produced generally positive feelings. That said, these feelings were not universal, even within restaurants where the initiative was generally a success, employees varied in their willingness to become involved. As shown earlier, some individuals merely wanted to complete their tasks as waitress, cook, etc. In restaurants where the initiative had never really bedded down, empowerment was seen as an unwelcome imposition, 'Just another trick to make us work harder'. In these situations, two features seemed to be common factors; either the Team Manager or Coach were reluctant to change their management style so as to empower staff, and high labour turnover prevented the development of work groups that supported employees.

Emotional labour can be stressful and produce negative behaviour in employees; however, by definition emotional labour exists in an environment of emotional dissonance. That is, having to display one set of emotions whilst feeling something else. If an employee experiences emotional harmony, they will be feeling and displaying the emotions expected by the company and social definitions of their role. It is here that empowerment has the potential to 'square the circle'. By managing people in a way that develops their sense of self-efficacy, convinces them that their tasks are meaningful and they are able to affect outcomes through the exercise of choice, employees are more likely to feel the emotions that have to be displayed. Hence emotional labour is no longer needed because the service worker is in emotional harmony. That said, case study evidence suggest that empower-ment is easy to discuss and hard to achieve. Being emotionally engaged in an empowered way requires careful and sympathetic planning by management. It is unlikely to come from a few superficial name changes that are driven by the need for a quick fix.

Conclusion

This chapter has explored the relationship between emotions at work and service organizations. Despite the opposition of both practitioner and academic communities, emotions are increas-ingly seen as inevitable features of working life that require more consideration. At a one level, emotions form the background to the realities of organizational cultural and political life. Thus fear and greed, jealousy, ambition, love and loyalty are all ingredients in the way organization members operate and respond to their colleagues, and to opportunities and threats. On another level, leading edge organizations are increasingly concerned to engage both internal and external customers on an emotional level. In some cases, humour is quite deliberately used to build customer loyalty. In other cases, employees' emotions are engaged by appeals to their emotional needs as a source of incentives that are more powerful than material rewards.

Service organizations have been driven to engage and consider emotions in service delivery. Customer care programmes of varying degrees of intensity all attempt, in one way or another, to engage the emotional experiences of customers and front-line service workers. These programmes require employees to display emotions that match the customer service offer. Employees are

Hospitality, Leisure & Tourism Series

said to supply emotional labour, particularly where they are required to display emotions that are different to the ones they feel. A permanent and unremitting period of emotional labour is stressful and can cause emotional dissonance that results in stress related behaviour. In other cases it can result in emotional deviance, which although less stressful to the individual, results in emotional displays that are deemed to be inappropriate to the service offer.

Empowerment appears to provide a means of managing people that helps overcome both emotional dissonance and emotional deviance. By managing people in a way that creates the psychological state of empowerment it is possible that service employees will achieve a state of emotional harmony. In Marriott's terms happy workers will be happy to create happy customers. Their emotions and drive will provide the necessary emotional backdrop from which the required emotional displays genuinely spring. Though few academics and practitioners speak in these terms and draw these precise links, they are implicit in much of the writings and case studies of practice. In these circumstances there is a symbiotic relationship; empowered employees are by definition in a state of empowerment that in turn produces the necessary emotional state that reduces emotional dissonance, and reduces the need to supply emotional labour.

CHAPTER 10

Improved business performance

- **Human resource management and business performance**
- **Empowerment and performance**
- **Measuring performance**

Fundamental to the argument that modern organizations should move to empowering employees is that the results make sense in commercial terms. Empowerment is not being exclusively advocated because it helps make work more appealing and beneficial to employees; such arguments would carry little weight outside an ethical, or employee led, agenda. The key justification is that improved employee performance results in improved organizational performance. Improvements in quality, customer care, repeat business, turnover and profits are at the heart of the interest in empowerment. Empowerment is said to involve a 'win-win' situation where both the employee and the organization benefit from the approach (Rosenthal *et al.*, 1998). By allowing more employee involvement and participation, employees gain greater job satisfaction and are thereby more committed to the organization's goals, and the organization consequently gains.

These benefits claimed for empowerment have to be set against benefits claimed for 'Human Resource Management' (Guest, 1995), 'high performance work practices' (Huselid, 1998) or 'high commitment HRM work practices' (Lowe *et al.*, 1996), or 'high involvement management' (Lawler, 1986). Although there are some subtle variations in the claims and use of each of these terms, the core assumption is that organization performance can be improved through the adoption of a cluster of techniques for the management of the organization's employees. In principle it is assumed that models of 'best practice' including the introduction of employee involvement and empowerment will result in benefits to all organizations. Others, (Purcell, 1996) argue that, far from being a universalistic approach, there will be an appropriate *fit* in the management of employees and the wider strategy of the organization. In some service organizations, a more participatory strategy is required, in other organizations a more consultative approach is required, whilst for some service situations, the nature of the service offer to customers is such that job design is based round highly standardized and repetitive work practices that present considerable barriers to this notion of high performance management.

Variations in the managerial intentions and the forms of empowerment introduced may be best understood through notions of 'fit' with wider business strategies, particularly as these match with the service offer being made to customers (Lashley and Taylor, 1998). If empowerment is to make the claimed improvement in organizational performance, working arrangements must result in the development of a sense of personal efficacy, which in turn results in working practices that positively impact on organizational performance. These links and developments are by no means naturally consequential. There may be other mediating factors that ameliorate the effects of employee performance. In some cases these may be outside the organization's control, whilst others are a direct result of contradictions in the organization's policy objectives and employment practices.

Attempts to link employee, or even manager, performance with organizational performance have not been easy to establish because there are some variations in the nature of the measures of organizational performance and the priority given to different measures. In the main, measures have tended to be based on rational economic, commercial outcomes – turnover and profit growth, return on capital, increases in market share, etc. These measures have two potential difficulties. Even within their own terms, it is assumed that all managers and owners have these as priority objectives, and they are shared equally by managers and owners. This may not be the case. Second, it is assumed that these commercial objectives are the only ones to be used in judging an organization's performance. It may be that other organizational members, employees, the organization's customers and suppliers, and the communities in which the organization trades will have different measures by which they assess successful performance.

Human resource management and business performance

The presumed link between employment practice and organizational performance has a long pedigree. Taylor's prescriptions which looked for the 'one best way' of production attached to a reward package which enabled 'economic man' to maximize income was an early attempt to couple employee motivation with productivity and output. Both contemporary and subsequent critics of scientific management were concerned with the narrow view of human motivation and needs in the workplace (Braverman, 1974). The 'content' theories attempted to explain motivation at work in terms of the pursuit of goals, needs and motivators, and 'process' theories were concerned with behaviour at work as the product of choices. The work of Maslow, Alderfer, Herzberg, and Lawler, Vroom and Adams, therefore, provide examples of attempts to give managers tools that '. . .reflect managerial concern with satisfaction and performance' (Thompson and McHugh, 1995: 224).

Current concerns, though reflecting these earlier links between employee satisfaction, are different in two important ways. First, 'high performance work practices', etc., extend the approach beyond this focus on employee motivation. Recruitment and selection, training, rewards and a whole host of practices in the management of personnel are deemed to be important in gaining improvements in organizational performance. The second difference, and related to the first, is that advocates of this approach claim that employers who use high performance work practices are able to gain a competitive advantage that cannot be replicated by the organization's competitors (Pfeffer, 1994). Increased productivity and improved quality are just two direct benefits of a 'multi-dimensional view on performance, because it takes into account the competencies and capabilities of (human) resources . . .' (Pauwe, 1996: 15).

Hospitality, Leisure & Tourism Series

Huselid (1995) suggests that an organization's human resources can provide a source of sustainable competitive advantage when four basic requirements are satisfied:

1 The contribution of individual performance must make a significant contribution to the production process.
2 The skills displayed must be rare.
3 The investment made by the firm in its human capital must be difficult to replicate. Finally, the contribution to production processes must not be easily replaced by capital investment, because this then allows the possibility for competitors to match the performance.

These conditions have particular relevance to the service sector, where many firms are recognizing the crucial value of their employees in providing a service quality edge over their competitors. Figure 10.1 represents the way in which 'HRM systems influence the principal intermediate variables that ultimately affect firm performance' (Becker *et al.*, 1996: 4). According to this model the employee management practices that prioritize employee skill development and motivation lead to improved productivity and organizational performance, which leads to improved sales, profitability and market value.

The key issue is how these organizations can liberate these potential resources in employees. The contribution of techniques such as empowerment is in providing a means of realizing employee potential and skills. The development of a sense of

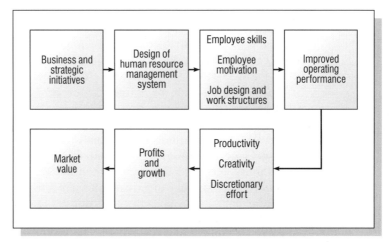

Figure 10.1 High performance work practices and business performance.
Source: Becker *et al.* (1996)

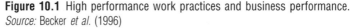

Hospitality, Leisure & Tourism Series

personal efficacy through a range of human resource management practices can affect 'discretionary effort through their influence on motivation and through organization structures that provide employees with the ability to control how their roles are performed' (Huselid, 1995: 636). A key point to consider is that human resource practices and organization structures can have both negative and positive effects. Thus if skills and knowledge possessed by the employees are not being exercised because the practices and structures do not enable them to be applied, the organization will not be making the optimum use of its human resources.

Huselid defines 'high performance work practices' as including 'personnel selection, performance appraisal, incentive compensation, job design, grievance procedures, information sharing, attitude assessment, and labor-management participation,' together with 'the intensity of recruiting efforts (selection ratio), the average number of hours training per employee per year, and its promotion criteria (seniority versus merit)' (1995: 645). Huselid organizes these factors reflecting concerns to improve employee skills and provide effective organization structures which will assist in maximizing employee contributions, and those practices that are concerned with employee motivation and 'reinforcing desired employee behaviours' (p. 647).

Using these measures of 'high performance work practice', Huselid claims that there are gains to be made by firms who invest in their employees through these practices. By comparing these firms with those who do not make such investment, he reckons that sales, profits and asset values increase and labour turnover falls by marked amounts. In a survey of several hundred US firms, Huselid comes to the conclusion that, 'A one standard deviation increase in these practices is associated with a relative 7.05 per cent decrease in turnover (*i.e. labour turnover, author*) and, on a per employee basis, $27,044 more in sales and $18,641 and $3,814 more in market value and profits respectively' (p. 667). Benefits can be gained from firms adopting these practices and he considers that the figures displayed might be underestimated where some of the investment is a one off – say in the case of recruitment. Apart from the gains to shareholders, employees gain through sharing in the benefits of increased productivity, etc., and the wider community gains through the reductions in labour turnover and increases in employee security.

Huselid argues in favour of a 'best practice' model that suggests that these practices can be beneficial to all firms. He dismisses the notion that employment practices may 'fit' with business strategies and external factors. Pauwee (1996), whilst agreeing with the broad thrust of the 'best practice' model, does provide an insight into the importance of contextual factors. In his review of the list of components in high performance work practices, he suggests that many of these practices have been consistent elements of employment practice in Holland for a couple of decades. In his case study of a Rotterdam-based container haulage firm, he suggests that a 'no compulsory lay-offs policy' (1996: 18) has promoted a situation where the firm has been able to gain considerable advantage through investment in employee training and flexibility in job design.

The context of high performance work practices might be an important issue in that they shape expectations and perceptions of what is regarded as a 'high performance' work practice. That said, both these and other writers link a 'bundle' of employment practices with improved organizational performance. Though not mentioned specifically, empowerment of employees is implied in much of these practices through both the direct practices involved in participatory management using 'quality of work-life programs, quality circles, and labor-management teams' (Huselid, 1995: 646). In a less direct form the development of a sense of personal efficacy is also implied through the reliance on selection and recruitment, training, performance appraisal and reward systems based on profit sharing and gain sharing plans.

Huselid is positive in his claims that these advantages can be gained by firms irrespective of the context or fit, '. . .recent research findings suggest strong main effects for adoption of High Performance Work Practices, and lends credence to the best practices viewpoint' (1995: 643). Later he goes on to say, 'All else being equal, the use of High Performance Work Practices and good internal fit should lead to positive outcomes for all types of firm' (p. 644). This claim for a universalistic application has been criticized on a number of fronts. Purcell (1996), for example, points to the fact that an examination of the contents of 'high performance' or 'high commitment' work practices involves slightly different bundles of practices, and thereby weakens its case for universal application.

Within the service sector, in particular, it is possible to see that different sets of employment practice are used by firms making different service offers to customers. The role and importance of employee performance and the discretion to be exercised by employees are two influential factors on the way that employees are recruited, trained, rewarded and supervised. This opens up some of the problems in the 'best practices' model that suggest universalistic applications. Often the check list of points covers such a wide range of differences in the means by which people are recruited, trained, rewarded and managed; and these have a key impact on the treatment and working experiences of employees. Even those critical of the 'best practices' approach sometimes miss the subtleties of the variations as they apply to service sector employment. Purcell (1996), in his critique of Huselid, points to an observation about the employment practices of steel mills being dependent on their low-cost or differentiated business strategies. The former were more likely to be control orientated whilst the latter were more commitment orientated. These observations are less relevant to service firms because the key drivers are standardization/customization and tangibility/intangibility. Firms who are delivering highly standardized, tangible service offers to customers will directly control employee performance and allow few opportunities for employee discretion. In other cases, the service offer is more customized to individual customers with a stronger reliance on the intangible aspects of the service interaction. Here managers will find it difficult to predict customer needs, and will be more reliant on the service employee being able to interpret and deliver the customer's service needs.

Bundles of high commitment practice may well cover activities such as recruitment and selection, training, appraisal and performance-related reward schemes, etc., but the devil is in the detail. Within the restaurants in this study, recruitment and selection practices range from being simple affairs undertaken by a manager using a pro forma supplied by head office, through word of mouth recommendation and team selection, to multi-staged events involving tests, role plays and several interviews. Training too includes a wide range, from training based on learning how to do the job in the 'one best way' through to training in a breadth of skills and internalized values through which to interpret service needs. Appraisal reward systems included those tied to consistent performance, through those that encouraged training, to performance related pay linked to sales and profits.

Similarly, employee involvement and participation practices are seen as elements in high performance practices, but they are rarely analysed in a way that highlights their impact on employees. Huselid, for example, includes 'quality of work life programmes, quality circles, and/or labor management participation teams' (1995: 646) as indicators of employee involvement, without recognizing the differences they represent for employee activity and ultimately for feelings involved.

Without going through the variations in both the service offer and types matching service operations, it is possible to detect two important considerations in the debates about the relevance of

Hospitality, Leisure & Tourism Series

'best practice' or 'fit' in determining organizational performance. The first point is that service organizations are generally concerned with both control and commitment, and that different approaches to managing people can be explained as shifts in the locus of control. The more the service requires employees to apply discretion, to meet difficult-to-predict service needs, the more the organization will need to rely on internalized forms of self-control, whereby the employees control their own behaviour to match in with a 'values driven' service offer to customers. This leads to the second related issue, in that it may be that the link needs to explore 'fit with what?' more than current research allows. In service organizations, there may be an appropriate fit between the employment practices and the nature of the service offer being made.

The work of Lowe *et al.* (1996) indicates some of the dilemmas and difficulties in attempting to link these 'high performance' work practices and organizational performance, even in manufacturing. Their work was based on a study of lean production methods, which is '. . . a universal method of best practices that is based on internal consistency and mutually reinforcing effects of "lean" low buffer factory practices, multi-skilled work practices and high commitment HRM practices' (1996: 4), and the potential impact on labour productivity as measured on output per hour. The sample of 71 motor components manufacturers in Japan, North America and Europe showed some wide variations in the output per hour across the production of exhaust systems, car seats and brake calliper parts. This far ranging and ambitious study concludes, 'However, the data with regard to work organisation and HR practices fails to offer convincing support for the universal applicability and efficiency of the lean production model' (p. 26). The evidence on the value of team organization as a means of organizing employees was ambiguous with some high performing firms successfully operating without teams and, '. . .a large number of plants with teams failing to perform to the highest standards' (p. 26). Of particular interest in the context of this book is their conclusion that 'there is little to suggest that high performance is necessarily concomitant with the devolution of responsibility to highly skilled, "empowered" line workers who actively engage in continuous improvement and problem solving activities' (p. 26).

The problem with this type of survey is that, in order to take out some of the complexities involved in international studies – cash values of goods produced and profits would be subject to the vagaries of exchange rate variations, etc. – the researchers concentrated on output of units. Though the design did allow variations in labour intensity through the study of three different products, it is assumed that the items produced in each product category were similar. There is no recognition that even within the production of exhaust systems there were variations in business strategies being followed by different manufacturers. It is possible that a low volume producer, by their definition, was actually producing a high value added and profitability. This research fails to recognize that job design, employee discretion and high value added may be integrated to produce a series of 'best fits' dependent on what employees need to do in the production process.

Within the service sector, the context of the type of offer and the links with appropriate human resources strategies are crucial. Any study of 'best practice' or 'fit' needs to be set within the context of what employees need to do and the discretion required of them. That said, these studies into links between human resource management practices and organizational performance are interesting. They suggest that empowerment might have an important part to play in improving profitability, sales, product quality and capital value, but there is a need to ensure that the form of empowerment is defined. The assumption that the introduction of empowerment can be brought in as a panacea is clearly naive. The context of the organization and the nature of the service offer made to customers will set parameters in which some forms of empowerment are more appropriate than others.

Empowerment and performance

Debates about the precise contribution that is made by an array of practices in the management of human resources, including empowerment, have been in part distorted by the generality on which the debate is conducted and about which the evidence is gathered. A lack of precision in identifying just what is meant by each of the practices, and the nature of the performance indicators to be used, has proved to be a key difficulty. This difficulty can be overcome by a more focused approach to the case studies under consideration. Harvester Restaurants, TGI Fridays and McDonald's Restaurants have all empowered employees in different ways and the results have to be assessed within the context of the objectives of the organization.

Harvester Restaurants introduced a flat structure by taking out one layer of managers at the senior management level and by removing the Assistant Restaurant Manager role within the restaurants. In addition, roles and responsibilities were redefined throughout the organization; Area Managers were organized into 'self managing teams' supported by a senior manager and regional administrative structure. Within the restaurants the employees were organized into 'autonomous work groups' where teams took on many of the 'accountabilities' that had formerly been the responsibility of unit managers. The specifically management positions were re-designated as 'Team Manager' and 'Team Coach' with a more co-ordinating, enabling and supportive brief with the teams in each restaurant.

Using the indicators of 'high performance work practices' recruitment and selection was frequently based on 'word of mouth', whereby existing employees recommend friends and relatives for job vacancies. Selection was typically done by the Team Manager, though in some cases team members might select the individual. Training is highly task focused, though the service offer meant that service values were an important aspect of the training. Individuals were also encouraged to take up additional training, which would help the team to be more effective. Appraisal and reward packages are largely focused on job performance with extra payments for trained employees. Bonuses on unit performance were only paid out to those who had successfully completed the basic training programme. Employee involvement was direct and largely task focused through the autonomous work groups.

Senior mangers believe that overall organizational performance has improved since the introduction of the flat structure. There has been a sales increase of 7 per cent, team member turnover has fallen by 19 per cent and liquor stocks have been reduced by almost £250,000. Wages costs were marginally reduced, from 24 per cent to 23.2 per cent, and administration costs have fallen by 41 per cent.

There has been an increase in understanding and commitment to the business objectives throughout the organization and communications were now more clearly directed to the appropriate people. Staff were now allowed to develop their talents and empowered to resolve issues. The organization could now respond more quickly to change by being more focused on the important issues and through processes of constant progress.

At unit level, Coaches and Team Managers in these units reported a great deal of satisfaction with the approach. They felt that it had generated much more commitment from team members and had freed them up to concentrate on business development and customer care. Labour turnover in the wider organization is low by the standards of this type of business, but high when set within a wider industrial context. Within these units in the study, labour turnover was particularly low at about 10 per cent. This is undoubtedly an important ingredient to success and one that is likely to produce a 'virtuous cycle'. Low labour turnover enables the development of strong teams, which in turn reduces labour turnover.

Unit management also reported a low level of guest complaints. One unit registered no formal complaints for three full quarters. This was due to the front line teams being able to resolve problems as they arose. So even if a customer received a meal that was not satisfactory, or was kept waiting too long, the immediate team member could resolve the situation to the customer's satisfaction. In a few cases, complainants wanted to see 'the manager' and didn't understand the flat structure. This could be a problem, though most dealt with it by bringing in a person from another department.

Problems were resolved more quickly without recourse to the manager. One member of the unit management team said, '*A few years ago, if the freezer broke and I was away for a couple of days, it stayed broken. Now we say to everyone in the kitchen, if the freezer breaks down what do we do . . . get it fixed. OK how do we get it fixed? . . . now we get it fixed, there is no alternative, even if it costs £1,000.*'

At TGI Fridays, the approach attempted to develop a sense of personal efficacy through strategies for the management of employees involving a package of recruitment and selection, induction, training, reward, and appraisal processes designed to deliver an offer to customers which is both 'McDonaldized' (Ritzer, 1993) and which allows customer choice within a limited framework. Employee empowerment to 'accept responsibility for the service encounter' is key to the success of the approach.

Recruitment and selection are directed at finding individuals who can exercise both consultancy skills in their interpretation of customer service needs, and creativity in their performance of service delivery. The process involves the use of psychometric tests, role plays or 'auditions' and several interviews. Training is largely focused on product knowledge and the service culture for front-of-house staff, and on immediate cooking skills related to their 'section' for kitchen staff. Appraisal and rewards are directed at sales generation through payment related to sales, or production, and customer satisfaction, as defined by reactions from customers (praise or complaints). A relatively high volume of tips also gives employees an incentive to prioritize customer satisfaction. Forms of involvement are more associated with consultation through team briefings, though the reward package also adds an incentive to develop a sense of ownership of the service encounter.

Observations of front-line personnel in practice show some interesting and proactive behaviours by employees. Employees will often take responsibility for providing hospitality for visitors

Hospitality, Leisure & Tourism Series

even when the unit is closed. One story told to me by a colleague is indicative of several other similar incidents. The person involved was visiting an unfamiliar city, took a wrong turning and ended up on the TGI Friday car park trying to discover where she had gone wrong. The TGI Friday restaurant was closed, but an employee came out, invited her inside, offered her a cup of coffee and directed her to her destination. On another occasion I was observing dinner service and witnessed several 'dub-dubs' in succession tying balloons to the chair of a young woman who was celebrating her birthday at the restaurant – much to her amusement. On another, a group of eight front-of-house and kitchen employees came and sang *'I'm getting married in the morning'* to a hen party. All these incidents happened spontaneously without the immediate intervention of a manager. In less dramatic ways, many of the employees witnessed engaged customers in a friendly way that clearly gained a positive reaction.

Whilst the mixed package of incentives might cause some tension amongst service workers, the package of rewards based on commission and tips did generally seem to produce a performance that combines a concern for sales and for service quality. The company reported that *'70 per cent of custom is repeat business'* and average customer spend is high compared to many similar businesses. That said, quality management techniques are basic, relying a great deal on internal processes via the immediate employees to detect and correct faults, and internal checks by managers. At the time of the study, the brand did not use 'mystery diners', focus groups or sampling questionnaires to gather feedback from customers. Clearly, the amount of repeat business implies a level of satisfaction, but there are no direct techniques used to build a picture of customer satisfaction.

Despite the levels of individual rewards, team briefings, rigorous selection techniques, and front-loaded training, labour turnover remains quite high in many units. A national average of 90 per cent was given by senior executives. That said, personal interviews showed a considerable group of core employees who had worked for the organization for several years. A consequence of the employee hierarchy, through which employees get to choose the best shifts and locations, might be that employees who cannot break into the elite group become dissatisfied. Another consequence of recruiting 'well qualified' employees is that they will frequently see this work as a stage before long-term employment.

Crew in McDonald's Restaurants work to highly standardized processes that limit their need to exercise discretion. Much of the company's offer to its customers is based on meeting customers' security needs through standardized products and services. Empowerment in these circumstances is based on the development of a sense of personal efficacy within crew members and thereby getting them to accept responsibility for the service encounter. In this case, interactions with customers are fairly short and simple, the exception would be for children's party hosts. However, this exception apart, most of the requirements of front line staff are predictable – to work quickly and interact with customers in a courteous manner. Over recent years, the company has developed a service strategy that recognizes the need to address customer service needs in a way that will encourage repeat business. As a consequence crew training now includes customer care, which supports front-line crew in their dealings with customers. This includes body language, eye contact, and dealing with customer issues.

In terms of high performance work practices recruitment and selection of part-time crew is a simple matter and is conducted by unit management using a pro forma supplied by head office. Recruitment of full-time crew members is almost exclusively from part-time employees, so that the company has a good chance to get to know the employee before any long-term relationship has developed. Approximately one half of McDonald's managers, including the European President, Paul Preston, started working for the company as part-time crew. Training is undertaken by all crew, irrespective of tenure, and is focused on the immediate job tasks, with some emphasis on functional flexibility so that each crew member can undertake at least two different jobs within the organization. Appraisal and rewards are chiefly focused on ensuring that employees continue to do the job as trained. A monetary bonus is paid to crew who consistently work in the manner laid down. The potential for promotion and a long-term career with the company is also a factor in the reward package. Involvement and participation of crew is limited to activities at team briefings, occasional rap sessions and the availability of a suggestion scheme programme. These latter devices can yield suggestions both for improvements in unit performance and new products – the 'Egg McMuffin' is reported by company executives to have been introduced as the result of a suggestion from a crew member.

Observations of crew performance do reveal examples of employees who engage with customers in a way that goes beyond mere service of food and drink. In one incident which I witnessed, a small child in a family party was getting restive and the parents were clearly embarrassed by the noise that he was making. A crew member quietened the child by giving him a balloon and a paper hat. On another occasion, a customer asked for a product that was not immediately available because it was before 10.30 a.m. and the restaurant was still serving breakfasts. The crew member explained this politely and said it would just take a few minutes. The customer was unreasonable and rude. He said, *'People like you should be wiped off the face of the world – women that is.'* The employee, seemingly unfazed by the outburst said, *'And will there be anything else, sir?'*

Executives at the company report that since introducing the customer care programme, reactions from customers have been positive. The company's quality assurance processes – which include mystery diner visits, customer contacts, comment cards, customer surveys, Area Supervisor checks and focus groups – register a general improvement in service quality as perceived by the company's customers.

McDonald's managers, in the delayered structure, are required to operate in a more entrepreneurial way. They formulate their own business plans and undertake analysis of their own profit and loss account so as to identify problem areas for action. Like crew members, they have to learn to work within a framework that is designed to deliver a consistent, standardized experience with a tightly defined brand specification. Through a form of involvement and participation that is best understood as responsible autonomy, managers need to absorb the company's values and policies so that they intrinsically know what will be allowed within the constraints set.

Manager recruitment and selection occurs chiefly through two routes. For about half, entry is through crew membership. Here the company is able to assess the individual and his/her potential over a prolonged period. The second route is via the management trainee programme that brings in people new to the company. Training includes a programme of work task familiarization – learning all the jobs in the restaurant followed by periods of work as Assistant Manager. In addition, the programme involves a suite of courses delivered at the company's training centres, and four self-study distance learning texts. All these materials build up the trainee's management knowledge and competence. Once appointed to a restaurant management role, the manager's reward packages include both a basic salary and bonuses that reflect the operation's successful achievement of service quality targets, and profit growth. The new General Manager role expands the manager's responsibilities and authority to make immediate operational decisions without reference to the Operations Consultant.

Interviews with managers in these changed roles reveals a degree of intrinsic and extrinsic satisfaction with the new arrangements. Experienced managers clearly welcome the opportunity to get on with the job, and the reward package can provide a considerable package of financial rewards. In some cases, it is possible for a manager to increase the basic package by another 50 per cent. Senior executives report satisfaction with the approach because the new roles and procedure focus on business performance, rather than operational performance. In the past, the reporting and management processes concentrated the unit manager's attention on service quality standards, and the management of the operational costs. Managers had to turn in good PACs (profits after costs), with limited knowledge about the performance of the unit as an investment. Now managers have to produce business plans and are measured against the financial performance of the business.

In summary, these different forms of empowerment have been introduced with different objectives in mind. This has resulted in empowerment taking a number of different forms and engaging the empowered in different ways. In each case the success, or otherwise, of the approach has to be viewed against the immediate business objectives set for the approach and the consistency with which the approach is applied through the organization. As some of the examples have shown, attempts to graft an empowering initiative on to a structure that is not compatible, or where managerial rhetoric sends mixed messages to employees, will be seen for what they are, and employees will not respond in a positive manner. If empowerment is to genuinely impact on the commitment and performance of employees, the approach, whatever its form, must result in the empowered feeling personally effective in the performance of their jobs.

Measuring performance

These attempts to link changes in the management of human resources are contentious. Even in their own terms, attempts to show that changes in the way people are 'all things being equal' responsible for changes in organizational performance are fraught with difficulties, because all things are rarely equal. For most organizations, the environment is dynamic and it is difficult to abstract the significant independent variable. On another level, the reliance on commercial criteria such as sales, profit and asset growth, etc., tends to be narrow and limited to assumptions about the primacy of entrepreneurial success as a driving motive for owners and managers. In addition, narrow definitions of commercial success tend to be unitary in focus and fail to recognize the plurality of interests that comprise organization life.

Claims for empowerment suggest that service organizations can improve service quality, generate more repeat business, improve profits and reduce employee turnover through increased employee commitment. As stated earlier, a more reflective view suggests that empowerment takes different forms and must fit with different types of service offer. Thus any attempts to link employee empowerment with supposed improvements in performance do need to consider issues of match and fit, which go beyond simplistic assertions that every initiative entitled 'empowerment' will inevitably lead to improvements in the organization's performance. For example, the introduction of autonomous work groups, with power to change the service and product offered to customers, works well in some service organizations, but would be a disaster in McDonald's where a deterioration in the standardized brand offered to customers would challenge a fundamental element of the business.

Apart from these differences in service types and the match with an appropriate form of empowerment, there are difficulties in attributing changes in an organization's performance to one (or a cluster of) change(s). The business environment is rarely static, and changes outside of the control of the organization's managers may be more influential on the organization's perform-ance than the internally generated initiative. For example, an up-turn in economic activity may be largely responsible for increases in sales. The closure of a competitor may have a beneficial impact on repeat business, and high levels of unemployment may be more responsible for reductions in labour turnover.

Even allowing for changes in environmental factors, there may be some doubts on the causal link between introducing an initiative and improving performance. Does the approach to managing employees cause the improvement in organizational performance, or is it the other way round? In other words do successful organizations empower employees? The success could be said to create a climate of confidence amongst managers that encourages different approaches to the manage-ment of employees. The link between empowerment alluded to earlier might be a case in point. The introduction of empower-ment needs an environment in which employees are already committed to the organization, unit or fellow workers. Uncom-mitted workers are unlikely to be receptive to empowerment and are more likely to respond unfavourably to being empow-ered. The case study at Parcelco provides a good example of how 'born to fail' empowerment can be in these circumstances (Cunningham and Hyman, 1999). Some employees at Harvester Restaurants expressed opposition to being empowered because they perceived it as being a management device for making them work harder for no extra reward. Where employee commitment is already well established, empowerment can build commitment even further. Again the Harvester Restaurant example is useful because it shows that the initiative was most successful where strong group bonds were already established. Autonomous work teams built on and used these natural dynamics of the work group. The initiative was successful where it built on already successful and stable work groups.

Much of the comment about the benefits for empowerment also assumes a common set of managerial intentions and ambitions for empowerment. Apart from the issues of form and fit mentioned earlier, there are clearly differences in how managers define the benefits for the introduction of empowerment. In some cases, the exercise of employee discretion is an important consideration and empowerment offers an apparent opportunity to provide more employees with more decision-making power whilst at the same time maintaining control. For others the intentions are to gain from employee experience and suggestions, whilst for others the intention may be to gain greater employee commitment, or to remove bureaucratic processes in the organization. In each case, evaluation of successful outcomes will be different.

It may be that these differences in managerial intentions vary over time. Foy's comments, mentioned in Chapter 1, hint at changes in managerial preoccupation. In the 1970s the problem was to reduce conflict, later the focus changed to one concerned with gaining from experiences of the workforce. Empowerment promises to deliver more committed employees and improved business performance. An empowered and committed workforce provides the organization with the ultimate competitive strategy – one that cannot be copied because the employees who comprise the organization are unique (Pauwee, 1996).

Management ideologies are themselves not uniformly held. Apart from the potential presence of different rhetorics being used in same the organizations, organization managers have different ideological conceptions of their role and relationship with employees. As stated earlier, empowerment and employee development might be a rhetoric that managers use alongside a rhetoric of cost reduction and profit maximization. Some organizations have clear managerial commitments to particular 'styles' of management, which either include employees in more participatory processes, or exclude them in a more directive style. Clearly issues of fit are important but also managers make choices that are shaped by their own perceptions and inclinations. Again, managers at Harvester Restaurants had a clear commitment to managing the organization in a participatory way. The reorganization was carried out thoroughly with clear and unequivocal commitment from senior management.

It is assumed in much of the literature which attempts to link business performance and the management of human resources, that business objectives pursued by owners are largely commercially driven and shared by managers. Both these assumptions need further discussion. There may be differences in organizational objectives depending on the size of the venture and the cultural setting in which it is set. Whilst large firms may be driven by economic considerations, particularly where investment funding is involved, small firms may have objectives other than profit maximization and growth. The Leeds Metropolitan University (2000) survey of small firms in leisure, hospitality and tourism, showed that just 9 per cent of firms employing four or less employees identified profit maximization and growth as key business objectives. Around 50 per cent were concerned with running the business for reasons of personal control and for life style reasons. Even among the firms employing 50 plus, a substantial minority prioritized these non-commercial objectives. Small organizations are a dominant feature of most service industries so attempts to link the management of people with business performance may need to reflect these wider lifestyle objectives.

Even the larger firms have some dilemmas around the interests of the investment community and the needs of the long-term business interest. In the UK, the City investment community is frequently accused of 'short-termism' that results in a management preoccupation with economic performance (Keep and Rainbird, 2000). In these circumstances, the rhetoric of profit maximization, sales growth, etc., may dominate the organizational decision-making culture so that initiatives like empowerment that require investment in people through training and development, are never properly developed. The result may be, as we have seen earlier, that initiatives are restricted to being labelling processes whereby empowerment is limited to being that which is labelled empowerment. In some cases, it is possible that senior managers 'introduce' empowerment for the benefit of investors without ever intending to thoroughly restructure the way that decisions are made or to involve employees.

Another issue for the link between human resource management practices and the performance of large firms is the narrow focus on 'hard' assets at the exclusion of other assets that make up the firm. Current financial reporting of organizational performance focuses on the monetary investment values and physical asset growth. With the exception of publicly floated soccer clubs that value players as assets, there is no requirement to value the human resources within an organization. The training and human resource development undertaken by employees and managers is not formally accounted or recognized in an organization's market value. Similarly, the levels of labour turnover and general levels of employee morale are not recognized in assessing value. As we have seen, some writers see these factors as important potential sources of competitive advantage (Pauwee, 1996; Thomson, 1998).

Leading from this, the evaluation of an organization's performance under capitalism remains formally that of the owners/shareholders. A wider view of organization life, which recognizes that other stakeholders might value organization performance by different criteria, might incorporate the nature of the organization as an employer. Apart from some of the 'bread and butter' employment issues, an employee audit might consider issues relevant to employee empowerment. These might include the degree and form of empowerment, an assessment of the sense of personal efficacy held by employees, the extent to which employees were able to use discretion, and were engaged in a culture of constant improvement. According to the claims of those who advocate empowerment, these matters should be important features of organizations committed to empowerment.

Eaglen *et al.* (1999), in their work building a cost and benefits model for training in hospitality retail organizations, suggest that attempts to build models in the past have failed because these have relied on overly financial measures. These have wanted to show that an investment in training would yield measurable financial gains. Eaglen *et al.* argue that not all gains can be measured in financial terms. They suggest that a 'balanced score card' approach is needed. This would involve both tangible and financially measurable benefits, and intangible benefits that are less easy to measure. Applying the model to a comparison of staff performance in different McDonald's Restaurants, they show reduced staff turnover, improved customer satisfaction, better employee satisfaction scores, more flexible staff and internal quality audit scores in restaurants that had a better training profile. They were also able to show that trained employees were more productive than those who were not formally trained. Whilst it is possible to put a financial value of the cost of losing fewer staff, improved customer satisfaction is harder to measure in financial terms. Though this research is concerned with the benefits flowing from formally training staff, the same arguments apply to calculating the business benefits of empowerment. In the first instance people are empowered, and we need to show

Hospitality, Leisure & Tourism Series

how empowerment changes the way they behave and from this, do changes in behaviour result in benefits to the organization? This has to cover an array of measures that take into account the range of stakeholder interests, not just shareholders.

Conclusion

Supposed improvements in organizational performance are at the core of claims for empowerment as a way of managing employees. Those promoting empowerment and managers who introduce it are rarely driven by ethical considerations about the power and reward structure of the capitalist enterprise. Even those writers, such as Bowen and Lawler, who do claim the empowerment is more democratic, are not advocating the spread of industrial democracy, they are concerned with making modern industrial commercial organizations more effective by tapping into the experiences and expertise of all the organizations' members. They recognize that modern competitive organizations are complex and can fail to learn from experiences unless they are able to capture the organization's experiences in its fullest sense. Empowerment is seen as a means of achieving the objective of employee involvement and participation without a loss of power. These potential benefits have particular attractions to the service organization, where employees delivering some services need to exercise discretion in their job, and empowerment offers a means whereby the employee makes the appropriate decisions but within a framework of control set by the organization.

Given the commercial intentions of initiatives that empower employees, it is necessary to consider the links between practices in the management of human resources and the impacts on organizational performance. Increasing numbers of authors are pointing to research that shows positive benefits from 'high performance work practices' or 'high commitment management'. The assumption is that there is a bundle of practices that can be applied by any organization which will increase profits and other financial indicators. Others are critical of this approach because they say that the universal nature of the best practice claims fail to recognize variations in organization environments and management ideologies within firms. It is likely that certain employment practices will be more appropriate than others in given circumstances and the employment practices have to 'fit' with a wider business strategy and organizational environment.

The issue of fit has particular relevance to service organizations where there are a number of different types of services being offered to customers and the employment practices need to fit with the nature of the customer offer. The form of empowerment introduced varies in different organizations and it is likely that there is an appropriate fit with the form of empowerment and the need of employees to exercise discretion in the delivery of the service task. The complexity of the service offer and fit with the operational needs of empowerment is further compounded by the difficulties of measuring organizational performance against a common set of traditional financial measures. Such measures fail to recognize the cluster of factors that may alter the realities of the introduction of empowerment and the variations in stakeholders' interests which these initiatives cut across.

CHAPTER 11

Empowerment and service quality management

- **Services and service quality**
- **Employees and customer satisfaction**
- **Empowerment and total quality management**

The delivery of services and service quality present managers with some difficult problems and tensions to manage. The nature of services themselves reflect difficulties of definition, standardization and control. The combinations of benefits and importance of employee and customer perceptions of service expectations and evaluations of successful service encounters all make for a complexity in managing service organizations that are not found in the management of manufacturing organizations. Mudie and Cottam (1999: 1) sum up the dilemma for service organizations, 'For the customer there may be little evidence, in advance, of what to expect. The service provider has often to produce the service under the watchful gaze of customers. Finally both parties may fail to agree what constitutes quality service'. Both academic commentators and practitioners have attempted to overcome these difficulties by the development of a range of analytical tools through which to measure customer assessments of service quality and service encounter success.

Allowing for the fact that services vary in the amount of interaction between the customer and the service organization, the service interactions that have been most under investigation in this text rely a great deal on the interface between employees and customers as key determinants of customer satisfaction and thereby repeat business, competitive advantage and commercial success. To varying degrees, the performance of the employee is the means through which the organization delivers service quality and customer satisfaction. Paradoxically, it is precisely these front-line staff who have been regarded by many service organizations as a key cost area and have used labour costs as a source of cost reduction and profit. Typically the person fronting the customer has been the lowest paid and least trained member of the organization (Barbee and Bott, 1991). Traditionally, many of these firms have adopted a cost leadership strategy that has been at the heart of policies relating to low levels of training, sloppy recruitment, poor induction and remarkably high levels of staff turnover (Rosenthal *et al.*, 1998).

Over recent years many service organizations have been concerned to gain greater competitive advantage by addressing issues of service quality, through initiatives such as total quality management and the development of service cultures, etc. An important ingredient in these strategies has been that employees need to be empowered to meet the customer need as it arises. Often these pronouncements have been over-simplistic. Few have considered what service workers need to do, or what form of empowerment best fits with the organization and its strategy. There is a need to understand these aspirations for empowerment through an analysis of service delivery problems and the role that front-line employees pay in different service operations.

Rosenthal *et al.* (1998) provide a useful example taken from the retail sector. Shopco introduced a quality strategy and saw employee empowerment and changed manager roles as key to success. The training largely concerned shaping perceptions and actions. 'The message of Service Excellence training was one of a new freedom (and responsibility) in staff dealing with customers' (p. 173). Training replaced more scripted approaches to customer service and employees were empowered to meet customer service needs as they arose and 'employees were continually search for new ways to *exceed* customer expectations' (p. 174). Through greater autonomy and use of discretion the company hoped that not only would customer service improve, it was also hoped that jobs requiring more discretion would also prove to be more interesting to employees. They conclude that, 'From senior management's perspective the programme does appear have had a positive impact on Shopco' (p. 178). However, they do suggest, like several studies (Holden, 1999; Collins, 1999; Cunningham and Hyman, 1999), the importance of managing the process of change with the state of empowerment as a primary objective, and that there can be significant differences in the workforce in the way they responded to the changes.

Services and service quality

The distinction between goods and services has been subject to a great deal of debate as different writers choose to argue that all goods contain some **intangible** elements (Levitt, 1972), or that services have distinct characteristics which cannot be captured by generic analysis (Lovelock, 1981). In practice, it is possible to see that there is likely to be a clustering on both tangible and intangible benefits associated with most goods and services. These differences are best demonstrated by Figure 11.1, which shows an array of goods and services that provide varying amounts of tangible and intangible services. This leads to a definition that service constitutes 'The production of an essentially intangible benefit, either in its own right or as a significant element of a tangible product, which through some form of exchange satisfies an identified consumer need' (Palmer, 1994: 3).

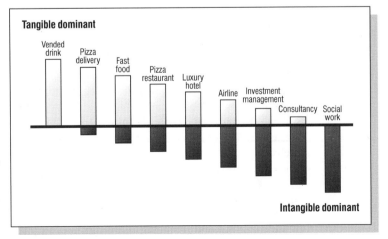

Figure 11.1 The continuum of tangible and intangible benefits

Hospitality, Leisure & Tourism Series

The core features of services of intangibility, inseparability, variability and perishability (Cowell, 1986; Mudie and Cottam, 1999) provide service organizations with some difficulties and dilemmas to manage in the delivery of services. The *intangible* elements of services make it difficult for customers to verify the benefits to be gained from a service prior to the purchase. This can only be done as a result of receiving the service. In addition, it is difficult to assess the expectations of customers, service employees, and managers in what the intangible benefits should deliver. Consumers face uncertainty when choosing between competing services, and the response of many service producers has been to increase physical evidence and to produce strong brands. In recent years many service organizations have begun to advocate competitive advantage through a focus on the intangible elements of the service encounter, because this is less easily copied by competitors. In particular, brand values that stress emotional benefits require employees to produce the emotional performance required. It is here that empowerment is said to be valuable.

The *heterogeneity* of services is also a feature that distinguishes them from typical manufacturing production. Service delivery is frequently variable and difficult to standardize because of the personal nature of the contact between the customer and the service deliverer. Thus individuals may well vary in their interpretation of customer needs. Elements of human 'chemistry' may interfere with performance, some individuals may be more personally committed to successful service encounters. Customer expectations of satisfactory service may well vary and be difficult to predict. Hence it is difficult to say the service delivery is homogeneous, even where the service is relatively simple.

Having made this general point, there is variety between different types of services and the degree of standardization and within the services provided. Some firms are able to standardize the tangible elements of the service encounter. Many fast food deliverers, branded restaurants, budget hotels, and others operate in businesses which supply standardized products to customers who demand the predictability and security of the branded service (Ritzer, 1993). Many of these firms have also attempted to standardize the 'intangible' elements of the service encounter by scripting employees, so that training included phrases and words to use during service. McDonald's Restaurants and Disney World are well known examples of organizations who have tried to homogenize the service encounter in this way.

Other service organizations are in positions where the encounters with customers are more individualized and difficult to predict. Obviously the pure intangible interactions within professional services will, to varying degrees, be individualized and thereby heterogeneous. Successful encounters will be dependent on the individual service deliverer being able to interpret the requirements of customers and adapt the service delivered to their wants. Other organizations may well require that front line staff deliver a standardized product in the tangibles but then require a more individualized, or personalized, service in the intangibles.

The third important feature of services is that the production and consumption of the service is *inseparable*. This creates a number of differences with typical manufacturing firms. Consumers of the service frequently are themselves participants in the service delivery, say as customers in a restaurant or a bank. They interact with the service deliverer, the environment and other consumers. Thus customers are party to the service interaction and will partially shape it, they will have their perceptions of the service encounter shaped through their perceptions of the service environment and their perceptions of fellow customers.

Whilst this general tendency is correct, not all services have the same degree of inseparability with their customers. Some services do not require customers to be physically present, say, where the service is primarily on objects – repairs on equipment, or where the service might be communicated – broadcasting, computer services etc. That said, many of these services do have contact points where service interactions take place. The inseparability issue even where services are largely provided away from the customer still requires careful analysis of customer expectations and empowerment can play a role in providing service workers with the sense of personal efficacy which enables them to interpret customer service needs.

Similarly, the relationship between customers and service deliverers is not uniform. In some cases the service interaction will be simple, requiring a limited range of short (and predictable?) transactions between customer and service deliverer: fast food or take-away operations are typical. In other situations the expectations of customers will require ritualized performance, where employees need to appreciate the expectations of customers: in haute cuisine restaurant or in banking services. An ability to balance customer expectations of formality with service accessibility is an important consideration. In other situations customers are buying into the service operation as theatre, and employees have to provide the appropriate performance: American bar and diner operations are examples, though to some extent employee 'performance' is a feature of most service interactions (Deighton, 1994).

Typically services are subject to *perishability* because they are temporal. Bed spaces in hotels or seats in restaurants represent capacity for a given period. Thus it is not possible to store up sales and satisfy them at another time. Nor can any loss of service output be made up at a later date. In many cases, the service is time specific and once lost is gone forever. Hence the empty hotel bed, or unsold restaurant meal represents revenue never to be regained. Unlike manufacturing output, service deliverers are not able to stock-pile services, or make up lost service production through overtime working, or multi-source services to allow for fluctuations in the demand and supply of services.

Perishability presents several key problems for service organizations. Service quality faults cannot easily be reworked and given back to the customer, as might happen with a manufactured product. Service demand has to be satisfied as and when it is required, so there is difficulty in planning service delivery to meet service demand. In some cases, service demand is not evenly spaced out over time. Not surprisingly, restaurants find that demand peaks at meal times. In other situations demand may be influenced by factors difficult to predict, such as the weather. This creates circumstances where there are limits to capital resources usage, and human resources are needed for short intensive periods.

Finally, many services are supplied to customers who do not 'own' the service as supplied, they cannot take it away or return it if unsatisfactory. Due to the intangibility and perishability features, customers are frequently buying the right to a service, or an experience. This creates problems of loyalty and memory; unlike the possessors of a tangible product, service consumers rarely have permanent reminders of the products features or benefits. Repeat purchases will be based on a bundle of remembered experiences and expectations. Individual perceptions and differences become important issues.

These features of intangibility, heterogeneity, inseparability and perishability present particular difficulties for service organizations. Different service organizations do confront different clusters of difficulties, stemming from the different service offers made to customers and different types of service encounter. Most services involve some element of interactions between employees and customers, in circumstances where both the production and consumption of services take place simultaneously. Both employees and customers are involved in personal interpretations of successful service encounters which are temporally specific and cannot be sampled or corrected in the event of a mistake. The personal and experiential nature of these interactions present problems for the definition, delivery and measurement of consistent service quality.

Early attempts to define service quality tended to distinguish between those aspects that were capable of objective measurement and those which are more subjective. Thus the former category might include the tangible aspect of the customer offer – say the size and quality of a meal or accommodation against standards, and those aspects of the service which can be measured – the time taken to be served, etc. Gronroos (1984) identified *technical* and *functional* elements to defining service quality. Technical aspects were those elements of the service that were quantifiable – time taken to answer the telephone, waiting times in a bank queue, etc. Here the customer is making judgements about the service on the basis of a set of personal standards that are capable of measurement. Functional elements were more concerned with customer judgements of service based on the interactions between the service deliverer and consumer. That is, on how the technical aspects of the service was delivered and might include the appearance and attitudes of staff, the physical environment in which the service is being delivered together with the management of the processes involved in delivering the service. In both cases, customer expectations form the basis on which they evaluate the success, or otherwise, of the service encounter.

The problem for management is in understanding what these expectations are and then sharing them with employees on the front line who will deliver the service in a way that matches with customer expectations. 'The general absence of easily understood criteria for assessing quality makes the articulation of customers' requirements and the communication of the quality level on offer much more difficult than is the case for goods' (Palmer, 1994: 175). Consumer expectations of service quality become an important definition feature of service quality when set against experiences of the service. Customers may vary in their expectations, customers with more experience of a service may well have higher expectations than those who have less experience of it. Organizations and their image may have a role in shaping expectations, advertising and other promotional activities may influence consumer expectations. Customers have a base level of expectations of the service – the minimum they expect. They have a level of expectations about what the service should be like – what they want. In addition, customers also predict what they expect the quality to be like (Zeithmal *et al.* 1993). The work of Herzberg (1966) on employee motivation has been used to explain aspects of customer expectations (Balmer and Baum, 1993). Thus it possible to consider states of service dissatisfaction, but an absence of dissatisfaction does not lead to customer motivation. There is likely to be a set of key (mostly intangible?) elements that will produce customer satisfaction and motivation to return.

Parasuraman *et al.* (1991) propose that service organizations need to be much more systematic about capturing their customers' expectations of the service. They suggest, 'Customer service expectations can be categorized into five overall dimensions: reliability, tangibles, responsiveness, assurance and empathy.' (1991: 41). These dimensions are reproduced in Table 11.1. They point out reliability is concerned with service outcomes, whereas the other elements are concerned with process. Interestingly, within a discussion about employee empowerment, three of the elements point to employee performance as key to customer expectations: responsiveness, assurance and empathy. These three elements are related to service process and '... the opportunity is present to surprise customers with uncommon swiftness, grace, courtesy, competence, commitment or understanding, and go beyond what is expected' (1991: 41). Using the Herzberg conceptual framework, reliability relates to the 'hygiene factors' whereby customers have an expectation of what the service should be like, but real motivation to use the service

Table 11.1 The five dimensions of service

Dimension	Definition
Reliability	The ability to perform the promised service dependably and accurately
Tangibles	The appearance of physical facilities, equipment, personnel and communication materials
Responsiveness	The willingness to help customers and provide prompt service
Assurance	The knowledge and courtesy of employees and their ability to convey trust and confidence
Empathy	The caring, individualized attention provided to customers

Source: Parasuraman *et al.*, 1991

repeatedly will be built through attention to the process element and service employee performance in particular.

Parasuraman *et al.* (1991) have developed a measure of service quality that asks customers 22 questions exploring the five dimensions outlined in Table 11.1.

SERVQUAL can be used by service providers to compare customers' expectations with their experiences and thereby show where service delivery has strengths and weaknesses. The performance of different competitors can be compared with the service organization's own performance. 'The SERVQUAL model highlights the difficulties in ensuring high quality service for all customers in all situations' (Palmer, 1994: 181). In particular it reveals 'five service gaps' where there may be a mismatch been the expectation of the service level and the perception of the service delivered. These gaps focus on the points at which expectations of service requirements by management, the standards set, the standards achieved, or the service standards communicated to customers produce a situation where customers' perceptions of the service delivered do not match with the

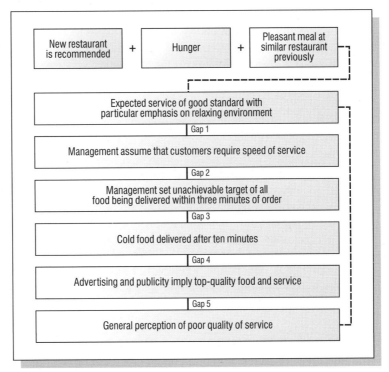

Figure 11.2 Source of divergence between service quality expectation and delivery. *Source:* Palmer (1994)

expected service. The diagram given in Figure 11.2 refers to an application to an imagined restaurant.

Rust and Oliver (1994) suggest that the management of service quality requires the recognition that 'Service quality is by nature a subjective concept, which means that understanding how the customer thinks about service quality is essential to effective management' (p. 2). Specifically they suggest a need to disentangle three related but distinct concepts – customer satisfaction, service quality and customer value. Customer satisfaction results from a service encounter and comparing the experience with expectations. Customer satisfaction relates to process theories and to the states identified earlier in which, '. . .satisfaction is viewed as largely based on meeting or exceeding expectations' (Rust and Oliver, 1994: 4). In essence customer satisfaction arises as a result of experience. Service quality can be judged against a set of ideals, 'Thus the SERVQUAL instrument illustrates the core of what service quality may mean, namely *a comparison to excellence* in service *by the customer'* (Rust and Oliver, 1994: 6). Service quality is said to be the customer's overall judgement about a firm's excellence or superiority (Bitner, 1990). Value includes quality and price, though might also include other economic and psychological benefits. 'Ultimately it is perceived value that attracts a customer or lures a customer away from the competition' (Rust and Oliver, 1994: 7). When arriving at a perception of the value of a service, customers are in effect considering the benefits received and the sacrifices made in the service encounter.

In summary, the nature of services in general, their intangibility, heterogeneity, inseparability and perishability, create difficulties for managers, employees and customers. The role of perception of needs, source of satisfaction, the success of the service encounter and differences in expectations provide many service organizations with service management difficulties. Recent research suggests that service organizations need to better understand customer expectations of service quality, the source of customer satisfaction and elements which shape customer evaluations of value. In particular, the performance of service employees in the service interaction appear to play a significant role in shaping customer evaluations of satisfaction, quality and service value.

Employees and customer satisfaction

Front-line employees have a key role in all services where customers' presence is required in the service encounter. As was stated earlier, some services make contact with customers through broadcast, electronic or other media; in some cases, the service interaction between customers and employees is brief, because the service is chiefly concerned with repairing a piece of equipment, etc. In most cases, however, the customer visits the premises of the service deliverer to receive the service – restaurant, hotel, supermarket, clothes shop, petrol station, theatre, etc. In these situations, employees have the key role in shaping customer perceptions of service quality and satisfaction. From the customer's point of view the service interaction with employees is the service. Even allowing for the point made earlier that customer perceptions of an organization's quality will be a product of the organization's image and its promoted offer to customers, the service interaction is an important point of contact where preconceptions and expectations result in either favourable or unfavourable evaluations of the service delivered. As we saw with Shopco (Rosenthal *et al.*, 1998), organizations wishing to adopt a quality competitive strategy need to address the management of people as a priority.

Paradoxically, many service organizations have failed to grasp the significance of the employee's role. Indeed service organizations have seen employees as 'the single most controllable cost' (Pannel Kerr Forster Associates, 1992). Given that labour costs do represent very significant proportions of total costs, cost reduction strategies have tended to be focused largely at labour. Many firms have paid low wages, invested little in training, and practised numerical flexibility through the use of large numbers of part time staff, or through the ready acceptance of high levels of labour turnover (Wood, 1992). The result has been that 'front-line employees are not trained to understand customers and do not have the freedom and discretion in the ways that ensure effective service' (Bitner *et al.*, 1990: 71). One of the key thrusts of this book is that these 'cost leadership strategies' are incompatible with a quality based strategy and with empowerment.

Barbee and Bott (1991) point out that the link between employee satisfaction and customer satisfaction has been understood for some time. They refer to the comment made by JW Marriott Senior, which gave high priority to employee satisfaction as a necessary ingredient to generating customer satisfaction. Firms that give high priority exemplary service delivery tend to pay attention to understanding how employee behaviour generates feelings of customer satisfaction even in adverse situations. Bitner *et al.*'s (1990) study of critical incidents in service delivery helps to build a picture of how employee behaviours can be crucial in determining customer satisfaction.

Bitner *et al.* describe a critical incident as one that, '... contributes or detracts from the general activity in significant way' (1990: 73). In the context of their study they specifically focused on those incidents that involved interactions between employees and customers, and which resulted in customers being *very satisfied* or *dissatisfied*. Their findings suggested three broad groups of incidents – employee responses to service delivery system failures; employee reactions to customer needs and requests; and unprompted and unsolicited employee actions. Each group represented a cluster of incidents in which employee behaviour could result in either customer satisfaction or customer dissatisfaction.

Employee responses to service delivery failure could be turned into incidents that employees use to advantage and that generate customer satisfaction, for instance, if an employee reacts quickly to service failure by responding sensitively to customer experiences – say by compensating the customer or upgrading a customer to a higher status service. More frequently, however, staff responses were likely to be source of a dissatisfaction – where the employee fails to provide an apology, an adequate explanation or argues with the customer.

Employee responses to customer needs and requests involved employee behaviour when faced with requests to provide a service not normally incorporated in the offer. Again, employee reactions can be both a source of satisfaction and dissatisfaction. Say where the customer has a 'special' need or preference, or where the customer has made a mistake. Employee responsiveness, flexibility and confidence that they can match whatever is needed by the customer are important sources of a positive customer response. Similarly, employee intransigence, inflexibility, and perceived incompetence are all potential sources of customer dissatisfaction. The Bitner *et al.* study suggested that generally employee responses were more a source of satisfaction than dissatisfaction when meeting unusual requests.

Unprompted and unsolicited employee actions incorporated actions that were outside of the customer's expectations of the service encounter. This might involve employee behaviours which made the customer feel special, or where an act of unexpected generosity took the customer by surprise. Customer dissatisfaction could be the result of a failure to give the customer the level of attention expected, or inadequate information, or might involve inappropriate behaviour such as the use of bad language, or drunkenness, etc.

In all these situations service interactions involved a number of critical incidents where employee responses were fundamental to the customer's satisfaction or dissatisfaction with the service provided. To effectively participate in the service employees need to be aware of customer expectations and perceptions, they must have a sense of engagement and concern for customer satisfaction and need to have a sense that they can make a difference to the service encounter. In another study, Bitner (1990) evaluating service encounters and the effects of physical surroundings and employee responses on customer perceptions of service quality, makes a number of conclusions for the managers of service organizations. It is important to manage and control each service interaction. If the service does not match customer expectations there are still opportunities to create customer satisfaction if the employee understands the processes through which customers lay blame for the incident. They are much more likely to accept a service breakdown if they are given a logical explanation for the service failure and are compensated in some way. Indeed these incidents can be turned into 'memorable incidents' if the employee response is swift in offering the explanation and compensation.

Apart from the role employees play in shaping customer experiences of service quality and generation of customer satisfaction through the service encounter, service employees play a key part in helping to 'personalize' services for consumers. It is possible to see some tensions in customer needs from service organizations. As we have seen, a service purchase can create difficulties for customers because it is difficult to know what the service will be like until it has been received. A consequence has been the growth of branded services, through which service providers send messages that help to establish customer expectations of the service encounter. Through a standardized offer customers are assured of the quality and attributes of the service to be supplied. The branded, standardized service helps to meet customer security needs, but can leave customers feeling unimportant and anonymous. Increasingly, branded and standardized service firms have been looking to various forms of personalization to help overcome these negative customer feelings. Suprenant and Solomon (1987) identify personalized service as occurring when the 'customer role is embellished in the encounter through specific recognition of the customer's uniqueness as an individual over and above his/her status as an anonymous service recipient' (p. 87). Again they point to appropriate employee performance to be matched with the forms of personalization being offered by the organization.

The issue of employee performance and customer satisfaction take on added urgency when firms begin to consider the costs of lost business and the benefits of generating customer loyalty. Leach (1995), Ansell's Finance Director, estimates that every pub customer spends an average of £785 per annum in public houses. A customer lost due to an unresolved complaint loses the business that amount directly. In addition it is estimated that a dissatisfied customer tells another thirteen people about their experience. 'The potential cost of one unresolved complaint is, therefore, fourteen times this amount – £11,032.' (p. 34). Harris (1991), using a US based retail industry context, estimated that if an organization lost one customer per day for a year, the total cost to the business could be over $94,000 per annum even if customers only spent on average $5 per week with the organization. Similarly it was estimated that repeat custom only cost one-fifth the amount needed to generate new customers. Within a hotel context Carper (1992) reported that the ratio was closer to 1:7. Heskett *et al.* (1990) maintain that 'Customer loyalty and profitability go hand in hand' (p. 31). They explain this through the reduction in costs of servicing new customers, and the effect that loyal customers have on recruiting new customers.

The financial implications of customer satisfaction, and the key role employees play in the service encounter, has brought about concern to ensure employees are equipped to maximize their effectiveness. Harris (1991) advocates the need to 'invest in your staff' (p. 236). Figure 11.3 provides a graphic representation for the links that are made between customer satisfaction, customer turnover, employee satisfaction and employee turnover. In the upper part of the diagram a virtuous cycle results in a continuous improvement in all the elements. The lower portion of the diagram, on the other hand, presents a vicious cycle in which declining customer satisfaction results in reduced customer retention, which results in employees having to work harder to recruit new customers which reduces employee satisfaction and increases employee turnover, which in turn impacts on customer satisfaction.

A result of all this analysis of the commercial imperative associated with service quality and service employee performance, particularly by service marketeers, has been the establishment of a metaphor that describes employees as customers. As such, they are involved in a value chain which interlinks the stages of the production of the service within the organization backwards with suppliers and forwards with customers. Internally, employees are both customers of other employees at an earlier stage in the production process, and suppliers to other employees who are at later stages. In addition, service employees have been subject to 'the tools of the marketeer' (Harris, 1991: 239). This notion of the employee as *internal customer* is one that has on one level a basis of sense in that, as we have seen, front-line employees are integral to customer satisfaction and employee morale is important in creating 'happy customers'. On another level, the inconsistencies and potential conflicts between

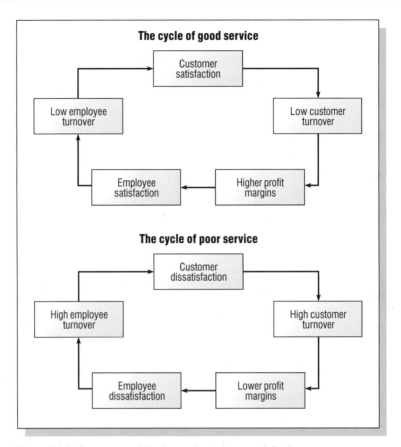

Figure 11.3 Customer satisfaction and employee satisfaction.

the needs of external and internal customers does limit this metaphor's usefulness. Rafiq and Ahmed (1993) point to the difficulties if internal customers in a restaurant do not want to work 'unsocial' hours. As with many of these pronouncements, the phrase 'internal customers' has a symbolic attraction but does not stand over-close attention and is of limited use as an analytical tool.

Managers of service organizations are faced with two key dilemmas. Labour costs represent, in most services, an important element of total operating costs. In the past many organizations have used the manipulation of labour costs as a source of cost reduction. Front-line service employees have been low paid, poorly trained with low motivation, high job dissatisfaction and high labour turnover (Bitner *et al.*, 1990) and this has resulted in customer perceptions that 'the observable symptom is decreasing quality in . . . the service encounter' (p. 71). As both academics

Hospitality, Leisure & Tourism Series

and practitioners have attempted to develop a better understanding of customer perceptions of service quality and the critical incidents in the service encounter that lead to perceptions of satisfaction, it has become obvious that those firms wishing to gain competitive advantage through service quality have to address the means by which they engage employees in the service encounter. To be effective employees need to be appropriately trained, given adequate information and develop a strong commitment to delivering successful service encounters. In some cases employers have developed reward packages which do give employees a material interest in successful service, e.g. TGI Fridays sales-related wage plus tips. In other cases, the dilemma for employers is how to keep the labour cost to a minimum whilst at the same time enhancing employee commitment to the service encounter.

The second dilemma relates to the need to control employee performance in a situation where service interactions are complex, interpersonal, and not easily subject to scrutiny. Given the importance of each service interaction in shaping customer perceptions of service quality and satisfaction, there is a need to re-examine the way that employees are managed and their performance controlled. In some cases, customer expectations are for a standardized and highly predictable service encounter. Here service delivery can be best planned using mass production techniques to deliver standardized experience. In other cases, service encounters may not be so easy to predict and opportunities to standardize interactions are limited. Here the very lack of predictability creates difficulties of control because managers have no way of either knowing what customers want, or being party to every transaction.

It is here that empowerment appears to offer the ability to square the circle. Empowerment, with its 'win-win' rhetoric, appears to be the device that will give employees the motivation to be involved and committed to customer satisfaction. Employee empowerment promises to be a technique managers can use to produce employee commitment, ownership and a sense of personal efficacy through which customer satisfaction can be delivered. It also seems to shift the locus of control from the supervisor/manager to the individual employee. Each person internalizes the service standards and works to these. Empowerment appears to offer the possibility of making front-line employees more responsive to customer needs, whilst at the same time providing a means through which management costs can be reduced.

In the chapter entitled 'Mobilizing People', Heskett *et al.* (1990) suggest that service organizations need to 'become employers of

first choice', 'develop and retain such people through ...
ministering', 'promote good managers towards rather than away
from the customer', 'dieting the organization, especially at middle
levels', and, 'empowering front-line managers while maintaining
adequate control' (p. 194). Much of these concerns and considerations were built into an apparently 'unified' body of ideas through
the advocacy of total quality management as the business strategy
for the management of service organizations in the 1990s.

Empowerment and total quality management

General concern for quality improvement, most prominently in
Japan initially, and then in most Western economies in the 1980s
and 1990s, resulted in an array of quality improvement techniques which moved beyond checking for and measuring faults.
The emphasis shifted, even in manufacturing, to the prevention
of quality breakdowns rather than the detection of faults that had
occurred. Given the nature of services, the fault detection avenue
was not a feasible option. Services cannot be sent back to be
reworked. Services have to be designed and delivered in a way
where faults are designed out of the system, or the points at
which faults are likely to occur are identified.

In some cases, service organizations were tempted to adopt
quality assurance systems which were based on 'designing
quality into the process' or 'getting it right first time' through the
production of standard procedures manuals which were verified
through later BS5750 or initially ISO 9000. 'BS5750 is a quality
monitoring process. You decide what you want to do, write it all
down and monitor whether you are doing it or not' (McDermid,
1992: 14). In fact few service organizations took up this approach,
and those who did tended to have marketing reasons for doing so
because it gave them access to customers. Many UK contract
catering organizations applied for BS5750 and IS0 9000 because
many of their industrial clients insisted that they would only
trade with organizations who had been similarly verified. The
problem with these systems is that they tend to focus on
consistency rather than customer satisfaction (Sutton, 1992).
Developed initially in the UK arms industry, BS5750 aimed to
limit the number of faulty parts when measuring against mass
production. Service industries require quality systems that are
holistic enough to allow for the characteristics of services and the
varied perceptions of customers. TQM appeared to offer service
organizations the system needed.

Almost every edition of *Service Quality Management* contains at
least one article advocating the use of total quality management
as a way of improving service quality. In many of these articles,

the link between TQM and employee empowerment is also made. Chopin has been a regular contributor on the subject and states that 'It is not helpful to define Total Quality Management. Such a definition would either be too simplistic leading to the cynical charge that it is all puff and no substance, while a detailed definition would be too prescriptive' (Chopin, 1994: 44). TQM, it appears, 'is for dreamers' (p. 44). Later, Chopin goes on to describe sixteen principles of TQM in services. These are summarized in Table 11.2.

Table 11.2 Principles of total quality management in service industries

1. Highest priority given to quality throughout the organization.
2. Quality is defined in terms of customer satisfaction.
3. Customers are defined as those who have both internal and external relationships with the organization – including employees, shareholders, the wider community.
4. Customer satisfaction and the building of long-term relationships are at the nub of the organization.
5. The organization's aims will be clearly stated and accessible to all.
6. Principles, beliefs, values and quality are communicated throughout the organization.
7. Total quality management creates an ethos that pervades all aspects of the organization's activities.
8. Core values of honesty, integrity, trust and openness are essential ingredients of TQM.
9. The total quality organization is intended to be mutually beneficial to all concerned and operates in a climate of mutual respect for all stakeholders.
10. The health and safety of all organization members and customers are given priority.
11. Total quality offers individuals the chance to participate and feel ownership for the success of the enterprise.
12. Commitment is generated in individuals and teams through leadership form senior management.
13. TQM results in an organization wide commitment to continuous improvement.
14. Performance measurement, assessment and auditing of the organization's activities is a common feature of TQM.
15. TQM aims to use resources more effectively and members are encouraged to consider ways of using resources more effectively.
16. TQM requires appropriate investment to ensure that planned activity can occur.

Source: Chopin, 1994

Even though there are several forms of total quality management (Wilkinson *et al.*, 1991), Chopin's list of principles covers several broad features of TQM that are found in most descriptions of the initiative. At heart, the initiative locates a commitment to quality services as a core organizational concern. The commitment of senior management is crucial and the approach has to permeate every aspect of the organization. The approach has been particularly attractive to service organizations because it aims to create a cultural environment in which employees, operating independently, are guided by a commitment to delighting customers because they have internalized the organization's objectives and values. These internalized values, beliefs and objectives ensure employees aspire to delivering customer satisfaction and quality improvement, without extrinsic controls or inducements. Total quality management philosophy has much in common with systems theory, particularly when linked to the metaphor of internal customers. Each subsystem is regarded as the customer of a supplier to other subsystems. 'The objective of TQM is to optimize these relationships at every subsystem boundary' (Johns, 1993: 13).

The similarities with aspirations for TQM and empowerment are not accidental because many of those writing about the benefits of TQM as an approach for managing service organizations also advocate the need to empower with authority to correct defects and respond to service failures as they occur. 'In this way an organization can continuously correct its performance, subsystem by subsystem, without the need for cumbersome, centralized or bureaucratic monitoring of subsystem quality' (Johns, 1993: 13). Furthermore, employee empowerment is important so that employees can respond to unusual customer requests, or use their experience and creativity to look for ways of delighting the customer. These aspirations for TQM and empowerment are relevant to the three employee customer interactions that Bitner *et al.* (1990) identified as critical incidents that could create, or damage, customer satisfaction. Dealing with service failures, responding to requests for unusual service and providing extraordinary interactions are all occasions when employee behaviour impacts either positively or negatively on customer satisfaction and perceptions of service quality. TQM provides an organizational setting in which empowered employees, through a heightened sense of their own personal efficacy, will respond in the desired way.

All the companies that have been used in this text have their own ways of dealing with the management of service quality, which incorporated many of the concepts of total quality management, even though they have not called it by that name.

McDonald's Restaurants for example, use **Q**uality, **S**ervice, **C**leanliness and **V**alue as core organizational aspirations. All the company's service quality monitoring processes assess QSCV, though recognizing that value is a psychological concept, this is assessed using different techniques from the other three. All restaurants are assessed on a regular basis using 'mystery diners', Area Supervisor audits, customer comment cards, customer complaints or praise, customer surveys and manager conducted assessments. All the sources of assessment are brought together in a series of grades, which are used to evaluate unit perform-ance. As we saw earlier, these quality assessments are used as points of entry for manager bonus schemes. Thus if a restaurant is increasing turnover and profits but failing to match quality targets, the manager will not be eligible for bonus payments. Only when service quality markers have been met will bonuses be paid. The McDonald's approach has much in common with the 'hard' version of TQM identified by Wilkinson *et al.* (1992). This definition 'places emphasis on the production aspects such as systematic measurement and control of work, setting stan-dards of performance, using statistical procedures to assess quality, this is the "hard production/operations management" type of view which arguably leads to less discretion for employees' (1992: 4). As we have seen, the form of empowerment is largely associated with winning commitment and developing the sense of personal efficacy, there is little by way of decision-making authority passed to employees.

Harvester Restaurants' approach, though similar to McDonald's in many ways, seemed to be informed by a different notion of total quality management. There were standard procedures manuals, which stated how dishes were to be cooked and presented, and standard service times for meals, in other words the technical aspects of service quality are defined. However, service employees were given a values driven approach to service delivery. Treating the customer as 'a guest in your own home' lays down few prescriptive behaviours, but does provide a guiding principle for front-line staff. The approach taken by Harvester Restaurants was similar to the 'soft' approach to TQM in Wilkinson *et al.* (1992). They describe the soft approach as incorporating the characteristics identified by Peters (1992), 'customer orientation, culture of excellence, removal of performance barriers, team working, training, employee partici-pation, competitive edge. From this perspective TQM is seen as consistent with open management styles, delegated responsibil-ity and increased autonomy of staff' (p. 2). Interestingly, much of the quality auditing was done by employees or management, and through consideration of customer feedback – largely complaint

Hospitality, Leisure & Tourism Series

monitoring. Here the approach to employee empowerment was through participation, particularly through the working of autonomous work teams. These teams played an important role in both controlling individual performance, and delivering employee commitment to organizational quality service targets.

In many ways, TGI Fridays incorporated elements of both approaches. Standard procedures manuals laid down production and presentation specifications, and service times were much more prescriptive than Harvesters. Employee performance was not quite so prescribed as at McDonald's though tests on product knowledge were used to ensure that front-line employees had the requisite technical knowledge to be able to advise customers. Employee performance was judged against time and behavioural service requirements, such as checking customers were happy with the dish as served. On the other hand, employee performance and the ability to identify customer service needs was evaluated at a more evaluative level. Ultimately, the company aimed to create a cultural environment through which employees could provide the performance to which customers would respond favourably. A mixture of both personal material rewards, through sales related bonuses and tips, and appeals to team working were elements through which individuals were encouraged to deliver the quality experience. Wilkinson *et al.* (1992) identified this as a third approach to TQM. 'The third definition is a mixture of "hard" and "soft", comprising three features: an obsession with quality; the need for a scientific approach; and the view that all employees are part of the one team' (p. 3). Empowerment was through employee involvement in that employees were encouraged to engage in the performance and identify with the performance of the unit.

The naming of initiatives that prioritize customer service quality vary; total quality management, customer service organization, total quality organization, are all variations of an approach which have similar intentions, conceptual origins and ideological roots. All basically suggest that service organizations can benefit from an organization-wide commitment to quality, the development of a customer quality dominated culture, employee empowerment, etc. Many of these approaches recognize that competitive advantage can be gained from delivering consistent service quality and ensuring customer satisfaction. Each identifies employee performance as playing a crucial role in identifying potential faults and thereby continuously improving performance, and in interacting with customers in ways that can either deliver customer satisfaction or dissatisfaction.

Ideologically these approaches have a somewhat distorted and temporally located management analysis of organizational behaviour and their relationship with employees in particular. The list reproduced in Table 11.2 has a unitary perception underpinning many of its prescriptions. The supposed even-handedness of stakeholder interests is a case in point. Share-holders, when push comes to shove, are the key interest group, and although it might be handy to promote the 'employees are our most important asset' philosophy when times are good, a trade downturn and a few resulting redundancies show just how important is the bottom line. Clearly there are times when labour market conditions elevate the ability of employees to resist managerial prerogatives, but the service industries, despite the potential that service perishability presents, have not proven to be fertile ground for collective employee power. That said, these current managerial concerns for winning individual commit-ment, resistance to employee collectives and the promotion of employer collectives can be located in what Ramsey (1977) has described as 'cycles of control'. As was discussed earlier, employer strategies tend to follow trends driven by labour market conditions and employee resistance, to pursue different tactics for managing and controlling employee performance. TQM and empowerment are current rhetorics that reflect a set of concerns and ideological hegemony of the 'New Right' (Tuck-man, 1995).

In service industries, TQM and employee empowerment can provide both managers and employees with benefits that can improve service quality and customer satisfaction, whilst giving employees more control over how they organize and complete their tasks. These techniques can produce win-win situations, but they can be used as a rhetoric which ultimately provide a situation where the 'route to TQM is integral to workforce consent to a new set – often far more intensified – of work relations' (Tuckman, 1995: 56).

Conclusions

Concern for service quality delivery and customer satisfaction provide employers with some intense difficulties and dilemmas. The first difficulty involves the nature of services, particularly those that chiefly involve customers being party to the service, because of the characteristics of services. Service intangibility makes it difficult for customers and service providers to agree a precise service definition prior to the interaction. Service insepar-ability means that customers are both actors and audience in the service drama, their perceptions of the encounter are individual and difficult to predict. The interpersonal nature of the service encounter means the services are difficult to standardize and tend towards heterogeneity. Finally, service perishability makes it difficult to rework or replace faulty services. In most cases, once the service has been undertaken, it cannot be returned by the customer for correction or reworking. This creates a need for service delivery to be 'right first time'.

Given these service constraints on customers, service employees and service organizations, there has been recent interest in the central role played by employees in the service interaction. In the past, service employees have often been regarded as key cost contributors to be manipulated as a way of controlling total costs. Current thinking suggests that employers need to pay attention to the recruitment, training, performance appraisal, rewards and empowerment of service employees. Service employees' understanding of the critical incidents which have an impact on customer perceptions of service quality, customer satisfaction, customer retention and ultimately profitability suggests employment policies need to be given high priority.

Total quality management and the empowerment of employees seem to be two approaches that provide a means of delivering consistent and improving service quality, through which to compete with other service providers. Total quality management provides an approach that establishes a cultural commitment to service quality, together with a set of techniques through which to monitor and continuously improve service delivery and responsiveness to changes in customer service expectations. Empowerment, on the other hand, suggests an approach to managing employees that will ensure employees are engaged in the service project. They internalize the objectives and policies of the organization and manage their own behaviour in a way that aspires to delight the customer.

In both cases, it is important to remember that the very vagueness of the terms allow a general application to very different tactics and contexts. Closer examination reveals that, like empowerment, TQM can be used to describe at least three different approaches to the management of service quality, and serious analysis needs to define terms. There is an urgent need to distinguish total quality management from that which is labelled total quality management. With that in mind, it may be that different forms of total quality management can be seen to match with different forms of empowerment, and are ultimately linked to different service offers to customers.

CHAPTER 12

Employment strategy and the service organization

- **Strategic human resource management**
- **The nature of services management**
- **Service employee discretion**
- **The management of human resources**

Employee empowerment is said to be a key component in revised approaches to the management of people in service organizations. The more strategic role played by people managers is also a fundamental innovation in those practices known by academics and practitioners alike as human resource management. In addition, earlier chapters have shown that the term 'employee empowerment' is used to describe a wide variety of different arrangements introduced by management in different organizations. It is likely that managerial intentions for empowerment are shaped by their perceptions of the nature of the service that their organization offers to clients. Taking the classical normative model, managers determine the strategic service offer to their clients and then shape the HRM strategy, including their intentions for and aims of empowerment, on the basis of this rational analysis. Fundamentally, an understanding of the nature of services and identification of key drivers in shaping the amount of discretion which employees need to exercise when delivering services to customers.

First, the chapter briefly reflects upon on the various debates about both the nature of human resource management (Storey, 1989; Guest, 1987, 1989; Legge, 1989) and typologies of business strategy (Whittington, 1993). Attempts to establish patterns of human resource strategy integrated with wider business objectives tend to employ normative definitions of HRM, and assume a traditional rational model of business strategy. Whilst it is possible to view both these assumptions as lacking critical dimensions (Legge, 1995), they do provide an insight into idealized models of strategy, and aspirations for human resource management to 'fit' with it, which are themselves flawed when it comes to the analysis of service organizations.

Chiefly, they fail to analyse managerial perceptions of the dilemmas posed in managing service organizations. The nature of the service encounter, imprecise customer expectations and the core role of front-line staff in producing customer satisfaction (Rust and Oliver, 1994) have resulted in a range of approaches to job design, recruitment, training, performance monitoring and control, etc. An idealized normative model needs to consider these approaches within the context of the services offered. Services are typified as being different from manufactured goods because of their intangibility, heterogeneity, perishability, and inseparability (Cowell, 1984), yet consideration of service organizations shows that not all organizations are in the same position with regard to these dimensions. Consequently the marketing offer to clients/customers varies (Buttle, 1986) and espoused competitive strategies vary (Johnston, 1989a). Any notion of 'fit' between these strategies and approaches to the management of human resources needs to thoroughly analyse these issues.

This chapter suggests a framework of analysis with which to explore the practices and approaches to the management of employees in the context of the service provided, the marketing offer and competitive strategy, and fundamentally, the role of employees in supplying the organization's services to its customers. Flowing from this it is possible to suggest that managerial perceptions of the offer to customers will shape their perceived requirements of employee empowerment, which in turn will influence the form introduced.

Strategic human resource management

According to Watson (1986) the study of employment strategy provides a useful concept in assisting in the study of the way organizations deal with employees. In particular, the study of employer strategies have a theoretical value in providing the relationships between organizational structure, organization culture, job design, attempts to gain employee commitment, leadership styles, recruitment, employee development and reward systems. Clearly, differing employer strategies regarding the empowerment of employees is also included. Though an aspiration for consistency and coherence is a key element of the claim for the strategic role for human resource management (Sissons, 1994), the study of employment strategy does not perforce validate the view that employment policies are arrived at in a rational-mechanistic manner. Employment policies can be said to emerge from internal political processes, and are shaped by managerial perceptions of the contextual factors within a cultural setting that predisposes managers to typical responses to the phenomena that they confront (Legge, 1995). Whether employment policies emerge deliberately in a coherent and planned way, or whether they emerge as a series of incremental steps, essentially managers make choices about their employment strategies and any attempt to understand the nature of those choices needs to be informed by the range of assumptions about the nature of business strategy, the nature of human resource management and the strategic role of human resource management.

Whilst the debates about the nature of human resource management will be touched on later, most commentators agree that human resource management implies a strategic position for the management of human resources – a position that matches the management of employees to wider business objectives. Guest (1987), in his model of HRM, suggests that the goal of integration and 'fit' with business strategy lies at the heart of human resource management. Purcell (1989) elaborates further by suggesting that business strategy can be seen as operating as a three-stage process in the organization. First-order strategies relate to the overall direction of the organization, second-order strategies are about the nature of the organization's internal relationships, and third-order strategies relate to the functional policies that support broad business strategies. The model is likened to a waterfall with policies cascading down stream from the strategic plan. At heart it assumes that strategic decisions are arrived at as a result of a rational and systematic analysis of the firm's environment and top-down implementation though the organization. Views of business strategy and the specific contribution of human resource management strategies tend to be 'normative' in that they describe how strategies 'ought to be', rather than analyse how they are enacted. Even within this frame of analysis, few writers give detailed attention to the needs of a human resource strategy within the service sector in general.

Attempts to analyse service organization's human resource strategies from this 'classical' (Whittington, 1993) perspective would be concerned with the 'fit' between human resource strategies and the organization's business objectives, together with, ultimately, the organization's environment. Whilst these will be discussed more fully later in this chapter, it is possible to speculate that Johnston's (1989a) suggestion that service firms follow business strategies aimed at price leadership, quality, service range, availability and uniqueness might have implications, under the rational normative model, for the policies for the management of employees. Similarly any attempt to establish a 'fit' with the human resource management strategies would need to analyse the service concept being offered to customers. Johnston suggests that there are three dimensions through which to identify the nature of the service being offered. Again, it is possible to speculate that the 'specialist v generalist', the 'standardized v. customized' and 'product v. process' dimensions might have appropriate human resource strategies.

Although the 'classical' perception of strategy is one shared by many who hold the view that human resource management should match with wider business strategy, it is but one perception of strategy. Several writers question this idealized model of the 'all seeing' strategic manager formulating strategic vision which is cascaded unsullied down through the organization. Legge (1995) uses Whittington's (1993) model of perceptions of business strategy to mount a robust challenge to the certainties of the classical model, and this might usefully inform analysis of strategies within service organizations.

Using two continua, Whittington identifies four perspectives on business strategy. The **'classical'** approach has been mentioned above and assumes that business strategy is both deliberate and aimed at profit maximization. The **'evolutionary'** approach suggests that attempting to create strategy is pointless, if not downright detrimental, because the marketplace determines success. Strategies are at best attempting to 'second guess' the market, and at worst will create inflexibility that will deny speedy response to new markets. Organizations need to try out new ideas, back winners and close down losers (Peters, 1992). This perspective assumes that business policies are aimed at profit maximization and are emergent rather than deliberate. The '**processual**' perspective assumes that business strategy is both subject to organizational adjustment through 'political' processes, and emergent as managers make small incremental changes in response to perceived market and environmental situations. Finally, the '**systemic**' perspective suggests that business strategy will be formulated via the perceptions and normative values of the cultural situations in which managers operate. Here the assumptions are that strategy is deliberate, but organizational objectives may well be shaped by considerations other than profit maximization.

Analysis of human resource strategies, and the introduction of empowerment practised by service organizations, needs to take account of these debates about the nature of business strategy because they assist in building a more sophisticated under-standing of employer intentions from the policies they formulate for dealing with employees. Blyton and Turnbull's (1994) doubts about the ability of managers ever to take rational strategic decisions in the face of external uncertainty and internal political mediating processes, is further compounded in Britain by the 'poor education and training' (p. 91) of managers. This latter point is exacerbated in the UK service industry because service industry managers are frequently less well trained than the national average; only 5 per cent of hospitality industry work-force have had a formal higher education (HTF, 2000). Taking the processual notion of strategy, it may be true that many service sector employers do not formally devise a set of human resource strategies devolved from wider business strategies in the classical manner, but it may be that a pattern of actions is apparent which might imply that labour is a cost to be minimized (Watson, 1986; Pannell Kerr Forster Associates, 1992). In effect, whether deliber-ately or not, many service organizations in the UK follow a 'cost leadership strategy'. Similarly the systemic perspective allows commentators to set an analysis of service industry HRM strategies against a national industrial culture of short-termism shaped by the nature of capital markets (Legge, 1995), the 'fall of a great power' continuing to hold ideologies which were relevant at the time of greatness but are no longer appropriate to the UK's current competitive position (Kennedy, 1988), and an industrial culture reflecting both entrepreneurial individualism (Purcell and Gray, 1986) and service perishability vulnerable to industrial action. The significance of perishability to the industry's employ-ment policies is discussed later.

The meaning of human resource management has also been subject to some considerable debate (Storey, 1989; Keenoy and Anthony, 1992; Legge, 1995). Whilst there are those who perceive human resource management as another (new fangled and faddish?) name for personnel management (Armstrong, 1987) concerned with the same catalogue of issues, there are also those who define HRM, albeit in a variety of ways, as being distinctly different from personnel management. Storey's (1992: 36) well publicized figure delineating dimensions of HRM and personnel management makes a case for differentiation and draws from the literature which emerged from the USA in the mid-1980s. Blyton and Turnbull (1992) view HRM as an 'umbrella term' describing a range of employment practices which became popular amongst both management practitioners and academics in the 1980s. Legge (1995) concludes that a comparison of personnel management and HRM reveals more similarities than differences, but that HRM provides rhetoric for corporate chief executives in the management of employees that incorporates the values of the 'enterprise culture', and in particular, reflects the values of the 'New Right'. Keenoy and Anthony (1992) argue that HRM is more than just a legitimation of 'management practice which treat people as a cost' (p. 238) whilst articulating a rhetoric that 'people are highly valued assets'. They say that HRM is a metaphor designed to reshape the social construct of the employment relationship. 'HRM reflects an attempt to redefine the meaning of work and the way individual employees relate to their employer' (p. 234). In particular, it is a device to establish and legitimize a unitary perspective of work organizations, and to de-legitimize employee collectives and pluralist analysis of organizational priorities. As argued in Chapter 3, the rhetoric of empowerment plays a key role in the legitimization of a unitary perspective.

Give this range of debates and disagreements about the nature of human resource management, it is essential that analysis of the topic applied to service operations reflects these debates and does not fall into the trap of assuming a single meaning for human resource management. Legge (1995) provides a range of four models in which to locate views about HRM. The *normative model* tends to state what HRM should be, or aspires to be; it provides a 'how to do' focus. The *descriptive functional model* focuses on the functions that HRM actually serves within organizations. The *critical evaluative model* locates HRM within a series of organizational and societal devices to gain commitment and win consent to managerial objectives and values, in particular in gaining support for a unitary perspective of organizational life. The *descriptive behavioural model* is concerned with examining human resource management in practice. Given the aspirations of the normative model, the search for coherence and consistency with business strategy, this model is concerned with the match between the practices of human resource management in organizations.

Hospitality, Leisure & Tourism Series

Much of the current published literature on both human resource management and employee empowerment in the service industries (Riley, 1991; Boella, 1992; Mullins, 1992) tends towards the normative model, and tends not to draw clear distinctions between human resource management and personnel management. To varying degrees, all of these texts interchange the terms as though they mean the same thing. The discussion being developed here aims to add to an understanding of the normative model by suggesting that service business objectives and the actual features of services being offered presents service organizations with contexts that may well shape and influence managers' perceptions of the 'problems of managing people' (Watson, 1986: 133).

Storey's 'hard' and 'soft' models reflect different emphasis and theoretical origins. The hard model suggests a 'utilitarian instrumentalism' (Legge, 1995: 66) given recent voice by the Michigan School and stresses the management of human resources as factors of production. The 'soft' model on the other hand reflects a 'developmental humanism' (Legge, 1995: 66) that emerged from the Harvard School and stresses the potential of people as a valuable resource. Certainly, the underlying rhetoric of our earlier studies of empowerment in hospitality operations has much in common with the soft model of HRM (Lashley and McGoldrick, 1994). It is also possible to detect approaches adopted within other organizations where the strategy is to 'treat labour as a variable input and a cost to be minimized' (Legge, 1995: 67). Firms operating in cost competitive markets, as many service sector operators, are typical of this approach. The adverse publicity about the use of variable contracts at a Burger King restaurant is typical (Bowcott, 1995). Having said that, there are numerous tensions within both hard and soft aspects of the model (Noon, 1992; Legge, 1995), and the distinction between hard and soft might be two rhetorics at work in the same situation (Watson, 1994). Certainly one manger whom I interviewed in my research with Harvester Restaurants talked about the approach as being based on 'hard love'. This matches with Legge's reference to 'tough love' (p. 88). The phrase suggests a preparedness to apply the hard perspective in controlling the labour cost, and exercise care in the management of the human resource. Indeed this merging of 'hard' and 'soft' is further evidenced in Harvester Restaurants (Ashness and Lashley, 1995) where employees will frequently decide to 'send someone home' when the business is quieter than anticipated. Here the 'hard' controls required by Burger King are delivered by 'soft' (committed?) employees themselves.

Guest (1987) has identified four key values or components of HRM – strategic integration of human resource and business strategies, employee commitment to organizational goals, numerical and functional flexibility of employees, and quality of product and service outputs. According to the normative model these core values then should inform organizational and job design, employee empowerment, recruitment and selection, training, appraisal, reward systems etc., as they apply within a given organization. For a more detailed outline of the cluster of policies which organizations 'should' adopt see Sissons (1994). However, it is possible to argue that within this normative framework different organizations will need to adopt different forms of empowerment to match these broader strategic needs.

That said, HRM as a distinctive approach expressed in normative terms has some major difficulties; it is informed by a unitary perspective of the organization, and it provides little by way of critical analysis within the employment relationship. Attempts to establish, through empirical research, its consistent and coherent application across industry have proved difficult to establish (Legge, 1995). Having said that, it is necessary to study the 'normative' model of HRM for several reasons. The normative model provides a model of expectations and aspirations for HRM on which to base any analysis of HRM and empowerment in practice. Thus it is necessary to establish what HRM 'should be like' before we study 'what HRM is or is not' in service organizations. Without this, analyses of initiatives in the management of people are in danger of treating HRM as that which is labelled HR, with little sense of the difference from that which was previously labelled personnel management.

A further reason for framing analysis in the normative model is that it does provide a managerial rhetoric that does guide, whether deliberate and planned or processual and pragmatic, the perceptions and actions of managers. In turn these actions shape the experiences of those who work in service industries, and is of sociological interest in the study of work. Particularly it provides the basis for critical evaluation of empowering initiatives introduced by management in service operations.

Finally, the normative model as expressed by writers in 'mainstream HRM' is flawed and limited in its analysis of industry in general and service industries specifically. The service encounter and the key role of front line staff, the recent emergence of a rhetoric espousing service quality as a now vital business strategy (Pannel Kerr Forster Associates, 1991), and the cluster of service features, particularly the role of intangibles, is largely ignored. For example, Legge's (1995) otherwise excellent book makes just sixteen references to service organizations and none at all to the hospitality industry, which employs 10 per cent of the UK workforce (Joint Hospitality Industry Congress, 1996). It is my view that a thorough analysis of service organizational HRM strategies can contribute to the wider debates about HRM by helping to establish a more rounded analysis of what HRM 'should be', against which to compare human resource management in practice. The following section argues that to understand the nature of fit between human resource management strategies, including the forms of empowerment, and wider business strategies, it is necessary to analyse the nature of the service offer to customers and the role of employee discretion in 'delighting the customer'.

The nature of services management

If one of the concerns of human resource management as an avowedly distinct means of dealing with the management of employees is the 'fit' with general business strategies, any normative model of HRM within services needs to explore those factors which are likely to shape the context of the 'fit'. Reflecting Purcell's (1987) hierarchy of strategies, the coherence of third-order strategies is of particular interest. How do human resource policies, including initiatives in empowerment, match with marketing policies in terms of the customer offer, and operational policies in terms of how goods and services are produced and delivered? Claims that services are distinctive when compared to manufacturing usually makes play of four features of services: intangibility; heterogeneity; perishability; and inseparability (Cowell, 1984). Whilst these features do present all service organizations with some specific difficulties, not all service firms are in the same position regarding these dimensions. As was shown earlier, different service organizations provide differing 'bundles' of service features and these impact on the nature of the operational management, marketing offer to customers and the way that front-line employees are managed, and consequently the best 'fit' for the forms of empowerment introduced.

Whilst the cluster of service features impact on the nature of the services offered, two dimensions have particular relevance to variations in the service offer and the organization of service operations. The intangible aspects of service and the heterogeneity of services pose difficulties for both customers and organizations supplying services to them. The intangible nature of service delivery makes it difficult for would-be customers to judge the nature of the service that will be provided prior to the receipt of the service. Many customers seek the security of prescribed expectations of branded services. The branded organization meets customers' security needs by making explicit what the service offer is and by delivering a standardized service consistent with customer expectations. At the same time many customers are looking for some confirmation of their individuality. To varying degrees many service customers object to mass produced services. Customer service wants therefore to represent a tension between fear of both the unpredictable and the anonymity of the standardized. The consequence of these tensions and dilemmas is that the key strategic drivers for many service organizations are tangibility/intangibility and the degree of heterogeneity, or standardization/customization, on the other. Figure 12.1 shows how these two continua intersect to produce four quadrants depicting four ideal types of service offer. The interplay of these two sets of influences impacts on operational, marketing and human resource management strategies (Lashley *et al.*, 1997).

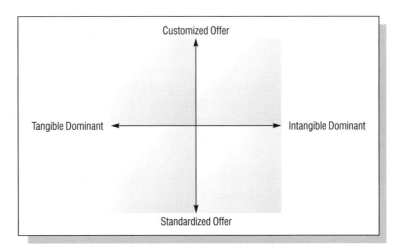

Figure 12.1 The degree of standardization and tangibility: the strategic drivers of the service offer

The management of front-line employees takes on a particular significance, because the intangible aspects of the offer are largely founded on employee performance and the interpersonal nature of their interactions adds a further dimension to the imprecision of the service encounter. Customer expectations and wants vary. Different customers have different expectations of the service situation and even the same customer may have different wants on different occasions (Rust and Oliver, 1994). Added to this, employees vary in their ability to predict and deliver customer satisfaction. The work of Bitner *et al.* (1990), discussed earlier, highlighted that the importance of the employee's reactions to various service situations was a powerful ingredient in determining service customer satisfaction or dissatisfaction.

The consequences of these variations and tensions, the difficulties of predictability and standardization together with the key role of front line staff create particular control difficulties with service organizations. Figure 12.2 represents these tensions and dilemmas. As was discussed earlier, service organizational policies can place service personnel in a difficult, if not stressful, position because they have to both ensure commercial, revenue and profits orientated organizational objectives, and at the same time meet customer service needs. Figure 12.2 indicates the 'three-cornered fight for control' frequently found in service situations (Shamir, 1980; Bateson, 1985).

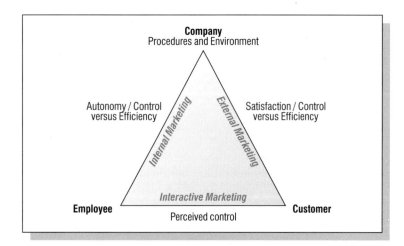

Figure 12.2 Control conflicts in the service encounter. *Source:* Adapted from Bateson (1985)

The consequence of these control tensions is that managers, in some operations, have to adopt different control strategies. The reality of the service situation is that it is not possible directly to control each interaction, and some control has to be reallocated to the employee. Empowerment can be a useful strategy in these circumstances because managers gain control by letting go of control.

The role of employees as 'boundary spanning' personnel in service organizations creates another feature of service management. The relationship between employees and customers, their significance in delivering the customer offer, and the amount of discretion that employees need to exercise in delivering customer satisfaction ensures considerable functional interdependence in service organizations. Typically, manufacturing based activities separate production from markets, both temporally and geographically. This is less possible in service situations. Services management require an interdependent relationship between service operations, services marketing and the management of employees. This relationship is represented in Figure 12.3.

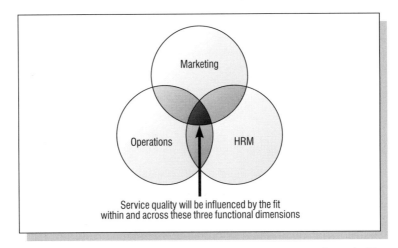

Figure 12.3 The functional interdependence of service delivery. *Source:* Lashley *et al.* (1997)

Heskett *et al.* (1990) link these together in the pursuit of truly world class business practice. Here the 'Strategic Service Vision' links the target market segment(s), the service concept, the service positioning, the operating strategies combining marketing, operational and human resource policies, and the service delivery system. Taking the classic traditional approach to strategy formation, and the subsequent cascaded policies in the management of people, the form of empowerment should be developed so as to match with the strategic objectives in relation to market positioning and the nature of the service offer. In particular, the role of employees in applying discretion in their delivery of customer satisfaction is likely to be key in determining the fit between the form of empowerment and these wider service issues.

Using the interplay of the key drivers of degrees of intangibility and standardization, it is possible to identify a number of different bundles of service, each representing a different set of market propositions and service offers to customers, different types of service operation and different approaches to the management of service employees. In each case it is possible to see how these elements interplay so as to establish a best fit between the management of marketing, service operations and people. Figure 12.4 suggests four different markets within services. Each represents a different configuration of the degrees of the tangibility/intangibility and standardization/customization. Each represents different bundles of attributes to the customer and requires different approaches to marketing the service.

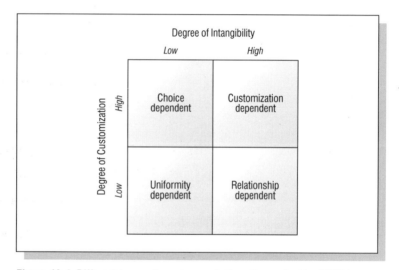

Figure 12.4 Different types of service marketing. *Source:* Lashley (2000b)

Uniformity dependent services are where the service delivered is highly standardized, involving a significant role for the tangible aspects of the service bundle. The quality of the rides and equipment in some leisure services, or the role of the food and drink in fast food operations are examples. Standardization is a key attribute, though bearing in mind Ritzer's (1993) observations, efficiency, calculability, predictability and control are dimensions of the attributes for customers. Within the case studies featured in this book, McDonald's Restaurants provides a clear example of a mass market service.

Choice dependent services are where services have many attributes in common with mass market services. The attraction is that of a branded offer that allows customers a reasonable chance to predict the outcome of the service interaction, but where there is sufficient variation with the service to meet some specialized customers' needs. To varying degrees the standardized formula is adjusted to individual customers, though the formula is such that customer segments are identifiable. Consequently, the customer has some sense of being given a personalized service, though within a framework of predictability. TGI Fridays is an organization with much in common with this marketing offer to customers.

The second two service market categories are more dependent on the intangible aspects of the service encounter, but represent variations in the degree to which the service received by customers is standardized or customized. *Relationship dependent* services represent fairly standardized service needs but require a more elaborate set of interactions with customers than in the more tangible driven mass market. Attributes to customers are met through the knowledge that there are likely to be few unexpected events, and branding helps to target specific benefits to customers. The service is more interaction focused and customer satisfaction is more dependent on the quality of the intangibles provided by front line employees. Harvester Restaurants and Marriott Hotels are examples of service operations that typify these services, and involved focused interaction based offers to target markets.

Customization dependent services are where services are highly customized to the individual customer's (client's) service needs. The attributes for the customer rest on the uncertainty of what the service need is in detail, but the security of knowing that the service organization can supply it. The service provider needs to develop a sense of trust, and reliability with customers. Business consultants provide examples of service providers in this category. Customers' needs are difficult to predict, and may require solutions across a wide array of needs.

Both Schmenner (1995) and Heskett *et al.* (1990) provide a matrix for identifying different processes in service operations management. In both cases they produce a four quadrant matrix by comparing the degree of customization and standardization in the service offer with a continuum relating to labour utilization. For Schmenner the key factor is the degree of labour intensity involved in the delivery of the service, whilst for Heskett *et al.*, the continuum considers the degree of customer contact required between employees and customers. Though approaching service operations management from slightly different viewpoints, the four types of service operations identified are remarkably similar to our own work which will be discussed in the next section. Figure 12.4 recasts the Schmenner model so as to better match the approach that we are attempting to build. That said, the types and terms used are unchanged.

By comparing the continua – degree of customization and the degree of labour intensity – four quadrants are produced by positions of high and low against the two continua. Each describes 'a reasonably distinct service process' (Schmenner, 1995: 11). *The service factory* represents service processes where there is low labour intensity and low customization (and thereby high standardization) of the service for customers. Fast food operations are typical of this operational type. *The service shop* involves a service delivery that requires more customization, but relatively low labour intensity. In other words, it may be difficult to predict individual customer needs, but when they are identified they involve relatively low labour intensity, or the application of one of a pre-arranged repertoire of actions by front-line staff. *Mass service* represents service processes which involve a relatively high degree of labour intensity, but with a limited amount of customization. Thus it is possible to predict customer service needs, but the nature of the service being delivered requires a fair amount of contact with staff. Finally, *professional services* are those in which there is a high degree of customization of the service to individual customer needs and a high degree of labour intensity.

These models by Schmenner and Heskett *et al.* are helpful in establishing types of service operational types that match with different marketing strategies for services. Most significantly they also impact on the management of human resources. They also

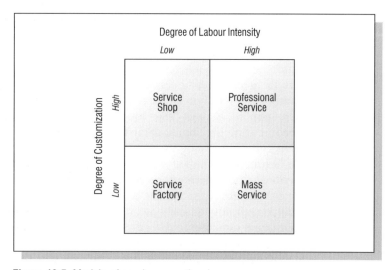

Figure 12.5 Models of service operational processes

Hospitality, Leisure & Tourism Series

establish a means by which firms might be graphically located at points within the quadrants. The tangible/intangible and standardization/customization drivers also create tasks that will require varying amounts of discretion to be exercised by employees in meeting customer service needs.

Service employee discretion

The previous section has shown that most services do involve to some degree issues related to tangibility/intangibility; heterogeneity/homogeneity; perishability; and separability/inseparability, but not all service firms provide services that are constrained by these factors in equal amounts. It has been argued that variations within tangibility and homogeneity have a key influence on variations in the service offer and thereby for the management of employees, and in the significance of employee judgement in predicting and delivering customer satisfaction. Any attempt to define a normative model for human resource management in services needs to take account of both the importance accorded by management to the discretion exercised by employees and variations the control of employee performance.

Where the service encounter is likely to be highly customized and largely intangible in its source of customer satisfaction, employees will be required to exercise a high degree of discretion in both interpreting and delivering customer service needs. In other cases the offer to customers may well be fairly standardized but requires a fair amount of contact between customers and employees, thus is intangible dominant. Here employees may need to exercise some discretion over the interpretation and delivery of the customer's intangible needs. In other services, the offer to customers is both highly standardized and tangible dominant. Here the employee typically exercises minimum discretion in fulfilling their duties. Operating systems are highly routine and designed to ensure the standardized service is delivered. In the final category, the offer is tangible dominant but there is a degree of customization round predictable requirements. Employees may need to exercise some discretion in interpreting customer service needs, or in performing the service act, but this is limited to reasonably well identified types of needs.

The amount of discretion to be exercised by employees raises the important issue of the control of employee performance. As has been shown earlier, services organizations are frequently managing tensions between standardization and customization. Customers want the security of a reliable brand, but do not want the anonymity of treatment that can accompany this approach. Organizations may want to control employee performance – so as to ensure commercial objectives, maintenance of the brand, quality targets, cost minimization and profits – but also allow employees autonomy to meet customer needs. Much of the literature on HRM stresses the broad choices open to management as being between concerns for controlling labour as a resource (hard) and gaining greater commitment from employees in increasingly competitive situations (soft). Whilst these models are helpful in suggesting that employment strategies may involve both commercial variation and managerial choice, a study of employment practices suggests that they are misleading for two reasons. Firstly, employment strategy in service organizations is concerned with *both* control and commitment. Given the nature of most service encounters within hospitality organizations, employee commitment to successful encounters 'should' under the normative model be of vital importance. This emphasis would be given further spin in situations where organizations are adopting a business strategy based on service quality. Given the sometimes contradictory nature of business objectives which stress the importance of 'delighting the customer' and maintaining the integrity of a branded concept, employees need to provide customer service within controls set by the organization. In these circumstances control and commitment are of equal importance, not two ends of a dichotomous scale. Figure 12.6 suggests that a range of control techniques are available to operators of services, and these techniques range along a continuum between exercising externally imposed managerial control over the employee and those which encourage employees to control their own behaviour by internalizing the objectives of the organization.

The second reason for suggesting that the control/commitment dichotomous scale is misleading is that it fails to recognize the importance of employee discretion as an element of job design crucial to an understanding of service delivery. As stated earlier, employee commitment to organizational objectives for service quality, fault detection, and operational improvements is as important to service operators as it is to their manufacturing counterparts, but in many operations employees have to be given discretion to make decisions about the service interaction. Front-line personnel in luxury hotels or in operations like TGI Fridays have, to varying degrees, to 'make it up as they go along'.

The amount of discretion to be exercised by employees, and the relative importance of tangible and intangible factors as sources of customer satisfaction, overlay the degree of standardization/customization of the service delivered and the forms of control to

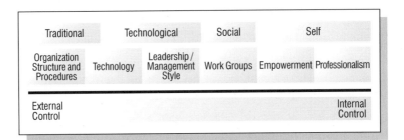

Figure 12.6 Variations in the locus of control of employees

provide a range of styles of human resource management which best 'fit' with different service processes.

The management of human resources

Thus far the model being developed has stated that the key drivers in service variation are in the degree of tangibility and standardization. These in turn create different types of service offers to customers, different types of service operation and different requirements for the amounts of discretion to be exercised by employees. These relationships are graphically displayed in Figure 12.7. This simple representation suggests that two continua are of particular inter-related significance in creating human resource management styles. Like the other models outlined above, the degree of standardization/customization of the service is important in determining much of what employees are required to do. However, the second influential factor is the form and locus of control of employee performance. These two continua create a matrix that identifies four key styles.

In *customization dependent services,* located in the top right hand quadrant, the strategy matches a highly customized service offer with a high degree of internal control by employees who also need to exercise a high level of discretion in their work. Traditional examples might be found in the 'professions' – medicine, accountants, consultants, lecturers, etc. This approach can be applied to other service deliverers but there appear to be few examples in the hospitality retail operations, for example.

The human resource strategy is based round employees exercising a high degree of discretion over their tasks, with responsible autonomy over the organization of work. There will be strong emphasis placed on selection and recruitment, with, in some cases, long periods of training as a means of both filtering entrants and ensuring internalization of appropriate values.

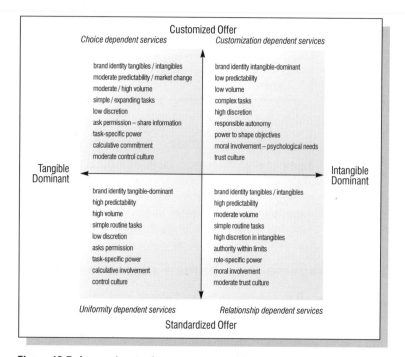

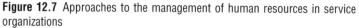

Figure 12.7 Approaches to the management of human resources in service organizations

There is no 'one best way' in undertaking tasks. Appraisal is linked to customer satisfaction, 'moral' commitment (Etzioni, 1961) in employees and leadership style that enables and facilitates employee performance. Employees are likely to be democratically involved and have power to influence the direction of policy above the immediate tasks.

The *relationship dependent service* occupies the lower right hand quadrant of Figure 12.7. It reflects the position where the customer offer is generally standardized, but the organization requires some degree of employee participation so as to meet customer service objectives because labour plays a key role in service delivery – mass service in Schmenner's model. The relationship between employees and customers assumes a major significance. Again internal controls will be most effective, because customer service is based in part on the speedy response to customer needs.

The human resource strategy involves low discretion over tasks. These are frequently standardized and based on 'one best way' of producing and serving the product. Training is simple and aimed at skills needed for narrowly defined tasks. Front line-staff have responsibility for customer service quality and have some discretion to respond to customer needs and complaints. Service values are provided to guide employees in their relationships with customers. Team working and team briefing may be a feature used to generate a sense of commitment and ownership by service workers. Often values based or role model training gives individuals guidance in how they are expected to act when situations are not easy to predict. Performance appraisal will consider customer satisfaction as measured by repeat business and complaints. Employee empowerment will be through participation, with opportunities to exercise authority and responsibility over task organization as well as service delivery.

The *uniformity dependent service* is located in the bottom left hand quadrant of Figure 12.7. It describes organizations that are providing highly standardized experiences to their customers and organize the management of human resources round a traditional approach that controls employee performance externally. The operational process is similar to Schmenner's service factory.

The human resource strategy involves low discretion for most employees. There will be limited responsible autonomy and most employees, even including managers, have their efforts closely supervised. Recruitment and selection is less important, because there is an emphasis on systems and 'one best way' of producing products. Service interactions will be trained and, in some cases, scripted. Employee appraisal will be based on performance of tasks against tightly defined standards, and linked to rewards. Managers will largely be concerned with monitoring the performance of subordinates so as to maintain adherence to predefined standards. Employee commitment will be largely based on calculative commitment (Etzioni, 1961). Employee empowerment will be limited because of the tight definition of the brand, and the limited opportunities for employees to exercise discretion. Initiatives will focus on empowerment through commitment to the service encounter and will involve some responsibility to deal with complaints.

The *choice dependent service* is located in the top left hand quadrant of Figure 12.7. It represents an approach that is customized in the intangible element of the customer offer, but is highly standardized in the tangible element. Employee performance is controlled through external processes as a means of ensuring the totality of the customer experience. Some discretion is exercised in matching the service expectation to the customer type. The service process closely matches Schmenner's service shop.

The human resource strategy involves some similar approaches to command and control styles. Systems define and shape the production process with little scope for discretion in the production process, though service interactions will require employees to spot performance types needed. Training for the production element is based on standard performance manuals and the skills relevant for the operation. Recruitment and selection is given high priority, particularly for service workers. These procedures involve the selection of individuals capable of giving the performance needed in the service interaction. Service workers have a degree of discretion in shaping the service encounter, but have limited responsible autonomy. Essentially this approach relies on gaining employee involvement and commitment to the service objectives with little power to influence decisions beyond this. Managers place high importance on the morale and motivation of employees, but remain in control of employee actions. Techniques may involve team briefings and suggestions aimed learning from employee experiences and ensuring employees understand organizational objectives. Employee empowerment is through involvement and is largely concerned with communication processes to ensure that the operation continues to be responsive to customer wants.

Whilst Figure 12.7 provides a simple outline of the styles that best fit with these service offers, marketing and operational management approaches, the relationship is somewhat more complex than the diagram suggests. Given the link with tangibles/intangibles, standardization/customization, and the level of discretion to be exercised by employees in meeting the customer service need, the relationships with the styles by which human resource management matches these variables is better

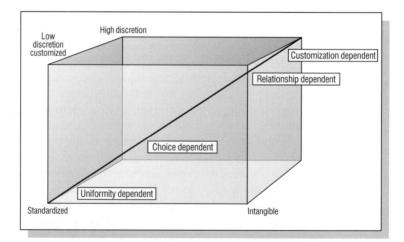

Figure 12.8 The management of human resource and key service characteristics

represented in Figure 12.8. Here the relationship with what employees have to do and the discretion that they exercise is shown to relate to the styles of managing people who deliver the service.

If the classical model of business strategy formulation and implementation is matched to the normative assumptions about HRM, managers will first decide on their broad service strategy – price, leadership, quality, availability. This in turn influences the nature of the service offered, particularly the tangibles and intangibles and degree of heterogeneity, which result in the offer to customers or brand features – customization/standardization, generalist/specialist, product/process. These features are then influential in the design of the service operation – the role and type of technology used; stages and complexity in the production process; stages and complexity in the service process; opportunities for economies of scale in production; quality definition and evaluation. Flowing then from these, the normative model suggests that human resource strategies are coherent with other strategies adopted by the firm; thus the job design including the amount of discretion exercised by the employees, the locus of control, the degree of responsible autonomy, recruitment and training, reward systems, appraisal of employee performance, organization structure, match with service characteristics, the marketing offer to customers and the nature of management operations.

The three case studies largely featured in this text do provide examples of service organizations that represent different service offers to customers and who do have approaches to the management of employees that seem to match the offers being made. McDonald's Restaurants Limited, is supplying a highly standardized service to its customers. The source of satisfaction is largely tangible driven, and linked to price leadership. Service operations closely match the service factory and people management is consistent with processes that deliver quality and product consistency by the application of 'one best way' job design and command and control approaches to people management. TGI Fridays represents a variation on the McDonald's approach. It is much more responsive to customer concerns for personalization of the service encounter. The brand itself is tightly focused at a well defined market segment, and within that identifiable types of service encounter where employees have to provide the appropriate service performance. The offer to customers involves mass customization and the operational process is typical of the service shop. The management of employees involves some elements of 'one best way' in the production of tangibles, but through close attention to recruitment and selection of employees and training, employees generate the required performances to meet customer needs. Harvester Restaurants made a decision to compete through the quality of its service encounter. The tangible product, like these other examples, is 'McDonaldized', the service encounter is also standardized and based on a simple set of interactions, but they require an employee performance that supports and delivers the 'homely' offer to customers. The offer is standardized but more intangible dominant. Customers are buying into a sense of British public house tradition, and employee performance requires an almost family style of relationship with customers. Treating customers as though they were 'guests in your own home' requires both a standardized approach but one which is also personalized to customers as individuals. Recruitment and selection therefore involves the recruitment of 'types' of employees who match these service relationships being marketed by the company.

These three case studies match each of three types of offer to customers and the associated operational, and human resource management approaches that fit. That said, these are not random cases studies; they were selected because they appeared to typify different approaches. The extent that they represent a consistency that is generally found in service firms is questionable and will require further work through the study of a wider range of organizations. In addition, whilst it has been possible to demonstrate fit in these three cases, there is no suggestion as to the causal link nor whether the management of employees was strategically designed to match the wider service features. Thus claims that human resource management is fundamentally strategic are not necessarily supported by these examples. Though it is possible that the senior managers recognize the symmetry involved and recognize a strategic role for human resource management, these approaches might equally evolve in a pragmatic way as grand 'strategic' approaches emerge as responses to short run problems.

Conclusion

This chapter has attempted to show that, under the normative model of the form of empowerment introduced into an organization, will be reflection of the wider business strategy under operation by the organization which will in turn structure the nature of the marketing offer being made to clients, the operational systems in place and the human resource strategies that best fit the organization's strategic choices. Under this analysis then, it is not surprising that empowerment is seen in different forms in different organizations. It is performing different roles and meeting different needs identified by different management teams.

Wider debate is needed in both the role, nature and development of business strategy in general and the role, nature and development of human resource management in particular. It has been argued that many of the contributions to these debates suffer from a limited view of organizational life in service organizations, where the nature of the service offer in some firms is such that employees need not only to be committed to the service objectives, but also have to apply their own discretion in anticipating customer needs and wants.

The chapter has provided an analysis of the key features of services and suggested how these both shape the constraints operating on service firms in general, and combine to influence the environment of individual firms differently. Using the variations in these features, this chapter has suggested that there might be four ideal types of HRM strategy matched to different combinations of service features. Professional, participative, command and control, and involvement styles all potentially represent different responses by mangers to the service features being offered to customers in their organization. Fundamentally, this chapter argues that researchers in the management of human resources within service operations need to reflect a wider range of debates about both business strategy and the nature of human resource management. That said, studies into the service industries can further inform these wider debates, because researchers in these mainstream debates frequently miss the specific context associated with service operations.

CHAPTER 13

Empowerment: another flash in the panaceas?

- **Inconsistencies and tensions**
- **Continuities of concern**
- **Management fads and panaceas**
- **Beyond the quick fix?**

In many ways employee empowerment has suffered from over-enthusiastic promotion by advocates and over-zealous application by practitioners. Advocates, frequently consultants or journalists, have tended to promote a simplistic and ill-defined notion of what employee empowerment means. They have tended to avoid any consideration of empowerment having different forms and meeting different organizational and employee needs. Similarly, there has been little consideration of the context or match most suited to particular situations. As we saw earlier, initiatives claiming to be empowering had much in common with initiatives that were called employee involvement or participation, and there were disagreements amongst commentators as to whether empowerment was associated with extending democracy, or not.

Practitioners, on the other hand have tended to adopt these simplistic versions of empowerment, with little attempt to identify what empowerment might deliver in a wider context. In some cases, initiatives have been half heartedly introduced, with little recognition of the full range of elements to be put in place, or most importantly with little consideration of the impacts of the initiative on the supposedly empowered. In some cases, managers have displayed a touching faith in the label empowerment – as though telling employees that they are now empowered was all that was needed to produce an array of organizational benefits.

Given this somewhat patchy record of promotion and adoption, it is perhaps not surprising that one commentator is reported as saying, 'Empowerment, in particular, has resulted in a perception by employees that their company has simply abdicated responsibility for their career development' (Dearlove, 1996: 4). Employee empowerment has all the hallmarks of a management fad, introduced in a blaze of unrealistic claims and expectations, which will be replaced by another 'quick fix' in the long term. That said, it need not be the case. Empowerment has much to offer service sector firms if it is carefully considered, matched to business needs, and fundamentally introduced in such a way that genuinely considered the impact on employee experiences and feelings.

This chapter aims to build a picture of the environment in which empowerment has became a popular management rhetoric by setting it within the context of the development of management fads. The chapter examines the factors that have represented barriers to the successful introduction of empowerment, not least of which are the pressures both within management and from consultants that lead to the introduction of initiatives that are likely to fail from the outset. Finally, the chapter suggests that employee empowerment might have positive benefits for both employees and employers, given a recognition of the ingredients necessary for its success – management commitment, and some stability in the short to medium term.

Inconsistencies and tensions

This text has argued that much of the comment on employee empowerment lacks precision and often attributes the same benefits and typologies to the same features to different forms of empowerment. Both critics and advocates alike tend to write about empowerment as though it means the same thing. As was shown earlier, the term has been used to describe individuals working within autonomous work groups, in job enriched work designs, quality circles, job enlarged work designs, and in circumstances where individuals had little or no control over their tasks but were encouraged to develop a sense of ownership and commitment to the organization's goals and offer to customers. I suggested that a more analytical framework reveals that these various arrangements have very different impacts on the relationships between employees and managers. To talk of employee empowerment in the form of an enriched job where all employees make decisions without recourse to a manager as being the same as quality circles where individuals representing employees as a whole make suggestions as to future actions and managers make the ultimate decision is unrealistic. Empowerment as a management technique is not universally the same thing. It may take forms that are participative, consultative or directive, and thereby involve a range of initiatives that need to be defined.

Even if it were possible to say that empowerment does have a clear and agreed meaning, there are some inconsistencies and tensions within the metaphor being created. A shared feature agreed by many writers is that empowerment is a management-led initiative. It is not being pushed by employee collectives or through trade unions. Although the rhetoric depends largely for its credence and acceptance as a democratic move, and some writers to claim it is about extending democracy (Bowen and Lawler, 1992), and it could encompass forms that empower individuals through their collective ownership of an individual enterprise, or through their collective control of organizational policies, these issues are not on the current agenda. Virtually all the forms of involvement that have been introduced under the banner of empowerment have been limited to task level arrangements, though in some cases there may be opportunities to make suggestions about issues that extend beyond the immediate task and workplace. Employees at Harvester Restaurants were able to make suggestions to the Team Manager at weekly team meetings, and quality circles can be required to make suggestions about non-task issues. As a solely inspired management initiative, empowerment then runs up against the issues that are fundamental to management techniques for the management of employees. To what extent can managers roll out these policies without resistance from, or at least the compliance of, the workforce? For that matter, to what extent do all managers share the concerns and agendas of senior management? To what extent are management policies consistent, giving the empowered clear and unambiguous

Hospitality, Leisure & Tourism Series

messages? The case studies by Cunningham and Hyman (1999), Proctor *et al.* (1999) and Holden (1999) all contain elements of these inconsistencies and describe failed attempts that might have been avoided had management thought through some of the issues more thoroughly.

Many of those who advocate empowerment insist that the empowered work within the boundaries set by management. The whole act of boundary setting can be a contentious issue in itself. Employees and managers may have different views of what is an appropriate boundary. There may be strong traditions within management to hang on to certain types of decisions. Middle managers in particular may have a vested interest in the existing location of authority and decision-making. For individuals who have followed a career path which has been structured on the hierarchical, with personal development and effort focused on progressing up the hierarchy, the removal of layers of management, perhaps their next promoted post, represents a major challenge to the very core personnel who will make the approach work or fail. The political impact of these decisions is rarely discussed. Both empowered employees and middle managers have to be convinced that the initiative will work in their interests and they have to support the arrangements introduced. It is difficult to see how individuals will generate the necessary levels of enthusiasm for changed working arrangements when they see themselves taking on extra tasks for no extra rewards, or where redundancies are taking place.

Another inconsistency related to these boundary setting aspects of empowerment is that the empowered's expectations of what is suitable as a working arrangement, and the extent to which they have their decision-making rights defined, may vary over time. There was a sense, coming from the interviews quoted in this text, that where employees were positive about the re-organization of work, it was because this was perceived to be an improvement on the traditional command and control of directive approaches. This too comes out clearly from the work of Kelly and Kelly (1990). It is possible to predict that, as expectations of appropriate management styles rise, employees will demand more participation and will want to see the boundaries extended to include non-task dimensions. Thus it is possible that empowerment will lead to demands for more empowerment. The notion that empowerment may be *dynamic* is rarely discussed in the essentially apolitical aspirations and pronouncements on empowerment.

It has been argued here that empowerment of employees has particular attractions for service sector firms. Service organizations face some difficult dilemmas and issues relating to the definition and delivery of service quality. Customers also face some difficulties in defining their expectations of service. In both cases, the growth of branded services has helped customers and organizations to develop a predictable offer and delivery of service. The enormous success of McDonald's Restaurants and other 'McDonaldized' services (Ritzer, 1993) has in large part been due to the development of standardized offers that extend predictability, control and calculability for customers and service organizations. In these organizations, employee performance has been also standardized through the use of 'one best way' job design, rigorous training and performance appraisal based on ensuring standardized employee performance – even to the extent of scripting employees in their conversations with customers. The problem with this approach is that it cannot be applied to all service markets. As the demand for services has grown, the market has segmented; many customers want the security of a brand, but also the personalized service encounter that helps them to feel important as individuals. To varying degrees, brand offers to customers require employees to be more flexible in their interpretation of customer needs, and the 'McDonaldized' approach has its limits. Employee empowerment and other techniques such as total quality management seem to offer the chance to manage employees that will both deliver the necessary service flexibility to customers yet remain within the commercial objectives of the organization.

This ambition for empowerment can expose the inconsistencies in the organization's offer to customers. Often the brand is tightly defined and although the organization instructs empowered employees to 'treat customers as though they were guests in your own home', the realities are that the organization has a commercial relationship with its 'guests' and this produces a number of tensions and feelings that the service employee has to manage.

The service brand requires for its success consistency and standardization so the customers know what to expect and are not confused by different experiences in different branches of the business. Staff are encouraged to 'delight' customers by producing service above the level of customer expectations. Several of the vignettes used by Marriott Hotels in their advertising campaign stress how empowered employees produce extra service to customers, but to what extent does this then shape a new set of expectations? Hubrecht and Teare's (1993) example of the hotel room attendant who washes the customer's clothing overnight, rather than tell the guest the laundry is closed, provides a useful example. The employee may have delighted the customer, but is the experience going to raise the customer's expectations, only to be let down at the next hotel in the chain, because the employee does not respond in the same way? One of the tensions in empowering employees is, therefore, in the loss of control of the service offer. Where employees interpret customer needs, there is scope for wide variation that runs contrary to both the expectations of customers and the control needs of the organization's senior managers. This latter point needs to be developed further. Freedom to deal with customer complaints, or to meet customers' special service needs through doing 'whatever it takes', can result in employees incurring costs which are both difficult to predict and control. Bowen and Lawler (1992) provide an amusing example. A doorman at a US hotel noticed that a customer had left a briefcase behind. The doorman, fired with empowered enthusiasm, followed the customer to the airport and on discovering the person had already flown out, followed him on the next plane. The customer was no doubt delighted, but one wonders about the reaction of the hotel's accountant, faced with these additional costs.

A third tension that the service employees have to manage in relation to customers is in the potential conflicts between customer service needs and commercial objectives. In some cases, the pace at which customers use the service may conflict with the organization's need to maximize revenue within a given set of assets. Thus customers may wish to linger over the service, whilst the commercial imperative is to encourage customers leave as quickly as possible so that new customers can be served. Restaurants provide a good example, where employees frequently have to manage the conflicting needs of customer and organization. In addition, there is clearly a tension between the number of employees on duty and the labour costs incurred. More staff may provide prompt service, reduce waiting time and ensure employees can spend the appropriate amount of time with each customer. Fewer employees on duty may increase customer waiting time, but increase operating profits by reducing labour costs. Operational management and immediate service employees may have to manage this tension. Both TGI Friday kitchen staff and Harvester Restaurants staff had a material interest in limiting the number of employees on duty, because it meant that bonuses (TGI Fridays) and tips (Harvester) were shared between fewer employees. In order to maximize their own incomes, employees potentially reduce service to customers.

This raises another key contradiction in the supposed workings of empowerment. Most advocates agree that one of the benefits of empowerment is the development of a more committed workforce. The problem is that the mechanism through which the empowered become more committed is ill defined and poorly conceived. Firstly, empowerment is said to require a committed workforce working in a trust culture (Barbee and Bott, 1991; Sternberg, 1992). If these ingredients are missing the introduction of empowerment results in barriers to the acceptance of the initiative amongst employees and managers. A second problem with the link between empowerment and commitment is that what it is employees are to be committed to is treated as unproblematic. As we have seen, service employees are being told to be committed to the customer. This can create tensions in the empowered employee as the employee has to manage a situation where their commitment to the customer may be contradictory to the commitment to the organization. The presence of tips, or non-material and relationship-based rewards, present outcomes that challenge the rewards coming from the employment relationship. Service employees have inter-personal relationships with their customers as a consequence of the human nature of the contact between the two. Creating situations in which customers leave the premises happy may be a source of satisfaction to some employees, which occurs in spite of the employment relationship and the organization. Empowered employees may therefore have personal interests in making customers happy at the expense of organizational policies and goals.

The advocates of empowerment suggest that this is the key management approach for the future. Service sector organizations have been told that empowerment of employees has particular relevance, because it enables the employee to meet customer service needs within the framework of policies set down by the organization's senior managers. These claims are seen to be somewhat overstated because there are some important inconsistencies and tensions within the 'model'. The generic nature of the term makes precision difficult because the empowerment seems to span a range of different forms and managerial intentions. In addition, the inconsistencies relating to the empowerment of individuals within a service brand create a number of contradictions and tensions that employees have to manage and which must create difficulties for consistency and control when employees interpret customer needs.

Finally the relationship between empowerment and employee commitment is difficult and ill defined. That said, empowerment has clearly caught the managerial imagination. Empowerment can be seen to both reflect a continuity of manager concerns and a modernity and currency that seems to produce new answers to older employee management problems.

Continuities of concern

Employee empowerment, like several initiatives in the field of human resource management (Legge, 1995), represented an expression of continuity and change in employer concerns about their relationship with employees. Where previous concerns had been about challenges to management from employee collectives (Brown, 1992), current managerial concerns are expressed in terms of winning greater employee commitment as a means of facing competition from other organizations. Taking empowerment as exemplifying 'high performance management' or 'high commitment management', there is a general message to employers that these practices will result in employees exercising discretion and developing commitment to the organization and its goals. Empowerment is an approach that fits comfortably with current widely argued approaches to business management that say that competitive advantage can be gained from close attention to employee development and management practices that recognize the unique contribution that employees make to business success.

Previous interest in employee consultation and participation had been advocated as a means of ameliorating employee dissatisfaction by a range of devices that involved employees in making some decisions, or at the very least commenting on management policy and objectives. Advocates were critical of the organization and management structures within Western firms and suggested that the wave of strikes and industrial conflicts in the late 1960s and early 1970s were due to alienating job design and overly directive decision-making procedures. Brown says, 'The ways in which work was organized, and the assumptions which underlay the design of many jobs, were seen as issues of practical importance as well as theoretical interest' (1992: 173). Job rotation, job enlargement and job enrichment were stressed as techniques for dealing with job design said to be repetitive, narrow and requiring limited employee discretion. Autonomous work teams and participative supervisor styles were also widely held to be appropriate ways of generating employee satisfaction. In addition, 'Industrial democracy, and greater opportunities for worker participation in decision making were also advocated as solutions to the *crisis* during the period' (Brown, 1992: 173). At the organization level, employee directors, joint consultation committees, works councils and extended collective bargaining all had their adherents and advocates as ways of dealing with organizational decision-making which would go some way to reflecting employee concerns and interests (Brown, 1992).

Using the model of analysis introduced by Tannenbaum and Schmidt (1973) and Marchington *et al.* (1992), it is possible to see that there is a limit to the forms of the relationship between employees and managers. The broad thrust of the way managers and employees work will be variations of a theme of directive, consultative and participative forms. There will be limits to the levels at which any involvement takes place, the range of issues to be included in the involvement and the power of employees to make their decisions stick. It is not surprising, therefore, that current concerns to win greater commitment from employees should turn to the array of forms that have been featured in earlier periods. Nor is it surprising that some commentators have suggested that empowerment is 'old wine in new bottles' (Lawler, 1986). In many ways employee empowerment has all the hallmarks of another management 'fad' or 'flavour of the month', but that also displays a continuity of concern to control and predict employee performance.

Braverman (1974) saw scientific management as a key development in the control of employee performance in manufacturing situations, which was then being applied to office work and other services. Certainly it is possible to identify much of Taylor's thinking in the processes employed by many fast food and themed restaurants. Indeed, we have seen 'one best way' approaches to much of the tangible, and significant aspects of the intangible, offer to customers. Despite the success of these highly standardized services, and the extension of the approach even to professional services, there are limits to the extent that this can be applied within all services. The difficulties of predicting and routinizing all services shows that some services require a different approach to managing employees. Like Braverman, Ritzer (1993) tends to stress a single trend within the management of services. The 'McDonaldization of society', though covering a wider set of issues, does share the assumption that there is just one approach to controlling employees.

This text has argued that there are a number of approaches that employers can take. The problem facing all employers is that the act of employment does not guarantee performance. In service industries the face-to-face relationship with customers adds another dimension to an old problem. Employers need to control service employee efforts in a way that allows them to exercise discretion, as well as to adapt to changing and unpredictable service needs. Empowerment offers a technique that gives employees the necessary status, autonomy and responsibility, but it is, in many ways, a reflection of approaches that were identified by Friedman (1977) as 'responsible autonomy'. Chiefly concerned with revealing alternatives to the

Hospitality, Leisure & Tourism Series

control of employee performance through responsible autonomy, it was an approach to the management of employees whose performance was central to the firm's long-term profits. Implicit in Friedman's notions of direct control and responsible autonomy for the control of employee performance is that each is applied to different elements of the labour market. Peripheral workers are subject to direct control, whilst core workers have responsible autonomy. Interestingly, many service industries have displayed many of the features of peripheral labour markets, with numerical flexibility, low skill, high labour turnover, etc. The recent emphasis on service quality and the significance of employee performance has been to raise the status of service employees in some organizations to that of core labour, essential for the organization's profitability.

Though employee empowerment in its participative form displays many similarities in common with the approaches identified as responsible autonomy, I have argued earlier that empowerment takes a range of forms and approaches to the management of employee performance that are best understood as representing a continuum between external (direct) control and internal (self) control. Friedman's responsible autonomy is located towards the internal end of the control of the continuum. Edwards' (1979) simple, technical and bureaucratic controls also fit within this continuum. Edwards does suggest that these approaches to employee control relate to different types of market situations in which organizations are trading. Though not quite matching with Edwards's analysis, I have suggested that different service offers to customers require the exercise of different degrees of employee discretion. Thus the nature of what employees need to do to necessitates different approaches to the control of employee performance.

Within the service sector, employee resistance to management has rarely taken a collective, trade union organized form. Resistance has been typically at an individual level, with employees working to their own agendas – either to develop extra service to customers because it gave them a source of job satisfaction, or to withdraw the levels of attention and emotional management needed for successful service encounters. In either case, the organization is faced with employee resistance to its policies and offer to customers. The direct control of the production line (command and control) approach has been an attempt to manage this and employees may be monitored to see if physical performance is as laid down and that their 'smile is genuine', but as we have seen, this approach has its limits, and there is a recognition that there is a need to employ more indirect control of employees.

Blyton and Turnbull (1994) claim that employers over the last decade have been persistent in their 'attempt to reconstruct forms of control and develop a new employee relations style' (p. 298). They point to trends in collective bargaining, approaches to trade unions, increased communication with the workforce, and in forms of consultation which tended to side-step employee collectives. These trends are also matched with continuities. It is possible to detect organizations that continue to conduct their employee relations in ways that are stable and relatively slow to change. Blyton and Turnbull also suggest that a more fundamental source of continuity is 'the persistence of a pragmatic and opportunistic approach to employee relations which elicits compliance rather than commitment' (1994: 299).

Within the service sector there appears to be complexity confirming different trends and directions in the approach to the management of employee relations. As stated above, this remodelling of employee relations has not been primarily concerned with the collective opposition of employees and the challenge to a management authority supposedly posed by trade unions; the need to control employee performance has been none the less real. The need to ensure that employee performance matches organizational commercial objectives, as expressed through the offer to customers, has been a common concern amongst many branded service firms. Ritzer's (1993) suggestions of McDonaldization to some extent bear witness to the process. In many cases, UK firms have borrowed approaches to the management of services from US origin firms that in turn used the concepts of scientific management to inform their approach.

Whilst these trends in the direct control of service employees' performance have been very influential, they do have their limits, even within their own markets, and have limited uses in other more difficult to predict service markets. Here it is possible to see the complexity of patterns of employee control with services. Some tendencies include deskilling, the extreme division of labour and detailed control of job content by the employer. Others are concerned with giving employees the flexibility and autonomy to meet customer needs. The case studies used earlier as exemplars show how firms can alter their approaches to the management and control of employees in different circumstances.

The model developed through observations of these cases and outlined in Chapter 12 implies that managers have a rational understanding of the part employees need to play in the delivery of the service to customers, and there is a conscious attempt to match the forms of empowerment to fit other business strategies.

The model also assumes that managers also believe, and act upon, the rhetoric that suggests 'employees are our most important asset'. That said, the extent to which managers address a strategy for the control of employees, in a systematic and carefully planned manner, is doubtful. None of the managers interviewed in these studies made these links directly, nor have any of the other managers with whom I have contact presented a clear and unambiguous vision of the links between employee discretion, forms of empowerment, and general employment policies designed to deliver a skilled and motivated workforce. Indeed there is rarely any consideration of the perceptions of employees and the detailed policies that meet their needs for stable jobs, good pay and styles of management that allows employees a say in the decisions which affect them. In the main, the link between employee costs and profits still seems to dominate service industry management concerns. A consultant recently quoted in *The New Innkeeper* (January, 1997) sums up many of these thoughts, 'If you pay staff £3.25 per hour and manage to save one staff hour a day over a year, this will increase net profit by £1,186. If you operate on 12% net profit, to achieve the same profit through sales would require an extra take of £11,615.' (p. 3). The impact of having one hour taken away from the employee in question is not taken as a significant issue in the calculation.

The current interest in empowering of employees represents a continuity of interests and concerns by practitioners and commentators. The concern to ensure predictable employee performance, levels and quality of output remains a key issue. Empowerment brings together a range of initiatives known by some as 'quality of work life initiatives' and the recognition that some employees require 'responsible autonomy'. In some organizations the service offer requires alternatives to traditional directive forms of control. In addition it seems to offer service organizational managers a chance to 'square the circle' by giving the employees more satisfying work whilst at the same time meeting commercial objectives. The lack of precision and detailed concerns for the impact of employer actions on employee motivation also represents a continuity in the employment relationship. In many ways employee empowerment looks like the latest in a long line of management fads and 'flavours of the month' that regularly reinvent the same ideas.

Management fads and panaceas

Whilst it is possible to detect the underlying continuity of ideas that support employee empowerment is not necessarily a

Hospitality, Leisure & Tourism Series

monolithic unified concept, empowerment is in fact linked with a number of ideas for the management of organizations. Together with an array of approaches, empowerment has been 'the battle cry of Britain's boardrooms of the 1990s' (Pandya, 1996), associated with team working, total quality management, and customer care, (Keenoy, 1994), as well as delayering, business process re-engineering, down-sizing and right-sizing (Caulkin, 1995, 1996; Dearlove, 1996; Pandya, 1996). In each case, the cluster of techniques have been chosen by management journalists as examples of management fads, 'flavours of the month' or 'management buzzwords'. Criticism of empowerment itself has fallen into either guilt by association with these other fads or into vague and anecdotal phrases about the impact of empowerment on employee attitudes. The impact of business process re-engineering, delayering and 'down-sizing' have come in for criticism for not delivering the benefits that were supposed to ensue. Pandya reports that, in a study of 1000 US firms that had gone through some form of down-sizing, fewer than 25 per cent reported an increase in the return on investment to shareholders. Similarly, business process re-engineering is a concept that has also failed to deliver the benefits that managers expected. Specifically empowerment is accused of resulting in employees 'having to do more for less' (Caulkin, 1996: 8), or 'working harder and longer hours for the same pay' (Pandya, 1996: 17), or 'developing a perception that employers have abdicated responsibility for career development' (Dearlove, 1996: 4).

The critics of empowerment frequently fall into the same modes of discussion as evangelical advocates. They fail to define what empowerment means, nor do they consider that forms are likely to involve different benefits and limitation to employees and employers. Empowerment can deliver genuine improvements in the workplace experience of employees. Being able to make decisions, or complete tasks in the way they seem fit without recourse to a supervisor, can be an improvement on traditional structures where employees are treated as having little to contribute other than their labour. In other cases, initiatives that claim to be empowering have paid little attention to the experiences and motivations of the supposedly empowered. A consequence has been that writers on empowerment have rarely considered whether the empowered have developed a sense of personal efficacy, nor have they recognized the need to consider how employees will become motivated by the change. Despite all the hype, empowerment has not brought a resolution of the tension faced by management, namely how to control employees and at the same time motivate them.

In many ways, the initial advocacy and subsequent criticism of empowerment reveals much in common with other trends, fashions and fads in management thinking. Huczynski (1993) says that despite the high volume of outputs on management, these ideas can be organized into six key families. 'Virtually all of the management fads that have been developed over the last hundred years are based upon these six families of management ideas' (p. 445). The rhetoric of empowerment plays an important part in several different current strands in management literature.

The precise contribution made by employee empowerment is rarely articulated. In many ways this lack of articulation and vagueness explains its appeal and utility to a variety of ideas and suggestions for improvements in organizational effectiveness. Managers of service sector organizations have perceived the need to engage the employee in mutual enthusiasm for delighting the organization's customers. The link between empowerment and total quality management is strongly pressed, and advocates have held employee empowerment up as the ideal adjunct to total quality management. Through empowerment the organization has a technique through which employee commitment can be generated, together with a mechanism for enabling employees to be involved in making suggestions that improve performance and to participate in those task-level decisions that will meet customer service needs.

A second stream to the enthusiasm for empowerment has related to initiatives that are aimed at the management structure. The advocates of 'delayering' or business process re-engineering also look to empowerment as a technique that can deliver the necessary coverage of managerial tasks at subordinate levels within the organization. Empowerment provides a means as both a technique and a rhetoric through which to manage the removal of tiers of management. As a technique, empowerment can assist managers in reformulating the responsibilities and authority distributed through the organization as a way of taking out levels of management that were thought to create barriers between senior managers and customers. As a rhetoric empowerment can be used as a way of justifying and explaining these changes. Thus the newly empowered subordinate is persuaded to regard the change as developmental and beneficial, rather than as intensifying their work through added accountabilities.

As we have seen in some of the specific cases study examples featured earlier, many of the initiatives introduced have links, in the current phase, to the work of Peters and Waterman (1982). Advice to organizations which, amongst other things, prioritized employee commitment, organization culture, customer orientation, and simple organization structures that eliminated bureaucratic controls on the ability to meet customer needs, underpins many of the initiatives that also incorporate an advocacy of empowerment. Guest's (1995) critical essay on the impact of *In Search of Excellence* states that the work has been responsible for 'spawning a number of other books, as well as research, consultancy and even a new managerial vocabulary' (1995: 5). The book became, in the 1980s, and still is in many ways, essential reading for managers, consultants and educators. Certainly, it held major influential sway over the later 1980s and early 1990s. Yet analysis of the research methods and conceptual model behind Peters and Waterman's text shows that it was poorly researched and raises questions as to how far their work should be 'treated as serious social science' (Guest, 1995).

Guest suggests that the success of *In Search of Excellence* might be explained in the nature of its message and the ease with which the message could be absorbed. The basic message, which emphasized, 'a shift in focus from the hard s's' of strategy and structure, to the soft s's' of style, system, staff, skills, and shared values' (Guest 1995: 10), represented a view that tells managers their intuitive judgements, particularly about people, are valid and essential for success. Watson (1996) makes a more general point about management education in general.

'Many of the myths, rituals and symbols of the managerial world serve to comfort managers as they face the confusions, moral uncertainties and ontological insecurities of a type of work which is based on the questionable assumption that they can readily shape, influence and indeed, control the thoughts and activities of other human beings' (1996: 463).

Huczynski (1993) reminds us of the post-1945 history management ideas. Apart from the identification of the endurance of the six families of management ideas, he suggests that these have produced four main techniques or solutions to business problems. Empowerment in its broadest sense can be seen to involve several enduring management ideas and up to three techniques. Many of the ideas underpinning empowerment link back to human relations, neo-human relations and management guru families of management ideas, and the solutions and techniques suggested encompass structural, employee and customer-focused classes of solution. Empowerment and the inter-links made with other techniques has the benefit for managers as having a familiarity, and linked to prior knowledge which, though now known by another name, requires little by way of conceptual development. Managers already understand the management theories behind the concept, they have familiarity with the solutions and techniques. As with the writings of Peters and Waterman, the lack of empowerment has been an easy concept for senior managers to understand, and the lack of precision in the meaning of empowerment has enabled managers to match their own meanings to perceived business problems – quality, bureaucracy, employee commitment, competitive advantage.

The future of empowerment as a management technique for service organizations will depend on senior managers' concerns and priorities. As we have seen, many commentators are suggesting that it has failed to deliver supposed benefits, and organizations are moving away from the techniques which incorporated employee empowerment. It may be that empowerment will be just another fad in the long history of management ideas and fashions. Along with management by objectives, management by walking about, transaction analysis, etc., empowerment may be replaced by yet another 'quick fix solution' that will persuade organizations and individual managers that their answer to their problems lies in this 'new approach'. Certainly Huczynski (1993) suggests that there are processes involved in modern organizations that make this pursuit of the latest fashion almost inevitable.

Supposedly 'new' management techniques help the organization's senior managers to create an environment in which middle and junior managers, and employees, are persuaded to support the organization's commercial objectives by seemingly new and innovative approaches – they relieve the boredom. As individuals, managers also have an interest in picking up and introducing new ideas and techniques. The new techniques enable individual managers to establish a name as a 'man (woman) with ideas', someone on the leading edge of the latest thinking. If there are processes within organizations which, together with individual managers' concerns, lead to a willing demand for 'new fads', then consultants are only too willing to act as eager suppliers. Huyczinski (1993) suggests that the collusion between those demanding 'new' ideas and those supplying the latest management technique leads to a typical pattern being established. The technique is first developed by a number of advocates who focus on some examples of the successful applications of the approach. A later wave of advocates try out variations of the techniques, or conduct studies where the approach is successful. After a while, critical voices are raised as the inevitable backlash sets in, and people question the value of the technique. Frequently, both advocates and critics conduct the debate without the benefit of evidence or data. Finally, a new technique comes along and the cycle is repeated.

Thus it is possible to predict that empowerment will ultimately fall victim to what Dearlove (1996) described as 'serial fad surfing' and will be replaced by yet another technique that will claim to provide managers with the answer to their problems. Whilst this pattern is predictable, it need not be inevitable, particularly if managers reflect on the potential benefits that empowerment can bring. Watson (1994b) points to the role of different management ideas in helping managers make sense of their position in the organization. Specifically, 'The concept of empowerment, for example, was seen by some managers as helping them articulate and put into practice certain personal values which they held with regard to how someone *in charge* of other human beings should relate to those people' (1994b: 904). From an organizational perspective, empowerment can provide benefits in the delivery of improved service quality, provided that the organization concerned develops a realistic understanding of what empowerment is and the precise applications that match with other organizational objectives.

Beyond the quick fix?

Managers of service organizations face some difficult dilemmas, which they attempt to manage. Whatever the precise term used to describe the approach, certain relationships with employees can be predicted. It is the relationship between the organization, its customers and employees that creates the context in which different techniques for the management of employees can be matched to wider business objectives. There is a limited array of possibilities and 'empowerment' is best located both within a range of approaches that are part of management traditions and a new variation on these themes. In particular, the link between employee empowerment and the development of a sense of personal efficacy is a new aspect of approaches that have much in common with consultative and participative styles of management. Blyton and Turnbull (1994) refer to these trends in management thinking as following a spiral pattern, representing ideas and trends being cyclical, yet not quite. This is a useful metaphor because it suggests that there is a complex relationship between the continuity of organizational concerns, and the variations and uncertainties that create new problems and uncertainties.

Cutting through the language and jargon, service organizations, particularly branded service organizations, frequently have to provide customers with standardized and predictable experiences which, at the same time, meet the customer's aspirations for a personalized experience. The control of employee performance requires the balance of a number of conflicting tensions. Employees need to be controlled so as to deliver the standardized aspect of the customer expectation, but allowed sufficient discretion to meet customer needs. Employee performance has to be controlled so as to minimize costs and maximize sales and profits, but employees need to be committed to the organization. Empowerment, for all its shortcomings and contradictions, does seem to offer service organizations an ideology and a set of techniques which suggest that management can control these tensions.

To be effective in these terms, however, empowerment in service organizations needs to be consistently applied. First, organizations must define the link between service delivery and the discretion to be applied by service employees. The discretion to be exercised by employees must match with the form of empowerment employed. Boundaries set should be realistic and represent an appropriate shift in the working arrangements being used in the delivery of the service. Fundamentally, the impact of these changes on the empowered is of key importance. The development of a sense of personal efficacy, and the willing support of the empowered to the changes, are crucial to its success. Involvement in the design and delivery of the changes, agreement about the boundaries within which the empowered work, and the rewards to be gained from changed working relationships, have to be agreed with the active participation of the empowered. Associated with this, the support needed by employees both in managing the change in their role and in being effective in the role has to be carefully managed and delivered. Once the system is up and running, employee performance needs continued support and feedback from managers who assist employees in developing their efficacy and removing barriers to its development.

All this suggests that senior managers of service organizations need to make some far-reaching changes in their ideologies and expectations of subordinates. On an ideological level, service organizations need to recognize employees as a key resource for commercial success. This has to be applied with consistency and vigour. If the organization is to move beyond achieving mere compliance to a position of building genuine employee commitment, the organization has to adopt employment policies that treat employees as though they were 'the most important asset'. In particular, employee reward packages, and promotion and development schemes need to be based on employee rather than managerial expectations. This assumes a more sophisticated set of procedures for consulting and making decisions with employees than are currently practised in most service organizations.

Above all organizations who follow the empowerment path need to take a long term view and evaluate benefits and gains using a wide array of performance measures which extend beyond commercial indicators. Employee and customer measures of organization success have to be brought in to consideration. Of course the extent to which this is possible in organizations 'twist round the spiral of capitalist economic development' (Blyton and Turnbull, 1994) may be questionable. When push comes to shove, service organizations are directly or indirectly commercially driven, and there are commercial, competitive and environmental pressures that managers are not able to control. Discussing the tensions between managers' need to control events, Watson (1994) says, 'Yet, in the reality of a world which is fickle and unpredictable, there is little opportunity for them readily to experience a sense of actually being in control of circumstances' (p. 904).

In these circumstances, whatever the name chosen, managers will look for techniques that vary the forms of control on employees. If employee empowerment is to have a future as a management technique it will need to be consistently applied and meet an array of manager, employee and customer aspirations. Service organizations will need to have a realistic set of expectations of what empowerment is and what it can deliver, its weakness and tensions as a technique, the circumstances necessary to make it work and the needs of employees.

References

Adelmann, M.B., Ahavia, A. and Goodwin, C. (1994) Beyond Smiling: social support and service quality. In Rust, R.T. and Oliver, R.L. (eds) *Service Quality: new directions in theory and practice*. London: Sage.

Ahanotu, N.D. (1998) Empowerment and production work: a knowledge based perspective. *Empowerment in Organizations*, Vol. 6, No. 7, pp. 59–67.

Alpander, G. (1991) Developing Managers' Ability to Empower Employees. *Journal of Management*, Vol. 10, pp. 13–24.

Anthony, P.D. (1990) The paradox of the management of culture, or 'he who leads is lost'. *Personnel Review*, Vol. 19, No. 4, pp. 3–8.

Antonacopoulou, E. and Kanampully, J. (2000) Alchemy: the transformation of service excellence. *The Learning Organization*, Vol. 7, No. 1, pp. 13–23.

Armstrong, A. (1987) Human Resource Management: the case of the emperor's new clothes? *Personnel Management*, Vol. 19, No. 8, pp. 30–5.

Ashness, D. and Lashley, C. (1995) Empowering service workers at Harvester Restaurants. *Personnel Review*, Vol. 24, No. 8, pp. 17–32.

Attaran, M. and Nguyen, T.T. (1999) Design and implementation of self-directed process teams. *Management Decision,* Vol. 37, No. 7, pp. 1–8.

Bach, S. and Sissons, K. (2000) Personnel Management in Perspective. In Bach, S. and Sisson, K. (eds) *Personnel Management: a comprehensive guide to theory and practice.* Oxford: Blackwell.

Baddon, L., Hunter. L., Hyman, J., Leopold, J. and Ramsay, H. (1989) *People's Capitalism? A critical analysis of profit sharing and share ownership.* London: Routledge.

Balmer, S. and Baum, T. (1993) Applying Herzberg's Hygiene Factors to the Changing Accommodation Environment. *International Journal of Contemporary Hospitality Management,* Vol. 5, No. 2.

Ball, S. and Johnson, K. (2000) Humour in commercial hospitality settings. In Lashley, C. and Morrison, A. (eds) *In Search of Hospitality: theoretical perspectives and debates.* Oxford: Butterworth-Heinemann.

Bandura, A. (1977) Self-efficacy: Towards a unifying theory of behavioural change. *Psychological Review,* Vol. 84, pp. 191–215.

Bandura, A. (1986) *Social foundations of thought and action: A social-cognitive view.* Englewood Cliffs, NJ: Prentice Hall.

Barbee, C. and Bott, V. (1991) Customer treatment as a mirror of employee treatment. *Advanced Management Journal,* Vol. 5, p. 27.

Barker, J. (1993) Tightening the Iron Cage: Concertive Control in Self-Managing Teams. *Management Science Quarterly,* Vol. 38, pp. 408–37.

Barry, T. (1993) Empowerment: The US Experience. *Empowerment in Organisations,* Vol. 1, No. 1.

Basset, P. (1996) Stakeholder economy at work. *The Times,* 21 January, p. 38.

Bassett, P. (1986) *Strike Free: New Industrial Relations in Britain.* London: Macmillan.

Bateson, J.G. (1985) Perceived control and the service encounter. In Czepiel, J.A., Solomon, M.R. and Superenant, C.F. (eds) *The Service Encounter.* Boston, MA: Lexington.

Becker, B.E., Huselid, M.A., Pickbus, P.S. and Spratt, M.F. (1996) Crisis and Opportunity: the Two Faces of Human Resource Management in the 1990s and Beyond. *ESRC Seminar Series,* Cranfield University.

Belbin, M. (1998) Foreword. In Johnson, R. and Redmond, D. (eds) *The Art of Empowerment: the profit and pain of employee involvement.* London: Financial Times Management.

Biddle, D. and Evenden, R. (1980) *The Human Aspects of Management.* London: Institute of Personnel Management.

Bitner, J. (1990) Evaluating Service Encounters: The Effects of Physical Surroundings and Employee Responsiveness. *Journal of Marketing*, Vol. 54, April, pp. 69–82.

Bitner, J., Booms, B.H. and Tetreault, M.S. (1990) The Service Encounter: Diagnosing Favourable and Unfavourable Incidents. *Journal of Marketing*, Vol. 54, January, pp. 71–84.

Block, P. (1987) *The Empowered Manager*. San Francisco: Jossey Bass.

Blyton, P. and Turnbull, P. (1992) *Reassessing Human Resource Management*. London: Sage.

Blyton, P. and Turnbull, P. (1994) *The Dynamics of Employee Relations*. London: Macmillan.

Boella, M. (1992) *Human Resource Management in the Hospitality Industry*. London: Stanley Thornes.

Bowcott, O. (1995) Burger King backs down and pays up. *The Guardian*, 19 December, p. 4.

Bowen, D.E. and Lawler, E.E. (1992) The Empowerment of Service Workers: why, how and when? *Sloan Management Review*, Vol. 31, Spring.

Bowen, J. and Basch, J. (1992) Strategies for Creating Customer Oriented Organisations. In Teare, R. and Olsen, M. (eds) *International Hospitality Management: corporate strategy in practice*. London: Pitman.

Braverman, H. (1974) *Labor and Monopoly Capital*. New York: Monthly Review Press.

Brown, R.K. (1992) *Understanding Industrial Organisations*. London: Routledge.

Bullock Committee of Inquiry (1977) *Report on Industrial Democracy*. London: HMSO.

Buttle, F. (1986) *Hotel and Food Service Marketing: a managerial approach*. London: Holt, Rinehart and Winston.

Carper, J. (1992) Strategies for winning guests in competitive times. *Hotels*, March, No. 52.

Caulkin, S. (1995) History Lesson. *The Observer*, 25 June, p. 8.

Caulkin, S. (1996) Hey, what's the big idea? *The Observer*, 21 July, p. 8.

Chopin, J. (1994) TQM – Let's Get Excited. *Management Services Quarterly*, Vol. 4, No. 6, pp. 44–47.

Christensen-Hughes, J. (1992) The Importance and Psychology of Personal Empowerment. Paper given at the Council for Hotel, Restaurant and Institutional Education Annual Meeting, Orlando, FL.

Collins, D. (1994) The Disempowering Logic of Empowerment. *Empowerment in Organisations*, Vol. 2, No. 2.

Collins, D. (1999) Born to Fail: Empowerment ambiguity and set overlap. *Personnel Review*, Vol. 28, No. 3, pp. 192–207.

Comen, T. (1989) Making Quality Assurance Work for You. *Cornell Hotel and Restaurant Quarterly,* November, pp. 23–29.

Conger, J.A. (1989) Leadership: The Art of Empowering Others. *Academy of Management Executive,* February, pp. 17–24.

Conger, J.A. and Kanungo, R.B. (1988) The Empowerment Process: Integrating theory and practice. *Academy of Management Review,* No. 13, pp. 471–482.

Cook, J.D., Hepworth, S.J., Wall, T.D. and Warr, P.B. (1981) *The Experience of Work: a compendium and review of 249 measures and their use.* London: Academic Press.

Cook, S. (1994) The Cultural Implications of Empowerment. *Empowerment in Organisations,* Vol. 2, No. 1, pp. 9–13.

Cooper, J. and Hartley, J. (1991) Reconsidering the Case for Organizational Commitment. *Human Resource Management Journal,* Vol. 1, No. 3, pp. 18–32.

Corsun, D.L. and Enz, C.A. (1999) Predicting psychological empowerment among service workers: the effects of support-based relationships. *Human Relations (USA),* Vol. 52, No. 2, pp. 205–225.

Cotton, J.L. (1993) *Employee Involvement.* London: Sage.

Cowell, D. (1984) *The Marketing of Services.* London: Heinemann.

Cunningham, I. and Hyman, J. (1999) The poverty of empowerment: a critical case study. *Personnel Review,* Vol. 28, No. 3, pp. 222–241.

D'Annunzio-Green and Macandrew, J. (1999) Re-empowering the empowered – the ultimate challenge? *Personnel Review,* Vol. 28, No. 3, pp. 258–278.

D'Egidio, F. (1990) *The Service Era.* Cambridge, Mass.: Productivity Press.

Dahl, R.A. (1957) The concept of power. *Behavioural Science,* Vol. 2, pp. 201–15.

Dahl, R.A. (1974) Power. In Potter, D. and Sarre, P. (eds) *Dimensions of Society,* London: University of London Press.

Dale, B.G. (1986) Experience with Quality Circles and Quality Costs. In Moores, B. (ed.) *Are They Being Served: quality consciousness in service industries.* Oxford: Philip Allen.

Dale, B.G. and Lees, J. (1986) *The Development of Quality Circle Programmes.* Sheffield: Manpower Services Commission.

Dearlove, D. (1996) No more new ideas please. *The Times,* 5 December, p. 4.

Deighton, J. (1994) Managing Service When Service is a Performance. In Rust, R.T. and Oliver, R.L. (eds) *Service Quality: new directions in theory and practice.* London: Sage.

Denton, D.K. (1994) Empowerment Through Involvement and Participation: Ford's Development and Training Programme. *Empowerment in Organisations,* Vol. 2. No. 2.

Drucker, P. (1988) The Coming of the New Organisation. *Harvard Business Review*, February.

Eaglen, A., Lashley, C. and Thomas, R. (1999) *Benefits and Costs Analysis: the impact of training on business performance.* Leeds: Leeds Metropolitan University.

Edwards, R. (1979) *Contested Terrain.* London: Heinemann.

Edwards, R., Reich, M. and Gordon, D.M. (1975) *Labour Market Segmentation.* Lexington, Mass: D.C. Heath.

Etzioni, A. (1961) *A Comparative Analysis of Complex Organisations.* New York: Free Press.

Fineman, S. (1993) *Emotion in Organizations.* London: Sage.

Flanders, A., Pomeranz, R. and Woodward, J. (1968) *Experiment in Democracy: a study of the John Lewis Partnership.* London: Faber and Faber.

Foulkes, V.S. (1994) How Consumers Predict Service Quality: what do they expect? In Rust, R.T. and Oliver, R.L. (eds) *Service Quality: new directions in theory and practice.* London: Sage.

Fox, A. (1974) *Beyond Contract: Work, Power and Trust Relations.* London: Faber & Faber.

Foy, N. (1994) *Empowering People at Work*, London: Gower Publishing.

Friedman, A.L. (1977) *Industry and Labour.* London: Macmillan.

Garwood, D.R. (1991) Empowerment: No Longer a Luxury. *Production and Inventory Review*, Vol. 11, No. 4.

Geary, J.F. (1994) Task Participation: Employees' Participation Enabled or Constrained? In Sisson, K. (ed.) *Personnel Management: A Comprehensive Guide to Theory and Practice in Britain.* Oxford: Blackwell.

Geroy, G.D., Wright, P.C. and Anderson, J. (1998) The strategic empowerment model. *Empowerment in Organizations*, Vol. 6, No. 2, pp. 15–27.

Goffee, R. and Scase, R. (1995) *Corporate Realities: the dynamics of small and large organisations.* London: Routledge.

Gordan, R. (1993) McDonald's explodes the myths over UK franchises. *Caterer and Hotelkeeper*, 12 August, p. 12.

Gronroos, C. (1984) *Strategic Management and Marketing in the Service Sector.* Chartwell-Bratt: Bromley.

Guest, D.E. (1987) Human Resource Management and Industrial Relations. *Journal of Management Studies*, Vol. 24, No. 5, pp. 503–21.

Guest, D.E. (1989) Personnel Management and HRM: can you tell the difference. *Personnel Management*, Vol. 21, No. 1, pp. 48–51.

Guest, D.E. (1995) Right enough to be dangerously wrong: an analysis of the *In Search of Excellence* phenomenon. In Mabey, C. and Salmon, G. (eds) *Strategic Human Resource Management.* Oxford: Blackwell.

Guest, D., Peccei, R. and Thomas, A. (1993) The Impact of Employee Involvement on Organisational Commitment and 'Them and Us' Attitudes. *Industrial Relations Journal*, Vol. 24, No. 3.

Hamlin, R. (1991) A Practical Guide to Empowering Your Employees. *Supervisory Management*, Vol. 36, p. 8.

Harley, B. (1999) The myth of empowerment: work organisation, hierarchy and employee autonomy in contemporary Australian workplaces. *Work Employment & Society*, Vol. 13, No. 1, pp. 41–67.

Harris, A. (1991) The Customer's Always Right. *Black Enterprise*, Vol. 21, No. 11.

Harrison, R. and Stokes, H. (1991) *Working With Organization Culture*. Roffey Park Institute.

HCTC (1993) *Meeting Competence Needs Now and in the Future*. London: Hospitality Training Foundation.

Herzberg, F. (1966) *Work and the Nature of Man*. Staple Press: New York.

Heslin, P.A., (1999) Boosting empowerment by developing self efficacy. *Asian Pacific Journal of Human Resource Management*, Vol. 37, No. 1, pp. 52–65.

Heskett, S.H., Sasser, W.E. and Hart, C.W. (1990) *Service Breakthroughs: Changing the Rules of the Game*. New York: Free Press.

Hirst, M. (1992) Creating a Service Driven Culture Globally. *International Journal of Contemporary Hospitality Management*, Vol. 4, No. 1.

Hochschild, A.R. (1983) *The Managed Heart: Commercialization of Human Feeling*. Berkley: University of California Press.

Hochschild, A.R. (1993) Preface. In Fineman, S. (ed.) *Emotion in Organizations*. London: Sage.

Holden, L. (1999) The perception gap in employee empowerment: a comparative study of banks in Sweden and Britain. *Personnel Review*, Vol. 28, No. 3, pp. 222–241.

Hopfl, H. (1994) Empowerment and the Management Prerogative. *Empowerment in Organisations*, Vol. 2, No. 3, pp. 39–44.

Horovirz, J. and Cudenne-Poon, C. (1990) Putting Service Quality into Gear. *Service Industry Journal*, Vol. 10, No. 2.

Hospitality Training Foundation (1996) *Training Who Needs It*. HTF: London.

Hospitality Training Foundation (1999) *Look Who's Training Now*. HTF: London.

Houtagers, H. (1999) Empowerment; using skills and competence management. *Participation and Empowerment in Organizations: an International Journal*, Vol. 7, No. 2, pp. 60–72.

Hubrecht, J. and Teare, R. (1993) A Strategy for Partnership in Total Quality Service. *International Journal of Contemporary Hospitality Management*, Vol. 5, No. 3.

Huczynski, A.A. (1993) Explaining the Succession of Management Fads. *The International Journal of Human Resource Management*, Vol. 4, No. 2, pp. 443–463.

Huselid, M.A. (1995) The Impact of Human Resource Management Practices on Turnover, Productivity, and Corporate Financial Performance. *Academy of Management Journal*, Vol. 38, No. 3, pp. 635–672.

Huselid, M.A. (1998) The Impact of Human Resource Management Practices on Turnover, Productivity, and Corporate Financial Performance. In Mabey, C., Salaman, G. and Storey, J. (eds) *Strategic Human Resource Management*. London: Sage.

Hyman, J. and Mason, B. (1995) *Managing Employee Involvement and Participation*. London: Sage.

Jacobi, O., Keller, B. and Muller-Jentsch, W. (1992) Germany: codetermining the future. In Ferner, A. and Hyman, R. (eds) *Industrial Relations in the New Europe*. Oxford: Blackwell.

Johns, N. (1992a) Quality Management in the Hospitality Industry: Part 1. Definition and Specification. *International Journal of Contemporary Hospitality Management*, Vol. 4, No. 3, pp. 14–20.

Johns, N. (1992b) Quality Management in the Hospitality Industry: Part 2. Applications, Systems and Techniques. *International Journal of Contemporary Hospitality Management*, Vol. 4, No. 4, pp. 3–7.

Johns, N. (1993) Quality Management in the Hospitality Industry: Part 3. Recent Developments. *International Journal of Contemporary Hospitality Management*, Vol. 5, No. 1, pp. 10–15.

Johnson, P.R. (1993) Empowerment in the Global Economy. *Empowerment in Organisations*, Vol. 1, No. 1.

Johnson, R. and Redmond, D. (1998) *The Art of Empowerment: the profit and pain of employee involvement*. London: Financial Times Management.

Johnston, R. (1989a) Developing Competitive Strategies in the Service Sector. In Jones, P. (ed.) *Management in Service Industries*, Chap. 7. London: Pitman.

Johnston, R. (1989b) Operations Management Issues. In Jones, P. (ed.) *Management in Service Industries*, Chap. 13, London: Pitman.

Joint Hospitality Industry Congress (1996) *The Vision for the Future*. London: Joint Hospitality Industry Congress.

Jones, P. (1989) *Management in Service Industries*. London: Pitman.

Jones, P. and Davies, A. (1991) Empowerment: a study of General Managers of four star hotel properties in the UK. *International Journal of Hospitality Management,* Vol. 10, No. 3.

Jones, P. and Pizam, A. (1993) *The International Hospitality Industry: Organisational and Operational Issues.* London: Pitman.

Kanter, R.M. (1989) *When Giants Learn to Dance.* New York: Simon & Schuster.

Karmel, B. (ed.) (1980) *Point and Counterpoint in Organisations?* Illinois: Dryden.

Keenoy, T. and Anthony, P. (1992) Metaphor, Meaning and Morality. In Blyton, P. and Turnbull, P. (eds) *Reassessing Human Resource Management.* London: Sage.

Keenoy, T. (1994) Performing somersaults. *The Observer,* 18 September, p. 8.

Keep, E. and Rainbird, H. (2000) Towards the Learning Organisation. In Bach, S. and Sisson, K. (eds) *Personnel Management: a comprehensive guide to theory and practice.* Oxford: Blackwell.

Kelly, J. and Kelly, C. (1990) Them and Us: Social Psychology and the New Industrial Relations. *British Journal of Industrial Relations,* Vol. 29, No. 1.

Kennedy, P. (1988) *The Rise and Fall of the Great Powers.* London: Fontana.

Kizilos, P. (1990) Crazy about Empowerment? *Training,* Vol. 27, pp. 47–51.

Koberg, C.S., Boss, R.W., Senjem, J.S. and Goodman, E.A. (1999) Antecedents and outcomes of empowerment: empirical evidence from the healthcare industry. *Group and Organization Management,* Vol. 24, No. 1, pp. 71–92.

Lashley, C. (1994) Is There Any Power in Empowerment? Conference Paper to Council for Hospitality Management, Research Conference, April.

Lashley, C. (1995a) Towards and Understanding of Employee Empowerment in Hospitality Services. *International Journal of Contemporary Hospitality Management,* Vol. 7, No. 1, pp. 27–32.

Lashley, C. (1995b) Empowerment through delayering: a pilot study at McDonald's restaurants. *International Journal of Contemporary Hospitality Management* Vol. 7, No. 2/3, pp. 29–35.

Lashley, C. (1996) Research Issues in Employee Empowerment in Hospitality Operations. *International Journal of Hospitality Management,* Vol. 15, No. 4, pp. 333–346.

Lashley, C., Taylor, S. and Lockwood, A. (1997) Aligning operations strategies for the service quality in hospitality operations. *Sixth Annual Hospitality Research Conference Papers.* Oxford: Oxford Brookes University.

Lashley, C. (1999) Employee Empowerment in Services: a framework for analysis. *Personnel Review*, Vol. 28, No. 3, pp. 169–191.

Lashley, C. (2000a) Empowerment Through Involvement: a case study of TGI Friday's restaurants. *Personnel Review*, Vol. 29, No. 5/6, 791–815.

Lashley, C. (2000b) *Hospitality Retail Management: a unit manager's guide*. Oxford: Butterworth-Heinemann.

Lashley, C. (2000c) Empowered franchisees? In Lashley, C. and Morrison, A. (eds) *Franchising Hospitality Services*. Oxford: Butterworth-Heinemann.

Lashley, C. (2000d) The case of McDonald's Restaurants Limited. In Lashley, C. and Morrison, A. (eds) *Franchising Hospitality Services*. Oxford: Butterworth-Heinemann.

Lashley, C. and Chaplin, A. (1999) Labour Turnover: Hidden problem, Hidden Costs. *Hospitality Review*, Vol. 1, No. 1, pp. 37–43.

Lashley, C. and McGoldrick, J. (1994) The Limits of Empowerment: A Critical Assessment of Human Resource Strategy for Hospitality Operations. *Empowerment in Organisations*, Vol. 2, No. 3.

Lashley, C. and Morrison, A. (eds) (2000) *Franchising Hospitality Services*. Oxford: Butterworth-Heinemann.

Lashley, C. and Taylor, S. (1998) Hospitality retail operations: types and styles in the management of human resources. *Journal of Retailing and Consumer Services*, Vol. 5, No. 3, pp. 59–84.

Lawler, E.E. (1973) *Motivation in Work Organizations*. Monterey, CA: Brooks/Cole.

Lawler, E.E. (1986) *High Involvement Management*. New York: Jossey Bass.

Lawler, E.E. and Mohran, S.A. (1987) Quality Circles: After the Honeymoon. *Organizational Dynamics*, Spring, pp. 42–54.

Leach, P. (1995) The importance of positive customer service to Ansell's. *Managing Service Quality*, Vol. 5, No. 4, pp. 31–34.

Leidner, R. (1993) *Fast food, fast talk: service work and the routinization of everyday life*. London: University of California Press.

Legge, K. (1989) Human Resource Management – a critical analysis. In Storey, J. (ed.) *New Perspectives in Human Resource Management*. London: Routledge.

Legge, K. (1995) *Human Resource Management: Rhetorics and Realities*. Macmillan: London.

Levitt, T. (1972) Production line approach to service. *Harvard Business Review*, Sept.–Oct., pp. 41–52.

Levitt, T. (1976) The Industrialisation of Service. *Harvard Business Review*, Sept.–Oct., pp. 63–74.

Likert, R. (1961) *New Patterns of Management*. New York: McGraw-Hill.

Lockwood, A. (1996) Empowerment: the key to service quality – an operations perspective. In *Conference Papers – Fifth Annual Hospitality Research Conference*. Nottingham: Nottingham Trent University.

Love, J.F. (1986) *McDonald's Behind the Arches*. London: Bantam Press.

Lovelock, C. (1981) Why Marketing Needs To Be Different For Service. In Donnelly, J.H. and George, W.R. (eds) *Marketing of Services*. Chicago: American Marketing Association.

Lowe, J., Delbridge, R. and Oliver, N. (1996) High Performance Manufacturing, Evidence from the Automotive Components Industry. *ESRC Seminar Series*. Cranfield University.

Mabey, C., Salaman, G. and Storey, J. (eds) (1998) *Strategic Human Resource Management*. London: Sage.

Mann, S. (1998) *Psychology Goes To Work*. Oxford: Purple House.

Mann, S. (1999) *Hiding What We Feel, Faking What We Don't: understanding the role of emotions at work*. Shaftesbury: Element.

Marchington, M., Goodman, J., Wilkinson, A. and Ackers, P. (1992) *New Developments in Employee Involvement*. Department of Employment, Research Series No. 2. Sheffield: HMSO.

Marchington, M. and Wilkinson, A. (2000) Direct Participation. In Bach, S. and Sisson, K. (eds) *Personnel Management: a comprehensive guide to theory and practice*. Oxford: Blackwell.

Maslow, A.H. (1954) *Motivation and Personality*. New York: Harper.

McDermid, K. (1992) Those in favour of BS5750. *Hospitality*, March, pp. 14–15.

McClelland, D.C. (1975) *Power: The inner experience*. New York: Irvington Press.

Merricks, P. and Jones, P. (1986) *The Management of Catering Operations*. Eastbourne: Wishart, Holt Rinehart.

Mitchell, D. (1979) *Control Without Bureaucracy*. Maidenhead: McGraw-Hill.

Morley, L. (1995) Theorizing Empowerment in UK Public Services. *Empowerment in Organizations*, Vol. 3, No. 3, pp. 35–41.

Morrison, A., (2000) Entrepreneurs or intrapreneurs? In Lashley, C. and Morrison, A. (eds) *Franchising Hospitality Services*. Oxford: Butterworth-Heinemann.

Mudie, L. and Cottam, J. (1999) Empowering the front line. *Participation and Empowerment: an International Journal*, Vol. 7, No. 8.

Mullins, L.M. (1992) *Hospitality Management: a human resources approach*. London: Pitman.

NEDC (1992) *UK Tourism: Competing for Growth*. London: National Economic Development Office.

National Westminster Bank (1990) *Survey of Small Firms*. London: National Westminster Bank.

Newell, H. (2000) Managing Careers. In Bach, S. and Sisson, K. (eds) *Personnel Management: a comprehensive guide to theory and practice*. Oxford: Blackwell.

Nicholls, J. (1995) Getting Empowerment Into Perspective: A Three Stage Training Framework. *Empowerment in Organizations*, Vol. 3, No. 3, pp. 5–10.

Nixon, B. (1994) Developing an Empowering Culture in Organizations. *Empowerment in Organisations*, Vol. 2, No. 1, pp. 14–24.

Noon, M., (1992) HRM a Map. Model or Theory? In Blyton, P. and Turnbull, P. (eds) *Reassessing Human Resource Management*. London: Sage.

Palmer, A. (1994) *Principles of Services Marketing*. McGraw-Hill: London.

Pandya, N. (1996) Delayering: the real meaning of business buzzwords. *The Guardian*, 23 August, p. 17.

Pannell Kerr Forster Associates (1991) *Hotel Profitability Critical Factors*. London: PFKA.

Pannell Kerr Forster Associates (1992) PFKA Column. *International Journal of Contemporary Hospitality Management*, Vol. 4, No. 2, pp. i–vi.

Parasuraman, A., Berry, L.L. and Zeithaml, V.A. (1991) Understanding Customer Expectations of Service. *Sloan Management Review*, Vol. 32, No. 3, pp. 39–48.

Parson, S.G. (1995) Empowering employees – back to the future at Novotel. *Managing Service Quality*, Vol. 5, No. 4, 16–21.

Pauwee, J. (1996) HRM and Performance: the Linkage Between Resources and Institutional Context. *ESRC Seminar Series*, Cranfield University.

Peters, T. (1992) *Liberation Management*. New York: Harper & Row.

Peters, T. and Waterman, R. (1982) *In Search of Excellence*. New York: Harper & Row.

Pfeffer, J. (1981) *Power in Organizations*. London: Pitman.

Pfeffer, J. (1994) *Competitive Advantage Through People*. Boston, MA: Harvard Business School Press

Pickard, J. (1993) The Real Meaning of Empowerment. *Personnel Management*, November.

Plunkett, L.C. and Fournier, R. (1991) *Participative Management: Implementing Empowerment*. Wiley, New York.

Poole, M. (1986) *Towards A New Industrial Democracy: workers' participation in industry.* London: Routledge & Keegan Paul.

Poole, M. (1989) *The Origins of Economic Democracy.* London: Routledge.

Poole, M. and Mansfield, R. (1992) Managing attitudes to human resource management. In Blyton, P. and Turnbull, P. (eds) *Reassessing Human Resource Management.* London: Sage.

Potter, J. (1994) Tapping the Iceberg: How to Get the Best out of Your People through Empowerment. *Empowerment in Organisations*, Vol. 2, No. 1.

Potterfield, T.A. (1999) *The Business of Empowerment: democracy and ideology in the workplace.* Westport, CT: Quorum.

Proctor, S., Currie, G. and Orme, H. (1999) The empowerment of middle managers in a community health trust: structure responsibility and culture. *Personnel Review*, Vol. 28, No. 3, 242–257.

Purcell, J. (1987) Mapping Management Styles in Employee Relations. *Journal of Management Studies*, Vol. 24, No. 5, pp. 533–48.

Purcell, J. (1989) The impact of corporate strategy on human resource management. In Storey, J. (ed.) *New Perspectives in Human Resource Management.* London: Routledge.

Purcell, J. (1996) Human Resource Bundles of Best Practice: a utopian cul-de-sac? *ESRC Seminar Series.* Cranfield University.

Purcell, J. and Gray, A. (1986) Corporate Personnel Departments and the Management of Industrial Relations: two case studies in ambiguity. *Journal of Management Studies*, Vol. 23, No. 2, pp. 205–223.

Purcell, J. and Sissons, K. (1983) Strategies and Practices in the Management of Industrial Relations. In G.S. Bain (ed.) *Industrial Relations in Britain.* Oxford: Blackwell.

Putnam, L.L. and Mumby, D.K. (1993) Organizations, Emotions and the Myth of Rationality. In Fineman, S. (ed.) *Emotion in Organizations*, London: Sage.

Rafiq, M. and Ahmed, P.K. (1993) The Scope of Internal Marketing: Defining the Boundary Between Marketing and Human Resource Management. *Journal of Marketing Management*, Vol. 9, pp. 219–232.

Rafiq, M. and Ahmed, P.K. (1998a) A customer orientated framework for empowering service employees. *Journal of Service Marketing*, Vol. 12, No. 5, pp. 379–395.

Rafiq, M. and Ahmed, P.K. (1998b) A contingency model for empowering customer contact services employees. *Management Decisions*, Vol. 36, No. 10, pp. 686–694.

Ramsay, H. (1977) Cycles of Control. *Sociology,* Vol. 11, No. 3, pp. 481–506.

Rawnsley, A. (1996) Stake and chips (hold the unions). *The Guardian,* 21 January.

Ray-Chaudhuri, J. (1998) Engaging in conversations: a tool for team identity empowerment. *Empowerment in Organisations,* Vol. 6, No. 1, pp. 45–61.

Rice, C. (1997) *Understanding Customers.* Oxford: Butterworth-Heinemann.

Riley, M. (1991) *Human Resource Management: a guide to personnel practice in the hotel and catering industries.* Oxford: Butterworth-Heinemann.

Ripley, R.E. and Ripley, M.J. (1992) Empowerment the Cornerstone of Quality: Empowering Management in Innovative Organisations in the 1990s. *Management Decisions* Vol. 30, No. 4, pp. 20–43.

Ripley, R.E. and Ripley, M.J. (1993) Empowering Management in Innovative Organisations in the 1990s. *Empowerment in Organisations,* Vol. 1, No. 1.

Ritzer, G. (1993) *The McDonaldization of Society.* London: Pine Forge Press.

Robbins, S.P. (1983) The theory Z organization from power-control perspective. *California Management Review,* Vol. 25, No. 2, pp. 67–75.

Rodrigues, C.A. (1994) Employee Participation and Empowerment Programs: Problems of Definition and Implementation. *Empowerment in Organisations,* Vol. 2, No. 2, pp. 29–37.

Rood, R. and Meneley, B. (1991) Serious Play at Work. *Personnel Journal,* Vol. 70, pp. 90–9.

Rosenthal, P., Hill, S. and Peccei, R. (1998) Checking out service: evaluating excellence, HRM and TQM in retailing. In Mabey, C., Salaman, G. and Storey, J. (eds) *Strategic Human Resource Management,* London: Sage.

Royle, T. (1996) Avoiding the German System of Codetermination: the McDonald's Corporation. *Conference Papers The Fifth Annual Hospitality Research Conference.* Nottingham: Nottingham Trent University.

Rust, R.T. and Oliver, R.L. (1994) *Service Quality: new directions in theory and practice.* London: Sage.

Salaman, G. (1979) *Work Organisations: resistance and control.* London: Longman.

Schein, E.H. (1988) *Organizational Psychology.* Englewood Cliffs: Prentice-Hall.

Schmenner, R.W. (1995) *Service Operations Management.* Englewood Cliffs: Prentice-Hall.

Sellers, P. (1990) What Customers Really Want. *Fortune,* Vol. 121, No. 13.

Senge, P.M. (1990) *The Fifth Discipline: the art and practices of the learning organisation.* New York: Currency Doubleday.

Senge, P., Kleiner, A., Roberts, C., Ross, R., Roth, G. and Smith, B. (1999) *The Dance of Change: the challenges to sustaining momentum in learning organisations.* London: Currency Doubleday.

Sewell, G. and Wilkinson, B. (1994) Empowerment or Emasculation? Shopfloor Surveillance in a Total Quality Organisation. In Blyton, P. and Turnbull, P. (eds) *Reassessing Human Resource Management.* London: Sage.

Shamir, B. (1980) Between service and servility: role conflict in subordinate service roles. *Human Relations,* Vol. 33, 741–56.

Shepherdson, I. (1996) Markets will have to get used to lower rates. *The Guardian,* 11 March.

Shirley, S. (1993) The Journey to Empowerment: total employee involvement. *Business Studies,* Vol. 6, No. 1.

Siegall, G. and Gardner, S. (2000) Contextual Factors of Psychological Empowerment. *Personnel Review,* Vol. 29, No. 5/6, 703–722.

Simmons, P. and Teare, R. (1993) Evolving a Total Quality Culture. *International Journal of Contemporary Hospitality Management,* Vol. 5, No. 3.

Sinclair, A. (1992) The Tyranny of a Team Ideology. *Organisation Studies,* Vol. 13, No. 4, 611–26.

Sissons, K. (ed.) (1989) *Personnel Management in Britain.* Oxford: Blackwell.

Sissons, K. (ed.) (1994) *Personnel Management.* Oxford: Blackwell.

Smith, A.C. and Moulay, V.S. (1998) Empowerment in New Zealand: insights into two cases. *Empowerment in Organisations: an International Journal,* Vol. 6, No. 3, 69–81.

Sosteric, M. (1996) Subjectivity and the labour process: a case study in the restaurant industry. *Work Employment and Society,* Vol. 16, No. 2, pp. 297.

Sparrowe, R.T. (1994) Empowerment in the Hospitality Industry: an Exploration of Antecedents and Outcomes. *Hospitality Research Journal,* Vol. 17, No. 3.

Spreitzer, G.M. (1995) Psychological empowerment in the workplace: dimensions, measurement, and validation. *Academy of Management Journal,* Vol. 38, No. 5 pp. 1422–65.

Spreitzer, G.M. (1996) Social structural characteristics of psychological empowerment. *Academy of Management Journal,* Vol. 39, No. 2, pp. 483–504.

Spreitzer, G.M., Kizilos, M.A. and Nason, S.W. (1997) A dimensional analysis of the relationship between psychological empowerment and effectiveness, satisfaction and strain. *Journal of Management*, Vol. 23, No. 5, pp. 679–704.

Sternberg, L.E. (1992) Empowerment: trust vs Control. *The Cornell Hotel and Restaurant Administration Quarterly*, Vol. 33, No. 1 (February), p. 69.

Stewart, A.M. (1994) *Empowering People*. London: Pitman.

Storey, J. (ed.) (1989) *New Perspectives in Human Resource Management*. London: Routledge.

Storey, J. (1992) *Developments in Management of Human Resources*. Oxford: Blackwell.

Storey, J. and Bacon, N. (1993) Individualism and Collectivism: Into the 1990s. *International Journal of Human Resource Management*, Vol. 4, No. 3, pp. 665–684.

Suprenant, C.F. and Solomon, M.R. (1987) Predictability and Personalization in the Service Encounter. *Journal of Marketing*, Vol. 51, April, pp. 86–96.

Sutton, A. (1992) Those Not So Sure About BS5750. *Hospitality*, March, pp. 12–13.

Tannenbaum, R. and Schmidt, W.H. (1973) How to Choose a Leadership Pattern. *Harvard Business Review*, May/June, pp. 162–180.

Taylor, F.W. (1947) *Scientific Management*. New York: Harper & Row.

Teare, R. and Olsen, M. (1992) *International Hospitality Management: corporate strategy in practice*. London: Pitman.

Thomas, H. and Logan, C. (1982) *Mondragon: an economic analysis*. London: George Allen and Unwin.

Thomas, R., Lashley, C., Rowson, R., Xie, G., Jameson, S., Lincoln, G. and Parsons, D. (2000) *The National Small Tourism and Hospitality Firms Survey: 2000 Skills Demands and Training Practices*. Leeds: Leeds Metropolitan University.

Thomas, K.W. and Velthouse, B.A. (1990) Cognitive Elements of Empowerment; an interpretive model of intrinsic task motivation. *Academy of Management Review*, Vol. 15, pp. 666–681.

Thompson, P. and McHugh, D. (1990) *Work Organisation: A Critical Introduction*. London: Macmillan.

Thompson, P. and McHugh, D. (1995) *Work Organisation: A Critical Introduction*. London: Macmillan.

Thomson, K. (1998) *Emotional Capital*. Oxford: Capstone.

Tredre, R. (1996) A reader rants: store poison pens. *The Guardian*, 25 February.

Tse, E.C. (1992) Development strategies for international hospitality markets. In Teare, R. and Olsen, M. (eds) *International Hospitality Management: corporate strategy in practice*. London: Pitman.

Tuckman, A. (1995) Ideology, Quality and TQM. In Wilkinson, A. and Willmott, H. (eds) *Making Quality Critical: new perspectives on organizational change.* London: Routledge.

van Goozen, S.H.M., van de Poll, N.E. and Sergeant, J.A. (1994) *Emotions: Essays on Emotion Theory.* Hove: Lawrence Erblaum Associates.

van Outdshoorn, M. and Thomas, L. (1993) A Management Synopsis of Empowerment. In *Empowerment in Organisations,* Vol. 1, No. 1.

Walsh, D. (1992) Recession forces US caterers to improve value for money. *Caterer and Hotelkeeper,* 30 July, p. 21.

Watson, T.J. (1986) *Management Organisation and Employment Strategy: new directions in theory and practice.* London: Routledge and Keegan Paul.

Watson, T.J. (1993) Rhetoric, strategic exchange and organisational change. Conference paper to the 11th EGOS Colloquium, Paris, July.

Watson, T.J. (1994a) *In Search of Management.* London: Routledge.

Watson, T.J. (1994b) Management 'flavours of the month': their role in managers' lives. *International Journal of Human Resource Management,* Vol. 5, No. 4, pp. 893–909.

Watson,T.J. (1996) Motivation: that's Maslow isn't it? *Management Learning,* Vol. 27, No. 4, pp. 447–464.

Whittington, R. (1993) *What is Strategy and Does it Matter?* London: Routledge.

Wickens, P. (1987) *The Road to Nissan, Flexibility, Quality, Team Work.* London: Macmillan.

Wilkinson, A. (1998) Empowerment theory and practice. *Personnel Review,* Vol. 27, No. 1, pp. 40–56.

Wilkinson, A., Marchington, M. and Goodman, J. (1991) Total Quality Management and Employee Involvement. *Human Resource Management Journal,* Vol. 2, No. 4, pp. 1–20.

Wilkinson, A. and Willmott, H. (1995) *Making Quality Critical: new perspectives on organizational change.* Routledge: London.

Willman, P. (1989) Human Resource Management in the Service Sector. In Jones, P. (ed) *Management in Service Industries,* Chap. 13. London: Pitman.

Wilson, T. (1996) *The Empowerment Manual.* London: Gower.

Wood, R.C. (1992) *Working in Hotels and Catering* London: Routledge.

Wyer, P. and Mason, J. (1999) Empowerment in small businesses. *Participation and Empowerment: an International Journal,* Vol. 7, No. 7, pp. 48–57.

Zeithaml, V.A., Berry, L.L. and Parasuraman, A. (1993) The Nature and Determinants of Customer Expectations of Service.

Journal of the Academy of Marketing Science, Vol. 21, No. 1, pp. 1–12.

Zhao, J. and Merna, K. (1992) Impact analysis and the international environment. In Teare, R. and Olsen, M. (eds) *International Hospitality Management: corporate strategy in practice*. London: Pitman.

Index

Hospitality, Leisure & Tourism Series

Hospitality, Leisure & Tourism Series